Global Shakespeare
and Social Injustice

GLOBAL SHAKESPEARE INVERTED

Global Shakespeare Inverted challenges any tendency to view Global Shakespeare from the perspective of 'centre' versus 'periphery'. Although the series may locate its critical starting point geographically, it calls into question the geographical bias that lurks within the very notion of the 'global'. It provides a timely, constructive criticism of the present state of the field and establishes new and alternative methodologies that invert the relation of Shakespeare to the supposed 'other'.

Series editors

David Schalkwyk, Queen Mary, University of London, UK
Silvia Bigliazzi, University of Verona, Italy
Bi-qi Beatrice Lei, National Taiwan University, Taiwan

Advisory board

Douglas Lanier, University of New Hampshire, USA
Sonia Massai, King's College London, UK
Supriya Chaudhury, Jadavpur University, India
Ian Smith, Lafayette College, USA

Eating Shakespeare: Cultural Anthropophagy as Global Methodology
Edited by Anne Sophie Refskou, Marcel Alvaro de Amorim and Vinicius Mariano de Carvalho

Shakespeare in the Global South: Stories of Oceans Crossed in Contemporary Adaptation
Sandra Young

Migrating Shakespeare: First European Encounters, Routes and Networks
Edited by Janet Clare and Dominique Goy-Blanquet

Shakespeare's Others in 21st-century European Performance: The Merchant of Venice *and* Othello
Edited by Boika Sokolova and Janice Valls-Russell

Disseminating Shakespeare in the Nordic Countries: Shifting Centres and Peripheries in the Nineteenth Century
Edited by Nely Keinänen and Per Sivefors

Forthcoming Titles

Reconstructing Shakespeare in the Nordic Countries: National Revival and Interwar Politics, 1870–1940
Edited by Nely Keinänen and Per Sivefors

Global Shakespeare and Social Injustice

Towards a Transformative Encounter

Edited by
Chris Thurman and
Sandra Young

THE ARDEN SHAKESPEARE
LONDON • NEW YORK • OXFORD • NEW DELHI • SYDNEY

THE ARDEN SHAKESPEARE
Bloomsbury Publishing Plc
50 Bedford Square, London, WC1B 3DP, UK
1385 Broadway, New York, NY 10018, USA
29 Earlsfort Terrace, Dublin 2, Ireland

BLOOMSBURY, THE ARDEN SHAKESPEARE and the Arden Shakespeare logo
are trademarks of Bloomsbury Publishing Plc

First published in Great Britain 2023
This paperback edition printed in 2025

Copyright © Chris Thurman, Sandra Young and contributors, 2023

Chris Thurman and Sandra Young have asserted their right under the Copyright, Designs and Patents Act, 1988, to be identified as editors of this work.

Cover design by Maria Rajka
Cover image: *Untitled* © Diane Harper

All rights reserved. No part of this publication may be reproduced or transmitted in any form or by any means, electronic or mechanical, including photocopying, recording, or any information storage or retrieval system, without prior permission in writing from the publishers.

Bloomsbury Publishing Plc does not have any control over, or responsibility for, any third-party websites referred to or in this book. All internet addresses given in this book were correct at the time of going to press. The author and publisher regret any inconvenience caused if addresses have changed or sites have ceased to exist, but can accept no responsibility for any such changes.

A catalogue record for this book is available from the British Library.

A catalog record for this book is available from the Library of Congress.

ISBN: HB: 978-1-3503-3509-7
PB: 978-1-3503-3513-4
ePDF: 9781-3503-3511-0
eBook: 9781-3503-3510-3

Series: Global Shakespeare Inverted

Typeset by Deanta Global Publishing Services, Chennai, India

To find out more about our authors and books visit www.bloomsbury.com and sign up for our newsletters.

CONTENTS

List of figures vii
List of contributors viii

Introduction: Global Shakespeare and its confrontation with social injustice *Chris Thurman and Sandra Young* 1

Part I Scholarship and social justice: Questions for the field 17

1 Re-thinking 'Global Shakespeare' for social justice *Susan Bennett* 19

2 Caliban in an era of mass migration *Linda Gregerson* 36

3 What makes Global Shakespeares an exercise in ethics? *Alexa Alice Joubin* 58

Part II Resisting racial logics 79

4 Making whiteness out of 'nothing': The recurring comedic torture of (pregnant) Black women from medieval to modern *Dyese Elliott-Newton* 81

5 Feeling in justice: Racecraft and *The Merchant of Venice* *Derrick Higginbotham* 102

6   Marking Muslims: The Prince of Morocco and the racialization of Islam in *The Merchant of Venice* Hassana Moosa 120

Part III Imagining freedom with Shakespeare 143

7   Shakespeare in and on exile: Politicized reading and performative writing in the Robben Island Shakespeare Kai Wiegandt 145

8   'Men at some times are masters of their fates': The Gallowfield Players perform *Julius Caesar* Rowan Mackenzie 166

Part IV Scrutinizing gender and sexual violence 185

9   The 'sign and semblance of her honour': Petrarchan slander and gender-based violence in three Shakespearean plays Kirsten Dey 187

10 Open-gendered casting in Shakespeare performance Abraham Stoll 207

11 Teaching *Titus Andronicus* and Ovidian myth when sexual violence is on the public stage Wendy Beth Hyman 230

Index 255

FIGURES

10.1 Hallie Peterson as Brutus and Yadira Correa as Cassius in *Julius Caesar*, directed by Allegra Libonati (The Old Globe Theatre, San Diego) 212

10.2 Bibi Mama as Viola and Claire Simba as Orsino in *Twelfth Night*, directed by Jesse Perez (The Old Globe Theatre, San Diego) 214

CONTRIBUTORS

Susan Bennett is Faculty Professor in Arts at the University of Calgary in Canada. She has published widely in theatre and performance studies with a particular interest in contemporary productions of Shakespeare's plays. Her most recent book, *Sound*, is published in the Bloomsbury series Theory for Theatre Studies, which she coedits with Kim Solga. A new project will examine the impacts of live streaming and other digital pandemic-era projects on the Shakespeare brand.

Kirsten Dey completed her PhD at the University of Pretoria in 2022. Her doctoral research focused on T. S. Eliot's *Four Quartets*. Her scholarly interests include Renaissance literature, Romantic poetry, Modernism, and South African short stories; her master's research was on Shakespeare's varying responses to Petrarchism. Her work has appeared in *Shakespeare in Southern Africa* and *Type/Cast*. She is FET Phase English teacher at Beaulieu College.

Dyese Elliott-Newton is a PhD student in the Department of English at UCLA. She is Teaching Associate for the English department and also the Inclusive Teaching Fellow for UCLA's Center for the Advancement of Teaching. Her current research considers the racial and gender politics of grief in early modern English drama. More broadly her courses and research discuss the intersections of race, gender, and disability in premodern and Black womanist literatures, especially as they relate to memory, law, and history-making.

Linda Gregerson is the Caroline Walker Bynum Distinguished University Professor of English at the University of Michigan, Ann Arbor. She is the editor, with Susan Juster, of *Empires of God: Religious Encounters in the Early Modern Atlantic* (2011) and author of *The Reformation of the Subject: Spenser, Milton, and the*

English Protestant Epic (1995), as well as seven books of poetry and a volume of essays on the contemporary American lyric. She has published numerous articles on Shakespeare, Milton, Spenser, and contemporary poetics.

Derrick Higginbotham is Associate Professor in the Department of English at the University of Hawai'i at Mānoa. Currently, he is finishing his book *Winners and Wasters: Queer Desires, Economics, and Theater in Premodern England*. He has published articles in *Exemplaria*, *Shakespeare in Southern Africa* and *Early Modern Black Diaspora Studies*. He coedits the Routledge book series Critical Junctures in Global Early Modernities with Nicolas R. Jones.

Wendy Beth Hyman is Professor of English and comparative literature and Chair of book studies at Oberlin College. She is the author of *Impossible Desire and the Limits of Knowledge in Renaissance Poetry*, editor of *The Automaton in English Renaissance Literature*, and coeditor of *Teaching Social Justice through Shakespeare: Why Renaissance Literature Matters Now*. She has published widely on Shakespeare, lyric poetry, and the history of science and technology.

Alexa Alice Joubin is Professor of English, women's, gender and sexuality studies, theatre, international affairs, and East Asian languages and literatures at George Washington University, where she serves as founding codirector of the Digital Humanities Institute. She is the author of *Shakespeare and East Asia* (2021), coauthor of *Race* (2018), editor and translator of *Sinophone Adaptations of Shakespeare* (2022), and coeditor of *Onscreen Allusions to Shakespeare* (2022), *Local and Global Myths in Shakespearean Performance* (2018), and *Shakespeare and the Ethics of Appropriation* (2014).

Rowan Mackenzie is both practitioner and academic, working with specialized communities. She is the founder and artistic director of Shakespeare UnBard, which facilitates collaborative theatre companies in a number of UK prisons, and co-chair of the Shakespeare Beyond Borders Alliance. She is the recipient of many national and international awards for her work, including the prestigious Butler Trust. Her monograph *Creating Space for Shakespeare* will be published by Bloomsbury/Arden in 2023.

Hassana Moosa is a PhD candidate, funded by the Commonwealth Scholarship Commission, in the English Department at King's College London. Her research explores early modern English dramatic representations of racialized slavery in the Mediterranean, as well as the racialization of Muslims in the literatures produced out of premodern Anglo-Islamic encounters. Hassana is on the steering committee of the UK-based Early Modern Scholars of Colour network. She is also an editor on the digital platform Medieval and Early Modern Orients (MEMOs).

Abraham Stoll is Director of the Theatre Program at Johns Hopkins University. He previously taught, and served as production dramaturg, at The Old Globe and University of San Diego Shiley Graduate Theatre Program. His most recent book is *Conscience in Early Modern English Literature* (Cambridge 2017).

Chris Thurman is Professor of English and Director of the Tsikinya-Chaka Centre in the School of Literature, Language and Media at the University of the Witwatersrand. He is the editor of *South African Essays on 'Universal' Shakespeare* (2014) and fourteen volumes of the journal *Shakespeare in Southern Africa*. He is president of the Shakespeare Society of Southern Africa and the founder of Shakespeare ZA (shakespeare.org.za). He writes a weekly arts column for *Business Day*.

Kai Wiegandt is Professor of literature at the Barenboim-Said Akademie Berlin. He is the author of the monographs *Crowd and Rumour in Shakespeare* (2012) and *J. M. Coetzee's Revisions of the Human: Posthumanism and Narrative Form* (2019). He edited a special issue of the *European Journal of English Studies* on *J. M. Coetzee and the Non-English Literary Traditions* (2016, with Maria-Jesús Lopez) and *The Transnational in Literary Studies: Potential and Limitations of a Concept* (2020).

Sandra Young is Professor of English literary studies at the University of Cape Town. She is the author of *Shakespeare in the Global South: Stories of Oceans Crossed in Contemporary Adaptation* (2019) and *The Early Modern Global South in Print: Textual Form and the Production of Human Difference as Knowledge* (2015), which traces the emergence of a racialized 'South' in early modernity. She is vice president of the Shakespeare Society of Southern Africa.

Introduction

Global Shakespeare and its confrontation with social injustice

Chris Thurman and Sandra Young

The field of Global Shakespeare has been well placed to appreciate the ambivalence that lies at the heart of Shakespeare scholarship in the twenty-first century. Because we focus on a figure who – as one of England's most celebrated exports for centuries – is associated with colonial inheritances and damning social hierarchies, Shakespeare scholars find ourselves implicated.[1] We have an obligation to reckon with that inheritance in some way; the obligation is also, however, an opportunity. Scholars of Global Shakespeare are in a good position to recognize the impact of Shakespeare's travels, and the ways in which creative innovations that take place beyond the anglosphere have imbued his work with sensibilities and perspectives on power that equip it to address histories of injustice. Yet questions remain about whether Global Shakespeare has been truly transformative, or whether a 'global' Shakespeare has been complicit in forms of cultural appropriation derived from a colonialist playbook, ultimately reinforcing Shakespeare's cultural capital and positioning a range of 'elsewheres' as 'exotic' distractions. Scholarly interventions thus need to allow Shakespeare's travels across the globe to make visible the kinds of inequities that pervade cultural and intellectual life within so many societies and across an interconnected, globalized world.

While Shakespeare studies has in recent years become more attuned to social injustice, the impulse to celebrate an already hegemonic figure undermines the work itself and its capacity to disrupt. Many institutions, both within the world of the academy and within the world of theatre practice, have troubling histories of exclusion and elitism or are located in communities that have experienced egregious historical injustice. The assumption that Shakespeare represents a kind of cultural and even 'moral' elevation is something that the field has worked hard to undo, but the persistence of the language of veneration and exceptionalism demonstrates the powerful cachet that attaches to the figure at the centre of our scholarship, a cachet that could be said to sustain even our most critical work. 'Global Shakespeare' as a field has benefitted from the same cultural capital that accrues to the figure at its centre, and despite an initial sense that a 'global' orientation could result in a more open-spirited approach to a wider world as well as a greater capacity for self-reflexive critical thought, the field has not aligned itself unambiguously with a social justice orientation. The moment calls for critical reflection.

Activist responses to the alarming manifestations of anti-immigration, misogynistic and racist discourses within mainstream politics have made the work of cultural studies urgent, timely and germane across many centres of scholarly and creative practice. In networks of bold activism a new generation of students has been unafraid to call 'BS' on the duplicity of political and educational institutions complacent to the status quo and the injustice, violence and catastrophic futures they tolerate. The academy owes a debt of gratitude to the invigoration of movements such as #RhodesMustFall and #FeesMustFall, #MeToo and #BlackLivesMatter, the Parklands survivors' #MarchForOurLives and the #ClimateStrike. These movements are global in nature – changing, vibrant and purposefully decentred. But they are also located in particular spaces, allowing them to address issues of injustice in their manifest materiality. The language used by these movements signals an orientation towards the future as well as an understanding of the entrenched histories that have given rise to the politics of the present.

For example, the unequivocal message on a placard in front of the White House in Washington, DC, showed that Black Lives Matter protesters saw clearly that systemic racism and the violence that it facilitates has a long history: 'Black genocide: 1619–2020'. The early date references the arrival of the first slave ship on the coast of Virginia in 1619 and, with it, the beginning of the enslavement of Black people in the United States.[2] This placard creates a clear link between the racist violence that pervades contemporary America and the racist violence that infused the British colonial project, as well as the exclusionary rhetoric of 'liberty' asserted in the 'Declaration of Independence' and the ideal of 'Union' celebrated in the post-Civil War era of so-called Reconstruction. Today's activists are alert to the duplicity of this language, both in its historical context and in its contemporary deployment, given the racist violence that it helps to shield. The clear-sighted critique emerging with the Black Lives Matter movement shines a light on the systems of governance and policing that authorize violence and entrench inequality. It recasts contemporary racial injustice as the legacy of slavery and the racism it depended upon.

This is an important moment for early modern cultural studies: at a time when calls for justice are all the more prevalent in public life across the world, the academy, too, is called to attend to questions of social justice. It may require a revision of the critical lexicon to be able to probe deeply the relationship between Shakespeare studies and the intractable forms of social injustice that infuse cultural, political and economic life, injustice that is made all the more visible through news cycles driven by social media. Student activism has helped to create the impetus for Shakespeare studies critically to examine the intellectual inheritances that continue to shape the academy and to renew and transform our curricula. This collection of essays represents a community of scholars asking probing questions of the field at a time when social justice movements around the world have drawn attention to injustice and made it impossible to look away.

The collection has its genesis in a conference on 'Shakespeare and Social Justice' held in Cape Town at the Fugard Theatre in 2019.[3] The Fugard, a beloved and vibrant independent theatre until the Covid-19 pandemic forced it to close its doors permanently in March 2021, was located in District Six. This area on the edge of Cape Town's 'City Bowl' had been home to a vibrant community and creative life that was devastated through forced removals in the 1960s when the apartheid government declared it a 'whites only' area. The construction of the theatre in 2006–7 entailed the restoration and transformation of a cluster of buildings that included a nineteenth-century church façade and a textile warehouse where many residents of District Six had worked during the first half of the twentieth century. In a sense the Fugard Theatre building was a living archive of precisely the kind of structural injustice that concerned the gathering of scholars seeking to probe the lingering effects of historical injustice, as well as the new forms of social injustice that pervade our worlds. The space also offered a palpable reminder of the transformative possibilities of creative work and its subversive and powerful affirmations. Located in a place that held in view both the sobering history and the transformative possibilities of challenging theatre-making and scholarship, the gathering functioned as a living archive, too, bringing to light the disturbing inheritances of the disciplines, practices and institutions associated with the longstanding field of Shakespeare studies and the revered figure at its centre. Shakespeare has a contested history in South Africa, where he is associated both with an educational system that advanced colonial and apartheid social hierarchies and with the struggle for freedom and justice. Scholars of Global Shakespeare might well argue that the same contestation – between Shakespeare as a tool of oppression and Shakespeare as a means of liberation – could be identified in almost any national or regional context.

This, if anything, is what makes Shakespeare 'global' in the sense that used to be inaccurately described as 'universal'. Shakespeare (the figure, the symbol, the body of work) is a shared point of reference, but that does not imply shared perspectives. Our collection of essays covers 'global' terrain but is in no way adequately representative of the range of national or regional perspectives that constitute Global Shakespeare – a narrowness that could be excused as a consequence of the vagaries of post-conference publication, but that readers may nonetheless discern as a limitation of the volume.[4] The contributors are based at institutions in South Africa, the United States, the United Kingdom and Europe; their cultural-political frameworks and paradigms, however, are not constrained to these territories. One could specify the geographical reach or scope of various essays, from the Caribbean (Linda Gregerson) to Bengal and East Asia (Alexa Alice Joubin), or even the many contexts of racialized Islam (Hassana Moosa). But if this volume seeks to address issues of injustice, such an undertaking must also entail some resistance to the demarcations of nation-based territorial categories.

A final observation may be offered about the terms employed in the title of this book and in its framing. At the time that the conference was held, the pairing of 'Shakespeare' and 'social justice' (and the productive tension that exists between these terms) had already been introduced into the lexicon of scholars and theatre-makers, but it was not widely employed as an explicit rubric for research and practice. Certainly, this pairing was not yet a common one in book-length studies. *Teaching Social Justice Through Shakespeare* (2019), edited by Hillary Eklund and Wendy Beth Hyman, was in press when Hyman travelled to Cape Town for the conference.[5] Some three years later, there are a handful of books that invoke these as the key terms in their title – with the *Arden Research Handbook of Shakespeare and Social Justice* (edited by David Ruiter, 2020) representing what is now an established sub-field.[6] But what happens when we place emphasis on manifestations of social *in*justice – and the ways in which these intersect with, or are exposed by, an interrogative and subversive approach to the field of Global Shakespeare? This is the question posed (and one that the contributors begin to answer) in these pages.

* * *

The essays gathered here demonstrate the potential for radically transformative work that more recent trends in Shakespeare studies and innovative theatre-making invite and enable. The collection thus constitutes a timely response to a world that has been forced to recognize the pervasiveness of racist violence and gender-based violence – a world in which inequality has been entrenched through the impact of a global pandemic, when access to healthcare, vaccines and income protection has been uneven, devastatingly so for the most disempowered and vulnerable of communities.

In the essay that opens the first section of this book ('Scholarship and social justice: Questions for the field'), Susan Bennett notes that 'it is timely to ask whether the category [of Global Shakespeare] is itself in need of decolonization':

> Traditionally defined, Global Shakespeare too easily offers the English-speaking world opportunities to act as consumers and

collectors of the exotic Other, extending still an Anglocentric and colonialist gaze on non-English-language examples of those who do things with Shakespeare.... Indeed, Global Shakespeare could fairly be accused of practicing an aesthetic colonialism that requires performances to surprise and thrill in how different they look, but at the same time remaining fully legible to Western audiences, critics and students familiar with the source Shakespeare text.[7]

The preoccupation with an expanding archive of 'productions from the Western world's elsewheres', evident in so much of what has been produced under the sign of 'Global Shakespeare', does little to address the hegemony of Anglophone culture.[8] It is time to think about how Global Shakespeare could be put to a different purpose, Bennett argues, to place questions of justice at the forefront of the field and to destabilize the colonialist histories that continue to shape aspects of its endeavours. To consider how a process of decolonization may be undertaken – or understood – Bennett suggests that we emphasize the definition of global as 'relating to, or involving the whole world'; such a Global Shakespeare 'would be concerned with and driven by properly global issues, with Shakespeare in a supporting role in illustrating any one or all of them. This Global Shakespeare archive would not always be arranged around nation or expressions of cultural difference but would pivot toward examples "involving the whole world"'.[9]

One phenomenon that is undoubtedly a 'properly global issue' is mass migration – the subject of Linda Gregerson's essay, which follows Bennett's, and which focuses on two novelistic invocations of the figure of Caliban: George Lamming's *Water with Berries* (1971) and Marina Warner's *Indigo* (1992). If *The Tempest* is a play that is 'haunted by displaced persons', then, as Gregerson shows, it is Caliban who forces us to ask questions acutely pertinent to the era of (forced) mass migration: 'Whose claims to sustenance and safety will be honoured? Who actively maintains the systems that deny such claims?'[10] The novels Gregerson discusses are both set in London but imagine and recall Caribbean histories that, re-read in our contemporary moment (and with the Windrush Generation in mind), evince the many ways in which the United Kingdom has refused to reckon with its own postcolonial history – never mind its colonial history. One of the tasks of a reconfigured Global

Shakespeare, Gregerson's essay reminds us, is to disrupt the centre-periphery model in the ways that Lamming and Warner do. In fact, Gregerson suggests, it is precisely *because* they are creative works that these novels are so effective in their treatment of subjects that might otherwise be somewhat reductively approached by 'polemical adaptation or analysis' that targets 'exemplary villains or liberatory role models'.[11] This observation leads Gregerson to a proposal about a Global Shakespeare methodology – one recognizing that 'literary and theatrical criticism is most trenchant when it remembers, and fully credits, the mediums it seeks to illuminate', whether the medium in question is a play, a novel, or another 'literary-performative mode of engagement'.[12]

In the essay closing the first section, Alexa Alice Joubin writes as if in response to this invitation. Her reflections on 'The Ethics of Global Shakespeare' are based on a survey of Shakespearean productions – adaptations, appropriations, translations – covering a broad sweep of geographies, languages, national contexts and political-ideological motivations. Joubin asserts that she is less concerned with 'who is more entitled to appropriate a particular culture' and more concerned with the 'deterritorializing effect of global arts': 'Transnational networks of collaboration and funding make it more meaningful to speak of a work's set of reference points rather than singular points of geographical origin.'[13] Nevertheless, she insists that ethical frameworks – 'mutually accepted guidelines on what constitutes a good action' – remain vital and include resisting easy recourse to 'a tacit narrative about how Shakespeare's universal moral values help artists in dire situations', not allowing Shakespeare productions from the Global South to be 'co-opted for their inspirational merit', and querying the Global North's investment in histories that appear to present 'performing or reading Shakespeare as a strategy to set things right': 'Shakespeare to the rescue', from apartheid South Africa to war-torn Afghanistan to diversity-snubbing America, with 'remedial Shakespeare' functioning in both personal (individual) and political (collective) capacities.[14] Instead, Joubin proposes an approach based on an epistemological consideration, one that requires Global Shakespeare practitioners and scholars to be always 'on the lookout for unconscious and discriminatory biases in the production and dissemination of knowledge' and to 'develop site-specific knowledge' based on 'location-specific cultural meanings', even when 'multiple localities are brought together to craft a new narrative'.[15]

Joubin warns us against perpetuating the misapprehension that the 'global' in Global Shakespeare is constituted by 'whatever the US and UK are not'.[16] Indeed, the risk that Global Shakespeare as a field may turn around an all too familiar Anglo-American axis remains constant. When it comes to questions about race, for example, there is a perception of friction (perhaps competition) between American or British scholars and scholars of/in the Global South. The approach of British and American academics to race in the early modern period tends to be filtered through – or expressed through an academic discourse on – race and racism in the Global North. As a result, academics from the Global South might feel that their analysis or even experience of race and racism in early modern studies is once again being marginalized by an imperial centre. But what happens if we place discussions about race (under the rubric of early modern or premodern critical race studies) emanating from or focusing on the United States and the United Kingdom within an already existing framework for considering how histories and legacies of racism merge with Shakespearean histories and legacies – that is, within the framework of what has previously been categorized as postcolonial Shakespeare studies? Distinctions between the Global North and the Global South are blurred in this process, and the United States and the United Kingdom are no longer understood as predominant or exceptional but are instead placed in dialogue with 'the global' in its most broadly construed sense.

This is arguably what occurs in Part II ('Resisting racial logics'), in which Dyese Elliott-Newton, Derrick Higginbotham and Hassana Moosa each draw on recent or contemporary events in Britain and America to facilitate their analyses of the operation of racial logic in *The Merchant of Venice* and the early modern world(s) it represents. Elliott-Newton takes as her starting point the abuse of Charlena Michelle Cooks, who in 2015 was violently arrested despite being pregnant – and whose persecution was premised on her 'monstrousness' and 'non-existence' as a Black woman in America.[17] The essay then turns to medieval and early modern texts (the Old Norse saga *Morkinskinna*, Shakespeare's *Merchant* and Jonson's *Masque of Blackness*) to discern precursors in the centuries-old practice of using the (pregnant) Black woman's body as 'a site of relief' of 'social anxieties', particularly through comedic violence.[18] This comic treatment is understood within the worlds depicted in these texts as a form of instruction via torture, a narrative that

> creates room for the normalization of violence towards certain racialized bodies, while simultaneously justifying the actions of the (white) torturers, by reframing these torturers as protecting themselves from the inherent monstrosity of blackness and other iterations of otherness. Once again, white anxiety provokes, justifies, and perpetuates the torture of non-white bodies.[19]

Higginbotham pursues a similar line of analysis in his discussion of the ways in which 'white fragility' (borrowing from Robin DiAngelo) among the Christian characters in *The Merchant of Venice* is evident in their treatment of Shylock. In this 'comedy of turbulent feelings', the simultaneous 'fragility and fierceness' of Antonio and his allies underscores how anger is tolerated and even encouraged in the behaviour of the (white) Christian Venetians while it is seen in ('dark') Jewish Shylock as evidence of his irredeemable difference.[20] Shylock, the outsider, asserts his similarity to the Christians – and the audience is invited to compare his behaviour to that of, say, Gratiano – but in fact this has the effect of further excluding him, as the play

> sanctions the anger of the white Christian Venetians via this comparative gesture. Their anger can appear more palatable, especially as a response to what they construe as unjust, and it can be productive in its capacity to underscore behaviour that they deem beyond the pale. By contrast, Shylock's 'darkness' characterizes his wildness as being of a different magnitude; this demonstrates the ways that racist thinking instantiates an exclusion that orders the world, determining who can and cannot be justly angry as well as who can and cannot belong.[21]

Moosa focuses on *Merchant*'s depiction of the Prince of Morocco, demonstrating the ways in which Islam is racialized on the early modern stage through an emphasis on putative cultural (rather than religious) characteristics. As with Higginbotham's discussion of Shylock, Moosa's analysis of Morocco's brief but significant role emphasizes the assertion of his 'sameness' – to Portia and to the other suitors – despite his apparent racial 'difference' and shows how, ultimately, the difference is confirmed and reinscribed. The Muslim-Moroccan-Moor nexus is teased out, and Moosa explains that Shakespeare's contemporaries were primed to respond to the Prince according to tropes associated with Islam circulating in Elizabethan England. Crucially, 'Shakespeare's portrayal of the Prince's Muslim identity reflects the early development of a problematic pattern of racializing Islam' – a pattern that persists today, allowing racists and Islamophobes to 'mark Muslims' and to 'enact forms of political and physical violence against them'.[22]

Part III in this collection consists of a pair of essays that engage with Shakespeare in the context of incarceration. Kai Wiegandt presents a new way of approaching what has become a signal point of reference in discussions about 'imagining freedom' with Shakespeare: the Robben Island 'Bible'. This copy of Shakespeare's collected works, circulated in secret among a number of the political prisoners who had been consigned to Robben Island by the apartheid South African government, is a site of contestation between those who seek to identify Shakespeare as part of the anti-apartheid struggle and those who are more cautious about narratives of Shakespeare and liberation. Wiegandt finds an alternative to this impasse by tracing thematic connections between some of the passages alongside which Robben Island inmates signed their names. When understood as reflections on exile and banishment, these passages present themselves in relation to the circumstances on Robben Island, and to South African history, through 're-readings' of Shakespeare that resonate with other (post)colonial 'rewritings'.

Rowan Mackenzie's essay, by contrast, emerges not from historical distance but from present practice; she gives an account of her collaboration with the members of the Gallowfield Players, a cooperative theatre company located in a British prison. In 2019, the Players staged a production of *Julius Caesar* – a play that, Mackenzie notes, found particular purchase in the populist era of Brexit and Trump, although such political overtones were not at the forefront of this project. Rather, the forms of social injustice that the Gallowfield Players seek to address are particular to the needs and aspirations of the members. Mackenzie's approach as Artistic Director of the company is based on the principles of trauma-informed practice, and various forms of trauma are brought into the rehearsal room: the inmates as previously traumatized individuals, the trauma that their crimes have caused, and the experience of imprisonment itself as a form of protracted trauma. In such a situation, Mackenzie acknowledges, 'Shakespeare is not a panacea' – indeed, 'choosing Shakespeare for this work may be seen as an affirmation of his cultural capital, established in a patriarchal, white-dominated culture which has facilitated the development of deeply entrenched social injustices over centuries'.[23] There is thus a risk that Shakespeare lends his authority to compound the hierarchies of incarceration, a mechanism that can perpetuate systemic injustice even as it is a central component of what we loosely refer to as the 'justice system'. Despite this, Mackenzie's essay gives us insights into the affirming experiences of individuals who, through their performance of Shakespeare, 'have been – at some times at least – masters of their own fates'.[24]

Joining the collective call for an end to gender-based violence (GBV), the contributors to Part IV, 'Scrutinizing gender and sexual violence', consider how to approach the staging, teaching and interpretation of Shakespeare's works at a time when GBV and gendered relations of power have been thrown into relief. In 'The "sign and semblance of her honour": Petrarchan slander and gender-based violence in three Shakespearean plays', Kirsten Dey examines Shakespeare's invocation of Petrarchan rhetoric to explore the link between gendered idealization and GBV, phenomena which, she argues, were 'as integral to his age as they are to our own'.[25] Through his creation of disenchanted Petrarchan lovers who either plan or perpetrate violence against their intimate partners, Shakespeare makes a case for justice for women, thereby calling upon his audience – then and now – to take urgent action. Dey proposes that Shakespeare's invocation of the Petrarchan tradition helps to 'reveal the dangers of gendered romantic idealization that is so rigid that the female beloved can be only wholly pure or wholly impure, and easily descend from idealized to despised'.[26] Dey's re-examination of *Much Ado about Nothing*, *Cymbeline* and *Othello* demonstrates how Shakespeare's works can help to expose the strange logics underpinning the long history of violence against women. In effect, the works constitute a call for urgent action, 'then and now'.

Abraham Stoll's essay turns our attention to the 'now' of twenty-first-century dramaturgy that is committed to non-binary praxis. In

'Open-gendered casting in Shakespeare performance', Stoll offers readers insights into what 'open-gendered casting' (as distinct from the older notion of 'cross-gendered' casting) offers to theoretical conceptualizations of gender as 'performative', and what recent gender theory might offer to progressive theatre practice.[27] At a time when the gender binary itself is under question, assumptions about gendered identity within theatre practice need revision. Stoll's essay is exploratory by design. It reflects on the theatre practice of the University of San Diego Shirley Graduate Theater Program and its Old Globe Theater, and the 'transformative' and 'radical' effects of open-gendered casting in enabling an understanding of gender beyond 'drag'.[28] Drawing on the later iteration of Judith Butler's vocabulary of performativity as 'citation', Stoll makes a case for recognizing the theatre as a space of theory, as well as practice: a space where the performativity of gender might be explored with infinite subtlety in the spirit of Butler's later work. At a time when open-gendered casting practice is emerging as normative, Stoll calls for critical reflection on how this can 'become a norm without losing its queer and feminist potential'.[29]

The imperative to place sex and gender in Shakespeare's plays under scrutiny – or to place sex and gender under scrutiny through engaging with Shakespeare's plays – is given new urgency in Wendy Beth Hyman's essay on 'Teaching *Titus Andronicus* and Ovidian myth when sexual violence is on the public stage'. At a time of media saturation with the reality of sexual assault, from the boasts of the former President of the United States and testimony at the trial of a Supreme Court nominee, to a slew of disclosures of historical abuse by high-profile figures across various industries, Hyman's course was scheduled to consider yet another instance of a woman being subjected to brutal sexual violence: Lavinia in *Titus Andronicus*. Hyman shares with readers some of the strategies she adopted to help her students to 'process these awful events while also doing intellectual justice to Shakespeare's plays and the Ovidian myths that inspired them'.[30] Hyman's account does not flinch from the tension emerging from a commitment to the classroom as a space of justice and truth, on the one hand, and as a space of safety and even healing, on the other. How to proceed when, as Hyman puts it, the 'goal of my teaching is . . . not just to do no harm, but to foster the confidence to undo harm'?[31] We are invited to bear witness, along with Hyman and her students, to the possibility that the 'sheer brutality' of a work of literature might enact 'an implicit validation': by making visible the suffering occasioned by violence, it may help to 'spotlight a thing that is too often hidden, suppressed, or denied'.[32] This 'making visible', Hyman suggests, is 'part of the work of revenge tragedy, the extravagant grammar by which it articulates a desire for justice'.[33] And yet to encounter this 'grammar' in the classroom requires particular tools, an attunement to the impact of misogyny and GBV on student experience both in the classroom and outside it, and a willingness to stay the distance. Hyman helps us think through the tools of conscious pedagogy that help to build students' 'resilience and sense of agency', tools that affirm the possibilities of care *and* justice, at a time when the disorder and distress of an unjust world is increasingly visible.[34]

Taken together, the essays in this collection help us to imagine what radical and transformative pedagogy, theatre-making and scholarship might look like. Their authors both invoke and invert the paradigm of Global Shakespeare, building on the vital contributions of this scholarly field over the past few decades but also suggesting ways in which it cannot quite accommodate the various 'global Shakespeares' presented in these pages. A focus on social justice – or, as the title of this collection frames it, on the many forms of social *in*justice that demand our attention – also allows us to reflect on the North/South constructions that have tended to shape Global Shakespeare conceptually, just as the material histories that the terminology of 'North' and 'South' represents have shaped global injustice as we recognize it today. At the same time, such a focus invites us to consider the creative ways in which Shakespeare's imagination has been taken up by theatre-makers and scholars alike, and marshalled in pursuit of a more just world.

Notes

1 See Gauri Viswanathan's *Masks of Conquest: Literary Study and British Rule in India*, the celebrated account of the role of English literature in entrenching colonial hierarchies in India (New York: Columbia University Press, 1989).

2 'The 1619 Project' proposes 1619 as the 'true birth date' of the United States of America, 'the moment that its defining contradictions first came into the world' (4). As envisioned by Nikole Hannah-

Jones, a staff writer at *The New York Times* and recipient of a 2017 MacArthur Award, 'The 1619 Project' is a work of public historiography that seeks to 'place the consequences of slavery and the contributions of black Americans at the very center of the story we tell ourselves about who we are as a country' (5). See the inaugural issue in *The New York Times Magazine* (18 August 2019). Online: https://pulitzercenter.org/sites/default/files/full_issue_of_the_1619 _project.pdf.

3   'Shakespeare and Social Justice' was part of the eleventh triennial congress of the Shakespeare Society of Southern Africa. It was held from 16 to 18 May 2019.

4   Two other publications collect essays and articles that developed out of papers presented at the 'Shakespeare and Social Justice' conference: a special issue of *Shakespeare Bulletin* (39, no. 4, Winter 2021) on 'Shakespeare and Social Justice in Contemporary Performance' edited by David Sterling Brown and Sandra Young; and a special volume of *Shakespeare in Southern Africa* (34, 2021) on 'Shakespeare and Social Justice in South Africa' edited by Chris Thurman.

5   Hillary Eklund and Wendy Beth Hyman (eds), *Teaching Social Justice through Shakespeare: Why Renaissance Literature Matters Now* (Edinburgh: Edinburgh University Press, 2019).

6   David Ruiter (ed.), *The Arden Research Handbook of Shakespeare and Social Justice* (London: Arden, 2020).

7   Susan Bennett, 'Re-thinking "Global Shakespeare" for social justice', pages 27–29 of this book.

8   Bennett, 21.

9   Bennett, 30.

10 Linda Gregerson, 'Caliban in an era of mass migration', 36–37.

11 Gregerson, 55.

12 Gregerson, 55.

13 Alexa Alice Joubin, 'What makes Global Shakespeares an exercise in ethics?', 61.

14 Joubin, 62, 65–66.

15 Joubin, 72.

16 Joubin, 71.

17 Dyese Elliott-Newton, 'Making whiteness out of "nothing"', 82.

18 Elliott-Newton, 83.

19 Elliott-Newton, 94.

20 Derrick Higginbotham, 'Feeling in justice', 102 and 110.
21 Higginbotham, 114.
22 Hassana Moosa, 'Marking Muslims', 135.
23 Rowan Mackenzie, '"Men at some times are masters of their fates"', 169.
24 Mackenzie, 179.
25 Kirsten Dey, 'The "sign and semblance of her honour"', 190.
26 Dey, 204.
27 Abraham Stoll, 'Open-gendered casting in Shakespeare performance', 209.
28 Stoll, 216–18.
29 Stoll, 225.
30 Wendy Beth Hyman, 'Teaching *Titus Andronicus* and Ovidian myth when sexual violence is on the public stage', 231.
31 Hyman, 233.
32 Hyman, 232.
33 Hyman, 238.
34 Hyman, 242.

PART I

Scholarship and social justice

Questions for the field

1

Re-thinking 'Global Shakespeare' for social justice

Susan Bennett

'Global Shakespeare' has developed as a significant and flourishing presence in the larger field of Shakespeare studies, a concept familiar not only to scholars writing essays, chapters and books but commonly used to title classes taught in English, theatre and drama departments across the English-speaking world and even beyond. At the same time, Global Shakespeare has also been widely adopted as a marketing category for performances seen outside their country of origin and as a register of appeal to a sought-after diversity of cultural consumers. Yet this sub-field of Shakespeare studies is, in many ways, still relatively new and all the more remarkable for the velocity and traction of its development. It is, of course, essential to the health of any disciplinary area that scholarly perspectives and emphases change over time, but I would be hard-pressed to name another focus within Shakespeare studies which has become so influential and has achieved this, academically speaking at least, as quickly. What I want to address here, then, is the emergence of Global Shakespeare at the end of the twentieth century and how this sub-field has come to be produced and understood. In the context of its history to date, I will propose some new protocols for thinking about Global Shakespeare, ones that I hope might sharpen our collective focus on matters of social justice.

Global Shakespeare found its scholarly inspiration, I suggest, in Dennis Kennedy's 1993 volume *Foreign Shakespeare* – a collection that was the first to consider performances in non-English-language theatres (almost all in Western and Eastern European countries, with a single essay, by an American academic, looking at Shakespeare and the Japanese stage). In the very first sentence of the book's introduction, Kennedy appears to anticipate a surprise, if not negative, reaction to his subject. He starts: 'Foreign Shakespeare? The moderately impertinent title of this volume implies a perspective on Shakespeare's stature, and on his place in world culture, which is normally obscured in the academic and theatrical enterprises that have adopted his name.'[1] Perhaps even more importantly, in an Afterword to the contributors' various accounts of non-English-language Shakespeare in performance, Kennedy specifically challenges the Anglocentrism of critical approaches dominant in Shakespearean interpretation. In other words, as a prelude to the development and expansion of a Global Shakespeare, *Foreign Shakespeare* set the parameters for future engagement, encompassing increased attention to contemporary performance and critical practices from across the world. What has followed in the twenty-five years or so since Kennedy's volume first appeared created Global Shakespeare as a broadly recognizable descriptive and organizational category. Global Shakespeare has become commonly understood not just as a topic for scholarly research but as a range of practices found on the stage, on screen, in other digital and print media and, increasingly, in the secondary and post-secondary classroom. In light of this rapid growth as well as an increasing familiarity with scholarly and performance examples that illustrate the term, it is timely, I think, to better calibrate its scope and usage as well as to outline in fuller detail the conditions of its formation. In this way, we might proceed with a more nuanced awareness of what exactly it is that has been booked for our stages, described in criticism and reviews, and archived in actual and virtual libraries in the guise of Global Shakespeare. Moreover, we might more carefully attend to how designating a critical or creative work part of the Global Shakespeare project determines, even overdetermines, its reception.

To start, then, in 1993: Kennedy's book was a field changer. It brought new recognition to how many productions of Shakespeare's plays could be found worldwide and in many languages far removed from the source English as well as from the Western European translations that had long been recognized and circulated (such as evidenced in the robust histories of Shakespeare scholarship and performance in France and Germany). Kennedy's volume stimulated a flurry of commissioned publications, usually crafted with the aim of introducing 'Shakespeare in [here fill in the name of a country or continent not previously considered and almost always non-English-speaking]'. Indeed, much scholarship claiming a place within the Global Shakespeare rubric continues to inhabit such single-country or single-continent critical silos. Two recent collections – Bruce Smith's magisterial *Cambridge Guide to the Worlds of Shakespeare* (2016) and Jill Levenson and Robert Ormsby's *The Shakespearean World* (2017) – offer examples that demonstrate this principle: in Smith, Alfredo Michel Modenessi's 'Shakespeare in Iberian and Latin American Spanishes' and Veronika Schandl's 'Shakespeare in Eastern Europe'; in Levenson and Ormsby, Margaret Litvin, Avraham Oz and Parviz Partovi's 'Middle Eastern Shakespeares' and Sandra Young's 'Shakespeare in Africa'. This is not at all to suggest that essays like these are other than valuable – rather, they go a long way to providing us with an archive that was for far too long unknown, neglected, or obscured (the very point that Kennedy made in *Foreign Shakespeare*). But I want to argue here that the sub-field of Global Shakespeare cannot merely content itself to keep contemporary this burgeoning archive of scholarship within Shakespeare studies, coupled with better records of productions from the Western world's elsewheres. This is a proposition to which I'll return.

The republication of *Foreign Shakespeare* in 2004, more than a decade after its first appearance, signalled both the book's impact and ongoing influence as well as Kennedy's place as the leading authority on Shakespeare outside the English-speaking world. His 'Shakespeare Worldwide' was included in the nineteen chapters comprising *The Cambridge Companion to Shakespeare*, edited by Margareta de Grazia and Stanley Wells (2001); other contributors to the volume addressed twentieth-century performance (Peter Holland) and cinematic adaptations (Russell Jackson) in only Anglocentric contexts, underscoring the idea that non-English-language Shakespeare was Kennedy's responsibility alone. At more or less the same time as *Foreign Shakespeare* appeared in its new paperback version, Barbara Hodgdon and W. B. Worthen's *A*

Companion to Shakespeare and Performance (2005) broke new ground in establishing performance as another significant and thoroughly legitimate concentration within the field of Shakespeare studies. Yet it is striking to realize now that the Hodgdon and Worthen volume (made up of thirty-four chapters) included only three that considered performance practices beyond the English-speaking world: one looked at *Othello* in India (Ania Loomba's 'Shakespeare and the Possibilities of Postcolonial Performance') and two turned their attention to Shakespeare and the intercultural (Yong Li Lan's 'Shakespeare and the Fiction of the Intercultural' and Joanne Tompkins' 'Conflicting Fields of Vision: Performing Self and Other in Two Intercultural Shakespeare Productions').

The first edition of *The Oxford Companion to Shakespeare* (2001) made no reference at all to the global; however, its second edition (2015) advertised 'Many new entries on the interpretation of Shakespeare's work in different countries and cultures, including Finland, Turkey, and Ukraine, as well as a lengthy essay on global Shakespeare', testament to the fact that the sub-field has, by this date, earned its place in an authoritative reference text.[2] In fact, global and the other words with which it typically interacts – local, worldwide, international, 'glocal', among them – are now commonplace modifiers in the discussion of contemporary performances of Shakespeare's plays. A case in point, James Bulman's *The Oxford Handbook of Shakespeare and Performance* (2017), the natural successor to Hodgdon and Worthen's earlier collection, is divided into four parts and devotes one – its largest – to Global Shakespeare. This section comprises twelve original essays on performances spanning Africa, Latin America and Asia, as well as several discussions of contemporary critical debates about the category. Since 2014, Alexa Alice Joubin has edited a Global Shakespeares series for Palgrave Macmillan: four monographs have been published to date and cover geographically specific topics in Australia, Cold-War Europe, the Arabian Peninsula and South Africa. Even the British Library has developed a webpage devoted to the subject of Global Shakespeare: 'Discover how Shakespeare's work was influenced by other cultures, and how in turn it's been interpreted in other nations over 400 years.' Significantly, the Library's description suggests how this critical sub-field has grown its ambit beyond the contemporary (the timeframe imposed by *Foreign Shakespeare*), tracking back through history to encompass interactions between Shakespeare's works and the world since the reign of Elizabeth I. As Laura Estill wrote in a 2014 essay: 'Although there is currently "much ado about" global Shakespeare studies, this field has been thriving for decades – even centuries.'[3] Thus, Global Shakespeare has loosened its emphasis on the contemporary and has become just as likely to swivel backwards in history to Elizabethan England, in the claim that Global Shakespeare was always already inscribed in colonial ambition.

The primer on Global Shakespeare prepared for the second edition of *The Oxford Companion to Shakespeare*, authored by Alexa Joubin [Huang], provides a usefully nuanced explanation of the term. She explains that the 'word "global" in global Shakespeare does double duty: it is an attributive genitive naming the stakeholder and playwright of the Globe Theatre, and it is a descriptive adjective signalling the influence and significance of that theatre and of Shakespeare. Shakespeare became both an author of the Globe and a playwright of global stature'.[4] Thus, the concept of Global Shakespeare is understood as produced by the binarized relationship of its two compositional terms. As critical theory has taught us about binaries, one word in the pair typically displays its confident power even as it requires its other in order to do so. In such a way, Huang's definition of global serves to elucidate and confirm the power of Shakespeare in his own time and since. The dynamism of meaning-making endemic to binaries has been more fully explicated by Judith Butler: 'The effort to *include* "Other" cultures as variegated amplifications of a global phallogocentrism constitutes an appropriative act that risks a repetition of the self-aggrandizing gesture of phallogocentrism, colonizing under the sign of the same those differences that might otherwise call that totalizing concept into question.'[5] In the case of the category of Global Shakespeare, viewed through this Butlerian lens, Shakespeare performs as 'that totalizing concept'. He is the field writ large, the cultural giant, the author of universally recognized plots, the most often produced playwright throughout history and today, the cinema's most prolific screenwriter, the figurehead of the English literary canon, the man who shares his birthday with England's patron saint, and perhaps that country's most reliable tourism generator. It is not at all surprising, then, that so much Global Shakespeare scholarship adheres overtly to the Shakespearean (phallogo)centre, as illustrated by essay titles such as Andrew Dickson's 'From Globe to Global' (2015), Sarah Dustagheer and Aleksandra Sakowska's 'Global Shakespeare for Anglophone Audiences' (2014) and Aneta Mancewicz's 'From Global London to Global Shakespeare' (2018).[6]

The volume *Shakespeare Beyond English* that I coedited with Christie Carson also participated in this exercise of assuming Anglocentric authority. The project asserted the importance of memorializing a six-week, complete works programme, the Globe to Globe Festival, held at Shakespeare's Globe in 2012 as part of London's Olympic Games celebrations. The event drew its distinctiveness from the fact that all the plays were staged in languages other than English and by theatre companies from as far away as the South Sudan and Brazil. Our editors' introduction to *Shakespeare Beyond English* made much of the excitement that non-English-speaking language communities living in London brought to seeing their 'national' productions in Shakespeare's own theatre (not everyone knows or is willing to recognize that the venue is a replica). But, at the same time, we emphasized the 'dangers that an enthusiastic and celebratory mode mask[ed] continuing inequities both locally and abroad'.[7] Dennis Kennedy offered an even harsher review of the Globe to Globe Festival, suggesting it demonstrated 'a cavalier approach to the idea of global Shakespeare': 'the Globe, claiming to be the Shakespearean centre, authenticated foreign Shakespeare; the individual companies went home with the cultural capital of having been centrally authenticated. That's not globalism so much as late-model cultural colonialism.'[8]

Kennedy's point of view was more than justified, given that the Shakespeare's Globe own company set out on a world tour not long thereafter (April 2014), taking their portable production of *Hamlet* to 197 countries over the next 2 years in a gesture they saw as sustaining Shakespeare's status as always already global. To illustrate the Globe to Globe *Hamlet* in its place in history, Dominic Dromgoole (then artistic director of Shakespeare's Globe) imagined the project as belonging to four centuries of a global Shakespeare:

> In 1608, only eight years after it was written, Hamlet was performed on a boat – the Red Dragon – off the coast of Yemen. Just ten years later it was being toured extensively all over Northern Europe. The spirit of touring, and of communicating

stories to fresh ears, was always central to Shakespeare's work. We couldn't be happier to be extending that mission ever further.[9]

As Joubin has written, the Red Dragon story has been widely debunked although '[e]nthusiasts of Shakespeare may very much want the anecdote to be true, as it encapsulates a dreamscape in which Shakespeare is making a difference'.[10] Dromgoole's enthusiasm for this 'dreamscape' is palpable in his conclusion that 'no country or people are not better off for the lively presence of Hamlet' (Globe to Globe). This speaks, certainly, to his belief in the project but it also underscores how the cultural power of Shakespeare – and England – is sustained even when, as Andrew Dickson has rightly and wryly commented, 'sending a British company on a world tour with the British empire's favoured playwright might come across as a touch neo-colonial – especially given they play in Jacobean English, usually without surtitles, and don't collaborate with local companies.'[11]

At more or less the same time as the Shakespeare's Globe tour of *Hamlet*, the Royal Shakespeare Company (RSC) was heralding its own international tour. Their initiative sent productions of Shakespeare's history plays to China, a cultural 'exchange' that saw the RSC supported by partnerships with the American bank and financial services company J.P. Morgan, German car manufacturer Mercedes Benz, Swiss luxury watch maker Rolex and the Bank of China, among others – an alliance between globally recognized prestige brands and the cultural icons of the RSC and Shakespeare, intimating shared value in the twenty-first-century consumer marketplace. The British government also provided support for the RSC's China tour via a £1.5 million contribution towards a new translation of Shakespeare's complete works into Mandarin. In the words of then UK culture secretary Sajid Javid,

> Creating stronger links with China is a top priority for the government and sharing the very best of our respective cultures is a brilliant way to make this happen. This funding means Western and Eastern cultures can learn from and be enriched by one another and what better way than using the works of Shakespeare. The package marks a really important step for both China and the UK to grow a strong and progressive relationship.[12]

Then Chancellor George Osborne also noted on the same occasion that 'Shakespeare is one of our greatest cultural exports' and 'the Globe is touring a *Midsummer Night's Dream* in China as I speak'.[13] The Sino-British relationships promoted by UK government officials demonstrate how Global Shakespeare has increasingly been instrumentalized to serve world markets. Javid proposed Shakespeare as both a model and a tool that can be deployed to encourage and activate other and more lucrative economic trade and outcomes. Thus, it is palpably important that the Shakespeare brand remains carefully controlled and marketed by powerful UK entities that include the British Council, the RSC, Shakespeare's Globe and the BBC, along with English educational institutions and programming.

At the same time, however, attachment to the proven cultural-economic value of the Shakespeare brand certainly exceeds the confines of the UK. This is amply illustrated by the hundreds of Shakespeare festivals that take place worldwide each year, the continuing proliferation of productions and adaptations of his works in varieties of media, and the sheer volume of Shakespeare-based publications from popular to scholarly – for example, Laura Estill notes that each Shakespeare play 'has 38 books and articles written about it per year'.[14] A potent illustration of the contemporary profitability of Shakespeare comes in the fierce competition for sales of editions of his work, including, among very many others, the prestigious *Norton Shakespeare* aimed at the undergraduate student and Bloomsbury's Arden Shakespeare, that the publisher promotes as having set 'the gold standard for editing and publication of Shakespeare's plays' for over 100 years.[15]

In this arena of publication, nourishment of the Global Shakespeare sub-field has proven increasingly important to and coincident with developments in teaching in secondary and post-secondary institutions not just in the UK but also in other English-language nations such as the United States, Canada and Australia. The history of Global Shakespeare I have outlined here has meshed seamlessly with an emergent imperative to diversify the curriculum and, more recently, the materialization of a call to decolonize Shakespeare.[16] It is no wonder that an expanded archive of Shakespeare productions drawn from all over the world has appeared to fit the bill. In particular, the availability of non-English-language performances – occasionally seen live by way of touring productions on theatre stages and at festivals, but more typically encountered via digital platforms such as MIT's Global Shakespeare, Digital Theatre+, the Asian Shakespeare Intercultural Archive (A-S-I-A) and Globe Player[17] – has facilitated these curricular ambitions. A newly invigorated, if not entirely liberated, classroom subject can utilize the case study examples the archives provide, buttressed by the robust output of Global Shakespeare scholarship.

For research and teaching, the World Shakespeare Bibliography (WSB), online since 2001, offers another indispensable resource as it indexes 'all important books, articles, book reviews, dissertations, theatrical productions, reviews of productions, audiovisual materials, electronic media, and other scholarly and popular materials related to Shakespeare'. That the WSB is not restricted to English-language entries has made it all the more foundational to the development of Global Shakespeare studies. WSB's coverage extends 'to more than 120 languages' and represents 'every country in North America, South America, and Europe, and nearly every country in Asia, Africa, and Australasia' (World Shakespeare Bibliography),[18] even as this inclusiveness serves to highlight that the vast majority of Shakespeare's global appearances in contemporary cultural production take place in the English language. Moreover, the WSB is restricted by access to a paid subscription. In common with digital performance archives, use of the bibliography is also fully dependent upon the availability of relevant technology and permissions as well as reliable bandwidth – conditions that are most likely to prevail in first-world educational institutions.

Given the vigour with which Global Shakespeare now circulates, and especially in the context of the purposes assigned to it within educational practices, it is timely to ask whether the category is itself in need of decolonization. Traditionally defined, Global Shakespeare too easily offers the English-speaking world opportunities to act as consumers and collectors of the exotic Other, extending still an Anglocentric and colonialist gaze on non-English-language examples of those who do things with Shakespeare.[19] Recognizing the alignment of Global Shakespeare with 400 years of history as well as with practices of colonialism, it is useful to include in my discussion here an analogous categorical term, Postcolonial Shakespeare. Like Kennedy's *Foreign Shakespeare*, criticism under this rubric was chiefly antecedent to the widespread uptake of a Global Shakespeare.

The turn to postcoloniality and Shakespeare had its beginnings in Ania Loomba and Martin Orkin's appropriately named *Postcolonial Shakespeares*, a collection published in 1998, and in Loomba's valuable essay on 'Shakespeare and the Possibilities of Postcolonial Performance', one of the three chapters in the Hodgdon and Worthen volume (2005) that looked outside the English-speaking world of Shakespearean production. The prompt for thinking about such possibilities was, I suspect, not only the experience or evidence of 'foreign' performance practices that Kennedy had promoted but even more so the burgeoning development of postcolonial theory and literature in English departments, inspired by the critical work of Gayatri Spivak, Edward Said, Frantz Fanon and others. An important topic for postcolonial literary scholarship was, not unexpectedly, the prominent role Shakespeare's oeuvre had played in the imposition of an English educational system on colonized peoples (brilliantly exposed in Gauri Viswanathan's *Masks of Conquest: Literary Study and British Rule in India*).[20] Loomba, Orkin and other postcolonial critics radically challenged the Anglocentrism of cultural materialist and New Historicist discourses within mainstream Shakespeare studies and amplified the long-lasting oppressive effects produced by the dissemination of Shakespeare's works across the colonized world. Postcolonial Shakespeares (deliberately plural), in a challenge to the status quo, illuminated practices that demonstrated little reverence for the Shakespearean centre and commonly saw Shakespeare's texts as blueprints for acts of resistance rather than subjects for devotion. Among other things, the study of postcolonial Shakespeare widened the geographic lens not just beyond England but beyond the largely Eurocentric focus in *Foreign Shakespeare*. Jyotsna Singh usefully captures this scope in her definition of postcolonial Shakespeare as an 'academic study of the cultural legacy of European colonialism'.[21]

By the beginning of the twenty-first century, however, the limits of postcolonial theories had been ably summarized by critics such as Michael Hardt and Antonio Negri. They argued that the postcolonial 'is entirely insufficient for theorizing contemporary global power'.[22] And the expansion of Indigenous Studies in Australia, New Zealand, Canada and the United States underscored that these countries were, even today, far from postcolonial. Thus, the merger of studies of putatively postcolonial Shakespeares into a seemingly more expansive category of Global Shakespeare not only respected trends in critical theory but also held out the promise of a more politically attuned set of interests – that scholars, teachers, theatre companies and professionals could set their work among a fuller range of contemporary artistic and critical practices worldwide. In this context, Singh describes the transformation of the study of postcolonial Shakespeare into a focus on 'global/local inter-cultural encounters' as 'a *legacy* of postcoloniality', even as the same vocabulary of critique continues 'to inform recent engagements within global, inter-cultural contexts'.[23]

As I've already suggested, the categorical move to the global has continued to reify the centre of Shakespeare (whether in critical studies, performance or curriculum) in England and the English language (lest we forget that the very many essays about Shakespeare in [non-English-language countries] are largely published in English). At the same time, performances acclaimed by Global Shakespeare critics (both within and outside the academy) are not typically valued for the translation of Shakespeare's texts into another language but for their display of aesthetic styles and cultural differences. I think here of the particular popularity of some Asian adaptations, including the National Theatre of China's *Richard III*, the Yohangza Theatre Company's *A Midsummer Night's Dream* and Vishal Bhardwaj's film adaptations of *Macbeth*, *Othello* and *Hamlet*. Indeed, Global Shakespeare could be fairly accused of practising an aesthetic colonialism that requires performances to surprise and thrill in how different they look but at the same time remain fully legible to Western audiences, critics and students familiar with the source Shakespeare text. As Seokhun Choi has trenchantly noted, to meet their audiences, these productions must '"show" rather than "talk"'.[24]

This begs the question, then, of how a decolonized (Global) Shakespeare might talk? How could the category of Global Shakespeare be reanimated in ways that destabilize its history so far? What new criteria might exceed those crafted by aesthetic, dramaturgical and broadly cultural practices? How can Global Shakespeare be dislodged from the grip of England, Anglocentrism and the English-language centre? To propose one possible response to these questions, let me return to Huang's definition in the second edition of *The Oxford Companion to Shakespeare* where the 'word "global" in global Shakespeare does double duty' in modifying the term's proper noun, Shakespeare. This double duty of 'global' to sustain the provenance of the Globe Theatre of the early seventeenth century and to assert the place of Shakespeare worldwide might be replaced with a focus on the term's own history. Specifically, we might turn to a definition that comes into common use in the mid-nineteenth century (not coincidentally the apex of European colonialism): the meaning that emerged in this period, according to the *Oxford English Dictionary*, was 'relating to, or involving the whole world'. If 'global' can be disentangled from its function(s) in modifying Shakespeare and instead granted at least a correspondence in value to the proper noun, then the weight of meaning that has historically too readily accrued to 'Shakespeare' might shift. In other words, this Global Shakespeare would be relevant to and driven by properly global issues, with Shakespeare in a more supporting role in illustrating any one or all of them. Such a Global Shakespeare archive would, then, not always be arranged around nation or expressions of cultural difference but could pivot towards examples 'involving the whole world'. This is the arrangement that Hillary Eklund and Wendy Beth Hyman proposed in their volume *Teaching Social Justice through Shakespeare*, where they helpfully set the stakes by noting 'each of us must also use our expertise to promote justice in more direct ways'.[25] New modes of Global Shakespeare interpretation, they suggest, would foster 'an expanded understanding of justice, one that resists the subjection and instrumentalization of learning and intellectual exchange' rather than simply invigorate discourses of Shakespearean interpretation.[26] In other words, Global Shakespeare would become the occasion to address human rights, climate crisis, language preservation, equitable access to health care and action towards more participatory democracy.

After twenty-five years of Global Shakespeare activities within the scholarly field and on (Western) stages and screens, this kind of critical stock-taking allows us to imagine what more the category might achieve and to insist that Global Shakespeare become more readily capacious. I have taken to heart an observation Katherine Steele Brokaw makes in her otherwise enthusiastic review of *The Oxford Handbook of Shakespeare and Performance*. She notes: 'there is no mention of eco-theater, of Deaf or other differently abled performers, or of several other kinds of marginal and community-based Shakespearean performance.'[27] Yet I know, as she does, that this kind of work happens globally. To take but one of the too-often ignored areas from Brokaw's list: the ASL (American Sign Language) Shakespeare Project has been active at Yale University since its launch in 1999; London's Deafinitely Theatre staged a British Sign Language production of *Love's Labour's Lost* at the 2012 Globe to Globe Festival; and Mexico's Seña y Verbo (Sign and Verb) theatre presented a sign language adaptation of *Romeo and Juliet* in 2016, which led to 'the signing of a historic MoU [Memorandum of Understanding] with the Institute of Social Security for Employees in Mexico (ISSSTE) to create an Arts and Disability programme together'.[28] *Teenage Dick*, Mike Lew's critically successful adaptation of *Richard III* (seen in New York, London and Chicago productions), exposed the rarity of seeing disabled actors on mainstream stages or in Shakespearean performances.[29] The lead character in Lew's play has been represented by actors with cerebral palsy and hemiplegia; his friend Buck (Buckingham) uses a wheelchair; the director of the 2020 Theater Wit (Chicago) production is also identified as disabled. Jenny Sealey, the artistic director of London's Graeae (a company that defines itself as 'a force for change in world-class theatre, boldly placing D/deaf and disabled actors centre stage') collaborated over several years with the Dhaka Theatre of Bangladesh to produce in 2016 *A Different Romeo and Juliet*, a performance by deaf and disabled actors that has since been filmed for national distribution. Even this limited evidence suggests what we too easily ignore and asks how Global Shakespeare scholars and students can bring their expertise and enthusiasm to support and encourage worldwide networks of theatres concerned with disability rights.

Instead of constructing a canon of favoured Global Shakespeare performances, we must rigorously seek out a fuller range of productions involving the whole world and, in that work, continuously track what we include and who we leave out. The history I have outlined here demonstrates how we in the West have profited from engagements with Global Shakespeare performances. It is now time to reciprocate. If Global Shakespeare is 'a field in which issues of appropriation, representation, and power are central', then we are obliged to confront our own considerable privilege and recognize a responsibility to reflect, engage and nourish those whose labour has created the objects of our study.[30] The challenge is to think anew about Global Shakespeare and to focus more effectively on those performances that enlist Shakespeare's plays to speak to the most pressing issues of the contemporary world. At the same time as the Global Shakespeare archive must become more inclusive, Global Shakespeare methodologies must be driven by a shared commitment to decolonize scholarly, theatrical and pedagogical practices.

In a poignant Afterword to *Teaching Social Justice through Shakespeare*, Ayanna Thompson challenges scholars, teaching units, colleges and institutions to do better in matters of what she calls communal care. To foster this work, she asks:

> What about our professional organizations? ... How can we build alliances with others doing this kind of work: medievalists, critical race scholars, education specialists, theater practitioners, and so on? If we manage to build these alliances, how can we sustain them? And how can we get our extra-institutional research centers ... to support this kind of work?[31]

In a similar vein, re-thinking Global Shakespeare provides the opportunity to care about social justice; it is our collective responsibility to work out exactly how this happens.

Notes

1 Dennis Kennedy, *Foreign Shakespeare: Contemporary Performance* (Cambridge: Cambridge University Press, 1993), 1.

2 Oxford Reference. Available online: https://www.oxfordreference.com/view/10.1093/acref/9780198708735.001.0001/acref-9780198708735 (accessed 20 March 2021).

3 Laura Estill, 'Digital Bibliography and Global Shakespeare', *Scholarly and Research Communication* 5, no. 4 (2014): 2.

4 Alexa Huang, 'Global Shakespeare', in *The Oxford Companion to Shakespeare*, 2nd edition, ed. Michael Dobson et al., Oxford Reference. Online (accessed 20 March 2021).

5 Judith Butler, *Gender Trouble: Feminism and the Subversion of Identity* (New York: Routledge, 1990), 13. Emphasis in original.

6 See Andrew Dickson, 'From Globe to Global: A Shakespeare Voyage Around the World', *The Guardian*, 25 September 2015. Available online: https://www.theguardian.com/books/2015/sep/25/

shakespeare-world-anti-apartheid-hero-nazi-favourite-bollywood (accessed 20 March 2021); Sarah Dustagheer and Aleksandra Sakowska, 'Introduction: Global Shakespeare for Anglophone Audiences', *Multicultural Shakespeare: Translation, Appropriation and Performance* 11, no. 26 (2014): 9–16; and Aneta Mancewicz, 'From Global London to Global Shakespeare', *Contemporary Theatre Review* 28, no. 2 (2018): 235–46.

7 Susan Bennett and Christie Carson, eds, *Shakespeare Beyond English* (Cambridge: Cambridge University Press, 2013), 4.

8 Dennis Kennedy, 'Globalized Performance', in *The Oxford Handbook of Shakespeare and Performance*, ed. James C. Bulman (Oxford: Oxford University Press, 2017), 450–3.

9 Globe to Globe Hamlet, 'About the Project', n.d. Available online: http://globetoglobe.shakespearesglobe.com/hamlet/about-the-project (accessed 20 March 2021).

10 Alexa Alice Joubin, 'Global Shakespeare Criticism Beyond the Nation State', in *The Oxford Handbook of Shakespeare and Performance*, ed. James C. Bulman (Oxford: Oxford University Press), 428.

11 Andrew Dickson, 'Hamlet, Globe to Globe by Dominic Dromgoole Review – Neocolonial Folly?', *The Guardian*, 14 April 2017. Available online: https://www.theguardian.com/books/2017/apr/14/hamlet-globe-to-globe-dominic-dromgoole-review-shakespeare (accessed 20 March 2021).

12 Gov.uk, 'UK takes Shakespeare to New Audience of one Billion People in China', 12 September 2014. Available online: https://www.gov.uk/government/news/uk-takes-shakespeare-to-new-audience-of-one-billion-people-in-china (accessed 20 March 2021).

13 See my essay 'Experimental Shakespeare' in Bulman, *Shakespeare and Performance*, 13–27, where I offer a more extended argument on the colonial impulses of these relationships and expand differently on the impacts of Javid's political speech in promoting Sino-British trade.

14 Estill, 'Digital Bibliography and Global Shakespeare', 9.

15 Arden Shakespeare, n.d. Available online: https://www.bloomsbury.com/academic/academic-subjects/drama-and-performance-studies/the-arden-shakespeare/ (accessed 20 March 20221).

16 See, for example, Katherine Gillen and Lisa Jennings, 'Decolonizing Shakespeare? Toward an Antiracist, Culturally Sustaining Practice', *The Sundial*, 26 November 2019. Available online: https://medium.com/the-sundial-acmrs/decolonizing-shakespeare-toward-an-antiracist-culturally-sustaining-praxis-904cb9ff8a96; three essays

in the 'Decolonizing Shakespeare' section of Hillary Eklund and Wendy Beth Hyman's *Teaching Social Justice through Shakespeare* (Edinburgh: Edinburgh University Press, 2019); and Maev Kennedy's report in *The Guardian* on decolonizing the English literature curriculum at Cambridge and other British universities, 'Cambridge academics seek to "decolonise" English syllabus', 25 October 2017. Available online: https://www.theguardian.com/education/2017/oct/25/cambridge-academics-seek-to-decolonise-english-syllabus (accessed 20 March 2021).

17 MIT's Global Shakespeare and A-S-I-A are free to use; Digital Theatre+ and Globe Player charge for rental/purchase of productions.

18 The WSB started out in 1960 as a single essay and has subsequently transferred to other formats (an issue of *Shakespeare Quarterly*, 1965; annual print volumes, until 2001; a CD-ROM, first available in 1996; online since 2001). For a comprehensive history of the WSB, see Estill, 'Digital Bibliography and Global Shakespeare'.

19 This is a point I make more broadly in consideration of what passes as 'experimental' Shakespeare. See my essay in Bulman, *Shakespeare and Performance*, 17.

20 See Gauri Viswanathan, *Masks of Conquest: Literary Study and British Rule in India* (New York: Columbia University Press, 1989).

21 Jyotsna G. Singh, *Shakespeare and Postcolonial Theory* (London: Bloomsbury Publishing, 2019), 3.

22 Michael Hardt and Antonio Negri, *Empire* (Cambridge, MA: Harvard University Press, 2000), 146.

23 Singh, *Shakespeare and Postcolonial Theory*, 129 (emphasis in original).

24 Seokhun Choi, '*Pansori Hamlet Project*: Taroo's New *Pansori* Shakespeare for the Local Audience', *Asian Theatre Journal* 36, no. 2 (Fall 2019): 352.

25 Eklund and Hyman, *Teaching Social Justice through Shakespeare*, 2.

26 Ibid., 9.

27 Katherine Steele Brokaw, review of *The Oxford Handbook of Shakespeare and Performance*, ed. James C. Bulman, *Shakespeare Quarterly* 70, no. 2 (Summer 2019): 170.

28 British Council, 'Shakespeare Lives in sign language theatre in Mexico', n.d. Available online: https://www.britishcouncil.ca/programmes/we-are-diverse/mexico (accessed 20 March 2021). Peter Novak's 'Signing Shakespeare (ASL)', in *The Cambridge Guide to the*

Worlds of Shakespeare, Volume 2, ed. Bruce R. Smith (Cambridge: Cambridge University Press), 1357–61 addresses, among other things, the history of ASL performances of Shakespeare's plays.

29 Theater Wit's production of *Teenage Dick* was curtailed by Covid-19 restrictions, so the company moved the play's 12-week run online, offering 98 tickets for each show – with the potential, then, for it to be seen by a global rather than a local Chicago audience.
30 Singh, *Shakespeare and Postcolonial Theory*, 127.
31 Ayanna Thompson, 'An Afterword about Self/Communal Care', in Eklund and Hyman, *Teaching Social Justice through Shakespeare*, 238.

2

Caliban in an era of mass migration

Linda Gregerson

In tandem with the scholarly field of postcolonialism there has emerged and continues to emerge a rich series of Shakespearean reimaginings by poets, novelists, dramatists, performance and visual artists, many of these centred around the figure of Caliban. Martinican Aimé Césaire's *A Tempest* (1969), Barbadian George Lamming's *Water with Berries* (1971), Barbadian Edward Kamau Brathwaite's 'Caliban' (1973), Sierra Leonean Lemuel Johnson's *Highlife for Caliban* (1974), Cherokee artist Jimmie Durham's *The Caliban Codex* (1992), Englishwoman Marina Warner's *Indigo* (1992) and French Canadian Robert LePage's First Nations production of *The Tempest* (2011) are but a few of the myriad examples that might be adduced[1]. Alternately construed as an African slave, an indigene, a poet and a rightful heir to nature and her bounties, Caliban has been configured time and again as a distillate figure of resistance to the depredations and oblivions of colonial subjection. These repurposings have profoundly enriched but by no means exhausted our meditations on power and its differentials in the Shakespearean canon. Can Shakespeare also give us leverage on the current phase of empire and its aftermath? Where is Caliban in an era of intensifying mass migration? Whose claims to sustenance and safety will be honoured? Who actively maintains the systems that deny such claims?

When the United Nations Refugee Agency[2] last updated its figures, in June of 2022, its statisticians estimated the number of forcibly displaced persons on the planet to be 89.3 million. Of these, 53.2 million were internally displaced persons, 27.1 million were refugees, more than 40 per cent of them under the age of eighteen, and 4.6 million were asylum seekers. Climate change, conflict, hunger, poverty and persecution have forced more than 1 per cent of the human beings on earth to leave their homes, more than double the 42.7 million who were forcibly displaced a decade ago.[3] Nothing suggests that this year's figures will present a more comforting picture. The global coronavirus pandemic and recent disruptions to food supplies have dramatically increased the vulnerability of migrant populations, and we have yet to see the true scale of displacements caused by climate change.

The Tempest too is haunted by displaced persons. Before their fates intersected on an island, ostensibly situated somewhere between the African and Italian mainlands but infused with tropes of European encounters in the New World, Sycorax had been exiled from Algiers, Prospero from Milan. Claribel, according to her uncle, has been 'banished' (2.1.122)[4] to Tunis, outside the bounds of known civilization. And this most recent exile is haunted by another, as Gonzalo's contributions to courtly praise remind us:

ADRIAN	Tunis was never graced before with such a paragon to their queen.
GONZALO	Not since widow Dido's time.
...	
ADRIAN	'Widow Dido', said you? You make me study of that. She was of Carthage, not Tunis.
GONZALO	This Tunis, sir, was Carthage.
ADRIAN	Carthage?
ANTONIO	I assure you, Carthage.

(*The Tempest*, 2.1.76–87)

Gonzalo is only partly confused. Tunis is not Carthage, not quite, but the two were closely linked in both ancient and early modern periods. Tunis was one of the first North African towns to fall under Carthaginian control in the first millennium BCE. By Shakespeare's era, both had been subsumed by the Ottomans. The Dido of legend was indeed a widow, though not originally 'of Carthage'. Born and raised in the Phoenician city of Tyre, she was, like Prospero, made a refugee by a brother's treachery. In Dido's case, she was forced to flee Tunis when her brother, the king, murdered her husband Sychaeus. In the *Aeneid*, Dido herself has become the agent of empire, founding a great city on land she obtains by means of a ruse.[5] At a later stage of the story, when Aeneas abandons her to fulfil his destiny as founder of Rome, Dido will in turn become one of empire's many discards.

The Aeneas of legend, like Dido, has been forced to flee his homeland after the fall of Troy. When he lands, with the broken remains of his fleet, on the shores of North Africa, he is astonished to see his own story, the story of the fall of Troy, commemorated on the walls of a Carthaginian temple. His calamity, and that of Troy, is a story the fleeing Tyreans have brought with them to a new land: those who suffer from displacement often take comfort and inspiration from the stories of earlier displacements. It is while the one-time queen of the Tyreans,[6] now Queen of Carthage, listens to Aeneas narrate the story she already knows, and narrate that story *from within*, that Dido becomes fatally enamoured. The story is in many ways her own – calamity followed by exile – and it is her hospitality to fellow exiles that arguably seals her fate. Hospitality to refugees was a fraught issue in Shakespeare's England as in our own unstable world.

When Leo Africanus (*c.* 1485–*c.* 1554) wrote his *Geographical Historie of Africa* in 1550 (trans. 1600 by John Pory), Carthage had been supplanted by Tunis as the hegemonic centre of North African trade and military power, but by 1604, as Englishmen knew very well, both cities had been subsumed by the Ottoman Empire. And the North African, or Barbary, Coast as it was then known, had absorbed new tides of exiles, including the Moors and Jews expelled by Spain as part of the Reconquista. In Shakepeare's *The Tempest*, Sebastian is emphatic in his characterization of Tunis as infinitely remote, in both geographic and cultural terms:

> Sir, you may thank yourself for this great loss,
> That would not bless our Europe with your daughter,
> But rather lose her to an African,
> Where she, at least, is banished from your eye,
> Who hath cause to set the grief on't . . . .

You were kneeled to and importuned otherwise
By all of us; and the fair soul herself
Weighed, between loathness and obedience, at
Which end o'th'beam should bow.

(2.1.119–27)

Thus is the distance between 'our Europe' and (their) Africa magnified to opposition and a royal alliance transformed to 'banishment' and 'loss'. When Antonio prompts Sebastian to regard himself as the heir apparent to Naples, he invokes the same exaggerated conceptual map, referring to Claribel as dwelling

Ten leagues beyond a man's life; she that from Naples
Can have no note, unless the sun were post –
The man i'th'moon's too slow – till new-born chins
Be rough and razorable . . .

(2.1.242–6)

Such are the perceptions of the European metropole, although the Neapolitans have recently sailed from Tunis and although, as Peter Hulme has pointed out, Naples is nearer to Tunis than to Milan.[7] Claribel's 'exile' is part of the diplomatic and dynastic traffic in marriageable daughters rather than the history of outright conquest or insurrection but, as various French marriages would have suggested to an early modern Englishman, combined and concordant kingdoms have a way of breaking apart. Whether she has neutralized a geopolitical threat or consolidated an advantageous alliance, Neapolitan mapping is the same: Claribel is now understood to be dwelling beyond the pale.

'Context too', writes Barbara Fuchs, 'can be polysemous'.[8] The overlay in Shakespeare's play of ancient and contemporary, Mediterranean and Caribbean, historical and legendary or utopian narratives, lays bare recurrent structures of imagination. 'Had I plantation of this isle', says Gonzalo, 'and were king on't, what would I do?' (2.1.139–40), and proceeds to posit an Edenic commonwealth of the sort that Montaigne had ascribed to Brazil: 'no kind of traffic . . . no name of magistrate . . . [no] letters, . . . riches, poverty, / Bourn, bound of land, tilth, vineyard . . . use of metal, corn, or wine, or oil; No occupation . . . no sovereignty'

(2.1.144–52). 'Yet', says Sebastian, 'he would be king on't' (2.1.153). 'The latter end of his commonwealth forgets the beginning', adds Antonio (2.1.154). Sebastian and Antonio presumably stand for the dark side of sovereign imagination – realpolitik versus benignant (and deluded) utopianism. But their machinations for power are no more practical, no less fantastical, than Gonzalo's. What can it mean to inherit the monarchy of Naples, or free Milan from tribute, when they are stranded on an island with no ships, no tools, no labourers, no knowledge of craftsmanship or navigation, indeed no more means of sustenance than the hapless settlers of Jamestown?

'This island's mine by Sycorax my mother', claims Caliban (1.2.331). A number of Shakespearean adaptors have been willing to take him at his word, but the unspoken premise warrants some scrutiny. Who counts as 'native'? By what logic does a refugee gain sovereignty over the place of refuge? By what further logic does sovereignty become heritable? Within the more limited parameters of Shakespeare's play, whence has Caliban derived his sense of ownership and command? He seems to be parroting a Prospero-like presumption of sovereignty-by-bloodline. But this is to occlude an earlier, contestatory phase. Sycorax, like Prospero on the island and Aeneas on the Italian peninsula, had arrived in this place as an outsider. Sycorax, like Prospero and Aeneas, had established dominion by imposing a coercive regime: witness the fate of Ariel, immured in a 'cloven pine' (1.2.277). We might wish, with Montaigne,[9] for a Caliban who construes native rights as a matter of intimacy with the ways and resources of the island, its freshwater springs, its nuts and berries – intimacies we associate with stewardship rather than sovereignty. But Shakespeare's Caliban does not exist outside ideology, or safely within our own. When he imagines rebellion, he can do so only within an inherited scheme, and by means of inherited vocabularies: 'I'll kiss thy foot', he says to Stephano. 'I'll swear myself thy subject' (2.2.147). He offers tribute, and he appropriates and confers regalia. He proposes to overthrow one master by means of another, and a lesser one at that. Stephano is a drunken butler, a manservant. Caliban sues to become a servant of servants, like the cursed offspring of Canaan. And worse, he calls this 'freedom': 'Ban, ban, Ca-caliban / Has a new master: get a new man. / Freedom, high-day, high-day freedom' (2.2.180–2).

* * *

More than thirty years ago, Rob Nixon published an important and influential essay celebrating the 'Calibanic lineage'[10] running from Toussaint Louverture (leader of the Haitian slave revolt of 1791–1803) through Fidel Castro and Franz Fanon. This lineage, Nixon explained, had been mapped by Caribbean and African writers during a decade and a half (1957–73) of intensifying resistance to colonial rule and imperialist hegemony. Adopting 'adversarial interpretations of [Shakespeare's] play', George Lamming, Aimé Césaire, John Pepper Clark and others had 'rehabilitated Caliban into a heroic figure' (564) and placed him at the centre of a 'vital, remedial tradition' (570) of resistance and revolutionary change. By 1987, however, when Nixon himself was writing, he felt the prospects for revivifying appropriation had dimmed: 'In [the present] climate', he claims, 'Shakespeare's play has been drained of the immediate, urgent value it was once found to have' (577). That climate is one in which the heady spirit of insurrection has been replaced by a generation of leaders whose concerns are 'technocratic'[11] rather than revolutionary, in which formal independence has brought not true autonomy but the dispiriting indignities of neocolonialism, in which Prospero continues his rule 'from afar' (577). But why should the disillusionments of postcolonialism have 'drained' this particular cultural text of 'urgent value'? Early in his essay, Nixon himself powerfully articulates the underlying principle of the drama's continuing vitality, to wit: 'the status of value as an unstable social process rather than a static and, in literary terms, merely textual attribute' (558). His unfolding analysis and the argument about diminishment, however, seem to reveal something far narrower about his expectations for usable appropriation. Nixon writes with refreshing candour about 'unabashedly refashion[ing]' Shakespeare's play 'to meet contemporary political and cultural needs' (559), but when he opines, for example, that '[t]he play's declining pertinence to contemporary Africa and the Caribbean has been exacerbated by the difficulty of wresting from it any role for female defiance or leadership in a period when protest is coming increasingly from that quarter', he seems to retreat from his own more supple definition of 'value as an unstable social process'. Admittedly, this essay was written long before Prospero was being played onstage by such powerful female actors as Harriet Walter. But why, as a general principle, should it be more difficult to reimagine Sycorax, or Miranda, or the ambiguously gendered Ariel as figures of power and defiance than to reimagine Caliban as a hero of liberation? And why, more fundamentally, should contestatory engagements with a classic text be measured exclusively by their ability to map a practical or inspirational course for action? Do the most significant powers of literature or theatre really lie in this direction? With respect, I would like to suggest that they do not, that literature's powers of subversion, estrangement, and leveraged critique, on the stage or on the page, may be better suited for other tasks. What if we think about the varieties of adaptation and appropriation as interrogatory encounters?

In his 1971 novel *Water with Berries*, George Lamming distributes trace elements of *The Tempest* across a broad spectrum of characters, events and prehistories. The traces are labyrinthine and deliberately cross-purposed, so I can only beg the reader's patience with a highly compressed sketch of them: at the centre of the novel and dominating its close third-person point of view are three London-based friends, Teeton, Roger and Derek, all of them immigrants from the fictional Caribbean island of San Cristobal. The island itself, in Lamming's rendition, is haunted both by the echoes of Shakespeare's island and by the impositions of the colonial imaginary (and thus by the recent history of critical and performance interpretation as well): 'Its history had been a swindle of treaties and concessions. Its sovereignty was no more than an exchange of ownership. There had been no end to the long and bitter humiliations of foreign rule' (*Water with Berries* 39).[12] Divided between the characters of Teeton's (white) English landlady (the Old Dowager) and her deceased colonist husband are the controlling powers, some subtle, some brutally tyrannical, of Shakespeare's Prospero. Bodied forth in the person of the Pilot, who is at once the Old Dowager's lover, the brother of her husband, and the biological father to the Old Dowager's daughter Myra/Miranda, is all the fraternal treachery of Prospero's brother Antonio. Unsettlingly, the Pilot's given name, Fernando, also associates him with Miranda's suitor Ferdinand, as does his, Fernando's, role in the sexual awakening of fourteen-year-old Myra/Miranda. Miranda's function as a pawn in the power competitions and alliances among men is manifested not only in Myra, whose history as a victim of rape both literalizes and horrifically multiplies the racialized anxieties of *The Tempest*, but also in the persons of Randa, the wife Teeton has left behind on San Cristobal, and Nicole, the (white)

English woman pregnant with Roger's child. In one of his most bitter anatomies of colonialism and its legacy, Lamming casts all three women as sacrificial victims of male will-to-power and the paranoia that attends it, in colonizer and colonized alike.

As to the novel's deeply problematic triple protagonists, Teeton, Roger, and Derek, their dark skin and their history as colonized subjects are only the most superficial of their links to the character of Caliban. More profound is the internalized colonialism that has drawn all three to England as to the true mother country, the source of all true cultural value and, by extension, the only horizon for self-realization. As Lamming put it in one of his essays, 'There is no escape from the prison of Prospero's gift. . . . This gift of Language meant not English, in particular, but speech and concept as a way, a method, a necessary avenue towards areas of the self which could not be reached in any other way.'[13] All three protagonists, like their author, are artists: Roger a composer, Derek an actor and Teeton, the main character, a painter. Teeton, we learn, had been imprisoned 'after a minor revolt' before fleeing San Cristobal seven years ago; tellingly, the nature and extent of his participation in that revolt are never specified. Equally obscure are the details of his secretive political life in London. Quite apart from and unknown to his circle of artist friends, Teeton belongs to an underground group of expatriates who refer to themselves as The Gathering and have for years been plotting an uprising on their native island. To what extent their plotting is meant to be of practical consequence the novel refuses to specify, but later narrative developments suggest that the real uprising (and there is one) occurs quite independent of their intrigues.[14] This murky disaggregation of purpose and consequence, repeated with variation throughout the novel, parallels the disturbed fragmentation and intermingling of its characters.

Water with Berries was not the first time Lamming adopted the figure of Caliban as a means of contemplating the powers and the dilemma of the colonial subject. In 'Caliban Orders History', which appears in his 1960 collection of essays, *The Pleasures of Exile*, Lamming pays tribute to the revolutionary figure of Toussaint Louverture, as celebrated in C. L. R. James's *Black Jacobins* (1938). In 'A Monster, A Child, A Slave', the essay cited earlier and also published in *The Pleasures of Exile*, Lamming makes Caliban the central figure in his contestatory reading of *The Tempest*. The latter essay is an extraordinary mixture of insight and imposition. 'It would not be difficult', the author speculates at one point, 'for Miranda to accuse Caliban . . . of having raped her; for she probably dreams about him' (*PE* 111). 'It is possible', he opines elsewhere, 'that Prospero envies and admires the passion [of Ferdinand and Miranda]. It is likely that he had never experienced any such feeling toward his wife' (*PE* 113). The problem with such interpretive moves is not that they are somehow 'wrong'. Lamming himself succinctly captures the inaptness of this category when he anticipates and counters the objection: 'It will not help to say that I am wrong . . . for I shall reply that my mistake, lived and deeply felt by millions of men like me – proves the value of such error' (*PE 113*). The problem with such interpretive moves is rather, I submit, that the satisfaction they provide – petty revenge against the white colonizers who themselves have a long history of sexually stereotyping the racial other – is both imaginary and fleeting. Far more powerful, far more courageous, and far more troubling are Lamming's explorations of these tortured intersections – racism, colonial displacement and sexual revenge – in *Water with Berries*.

Lamming's novel begins quietly, with mundane moments in mundane settings, but gradually discloses an escalating series of lurid events, including but not limited to racist and misogynist exclusion, suicide, arson, incest, rape and murder. Point of view, that shifting close third person, renders the narrative almost hallucinatory at times, a sort of fever dream or hellscape. The genre, in other words, is expressionist rather than realist. Within the fiction, however, even the most melodramatic developments are meant to be construed as 'real'. Teeton murders his landlady and sets her cottage on fire. Roger drives his wife to suicide. Derek rapes a young actress in full view of a theatre audience. A woman narrates the story of her childhood: abducted by her father as three-year-old child, brought up on an island under his exclusive and ambiguously incestuous tutelage, gang raped by servants and dogs. Action unfolds against a shadowy backdrop of Shakespearean leitmotifs: multiple Calibans; Prosperos male and female; a crossbred Ferdinand/Antonio; a crossbred Caliban/Othello; a crossbred Caliban/Lear; sacrificial incarnations of Miranda, Desdemona and Cordelia; islands West Indian, Orkneyan and doubling as a darkness-shrouded heath. Shakespeare haunts the London of Lamming's novel as the dead haunt the living in the Ceremony of Souls.

Lamming first witnessed the Ceremony of Souls during a trip to Haiti, and he describes it in some detail in the Introduction to *The Pleasures of Exile*. 'The celebrants', he writes,

> are mainly relatives of the deceased who, ever since their death, have been locked in Water. It is the duty of the Dead to return and offer, on this momentous night, a full and honest report on their past relations with the living . . . their release from the purgatory of Water cannot be realized until they have fulfilled the contract which this ceremony symbolizes. . . . The living demand to hear whether there is any need for forgiveness, for redemption; whether, in fact, there may be any guide which may help them towards reforming their present condition. . . . Revenge, guilt, redemption, and some future expectation . . . [bind] the Dead and the living together. (Introduction, *PE*, 9–10)

To what extent the title of *Water with Berries* is meant to evoke this purgatorial realm in Haitian cosmology, as well as the line from Caliban's monologue, I do not know, but within the novel Teeton sees, or imagines he sees, a Ceremony of Souls on the heath never named as Hampstead, the better to allow its watery transfigurations. 'It was familiar . . . this annual parliament of the dead. . . . That's where he had met Randa' (*WB* 129). Randa is the wife Teeton has left behind on San Cristobal. We have just learned, and Teeton has been forcibly reminded, of his cruelty to her, the 'seven years of spiteful silence' (*WB* 138) with which he punished her after she helped him escape from prison. 'You wouldn't have been alive today', says a compatriot, '[h]ad it not been for Randa' (*WB* 125). It is the shock of this interlocutor's next statement, news to us as to Teeton himself, that sends the latter onto the heath: Randa has that very morning committed suicide (as Roger's wife will be driven to suicide some sixty pages later, another recurrent theme in this book of tangled guilt).

In its ethical and emotional contours, *Water with Berries* is extraordinarily complex. Its protagonists have found their island homeland thwarting: composer Roger 'has never heard any music' in the landscape of his birth (*WB* 92); he and Derek 'had been educated for escape' from their earliest stirrings of ambition (*WB* 90); Teeton's failed efforts at direct political action have made him a 'deserter' (*WB* 118). Yet the English metropole to which these three are drawn is the site of profound disillusionment. After one notable season playing Othello with the Royal Shakespeare Company, Derek has been reduced to playing corpses on the London stage; Roger has given up music; Teeton has earned a living by selling paintings of remembered Saint Cristobal landscapes, commodifying his homeland in an act of 'innocent betrayal' (*WB* 39). The novel's intricate relationships – between Black lodger and white landlady-and-protector, Black composer and white wife, Black actor and white theatrical tradition – are characterized by genuine intimacy and nurture as well as exploitation. 'I am a direct descendant of slaves', wrote Lamming in *The Pleasures of Exile*. 'Moreover, I am a direct descendant of Prospero, worshipping in the same temple of endeavor' (*PE* 15), which is to say, in the temple of language. In its every turning, *Water with Berries* manifests the reciprocal if hierarchical nature of postcolonial subjectivity. The novel's real protagonist, from this perspective, is interpersonal and transhistorical.

'Caliban cannot be revealed in any relation to himself', writes Lamming in *The Pleasures of Exile*, 'for he has no self which is not a reaction to circumstances imposed upon his life' (*PE* 107). What *The Pleasures of Exile* explores discursively, *Water with Berries* explores 'in the flesh', less hampered by political agenda or polemical intent. Or to put the matter more precisely, its mode of exploration allows the novel to subject political purpose and polemical strategy to the same scrutiny it applies to characters and their motives. Riddled with ambivalence, the novel powerfully renders the *felt* legacy of oppression and displacement, for Caliban above all and, to a lesser extent, for Prospero and all those who have benefitted from colonial exploitation. 'That experiment in ruling over your kind', says one of the doomed white men in *Water with Berries*, 'It was a curse . . . And it will come back to plague my race' (*WB* 254). Lamming's novel does not lend itself to easy optimism. Rather, its vision is that which Lamming found in the Haitian Ceremony of Souls, where the dead and the living, Prospero and Caliban, the refugee and the 'native', who is himself an earlier refugee or forced migrant, have no way forward but together. Those who have endured self-alienating harm and those who have visited such harm upon others have both been irrevocably changed by the 'experiment in ruling'; there is no returning to a theoretical state of innocence or origin. 'Reconciliation' in the fullest emotional, structural and moral sense may be wishful thinking, but co-existence and negotiated futurity require, at the very least, reciprocal acknowledgement of that constitutive change. This itself, I would argue, may be a significant contribution to political thought and is also, of course, a central proposition of much recent cultural and historical criticism.

* * *

Perhaps the boldest and most shocking feature in Lamming's anatomy of (post)colonial subjection is the role he assigns to violent misogyny. Forced abortion, psychological manipulation, venereal disease, abandonment, rape and quasi-prostitution: these are visited upon his female characters like so many plagues. 'Grab what c[---] you can', says one of his minor characters; 'Hit it and run' (*WB* 151). Layer by poisonous layer, Lamming excavates the self-loathing instilled in men by successive epochs of forced displacement, physical and sexual exploitation, racial contempt, cultural subordination, 'the long and bitter humiliations of foreign rule' (39).[15] And the natural guise of self-loathing in men, he seems to argue, is hatred for women.

Two decades after the publication of *Water with Berries*, novelist Marina Warner turns these powerful indictments on their head in her own, feminist reimagining of Shakespeare's play. In *Indigo* (1992), Sycorax is a wise woman of the fictional Caribbean island Liamuiga, knowledgeable in all its ways, including the cultivation and processing of indigo, and consulted by its inhabitants as a healer of body and mind. She chooses to live as an internal exile only when her fellow islanders begin to fear that she can raise the dead. And why do they fear this? When a group of corpses washes up on the island one day, we are meant to recognize what the islanders will later learn: these were slaves thrown overboard during the voyage from West Africa; the Middle Passage has come to Liamuiga. Among the castaway Black bodies is one with a living child in its womb, a child Sycorax delivers and adopts as her own. This child is Dulé (later Caliban); his younger sister will be Ariel, adopted when she has lost her Arawak family and been separated from her Arawak tribe. Three figures, variously displaced. And it is they who resist when a company of English colonizers arrives on the island. Warner does not rewrite history in its broadest strokes: her colonizers still 'succeed', if their legacy of oppression and ruinous depredation can be called success. But the reliable centres of cognizance and ethical stability, the characters with whom we are invited to identify, are Sycorax and Ariel and, three and a half centuries later in the contemporary London of the novel, the mixed raced descendant of the island, Miranda.

Structurally, Warner's novel consists of thirty-three chapters and six main sections, which alternate between the sixteenth- and seventeenth-century 'then' of the island and the twentieth-century 'now' of London and the-world-as-seen-through-English-eyes. Woven throughout is a complex web of tropes and traces from *The Tempest*, along with elements drawn from other tales of English exploration in the New World. Parallels are legion, but the novel's relation to its antecedents is never merely schematic: imagined through the intimate lens of character, every inherited echo has undergone a sea change. 'Then' is the story of Sycorax, Caliban/Dulé and Ariel and the profound disruption of colonial settlement in the person of Christopher (Kit) Everard. 'Now' begins in the pea soup fog of postwar London and continues through the interconnected, late twentieth-century momentums of political radicalization (Black Power, 'free love', broad-based anticolonialism) and imperialism-by-other-means (tourism, environmental exploitation, international finance).

London, November 1948: the present-day Kit Everard, descendant of the colonial settler, is trying to make his way on foot through the blinding smog and bitter cold of nighttime London. With him are his wife and six-year-old daughter. The way is difficult, even menacing: speeding cars emerge from the darkness in a city whose poisoned air seems only to deepen the deprivations of postwar rationing. And the tube station they've sought turns out to be no haven at all: the gates are locked, the trains not running. At which point, the Kit we have heretofore seen as a sympathetic character, humiliated by a withholding father and beleaguered by an unstable wife, turns on the 'slight . . . middle-aged black man' who operates the station lift and begins to bully him in shockingly racist terms. The scene is pivotal for a number of reasons. We know that Kit himself had been taunted at school for the complexion and the hair he inherited from his Creole mother: 'N[-----] Everard', they called him behind his back (*Indigo* 67); Caliban has left his trace. Even now, in adulthood, acquaintances speak knowingly about the 'touch of the tar brush' (*Indigo* 22) that marks this heir to Prospero as not-quite-fully-British. Furthermore, like the man he so viciously turns on, Kit has come to England as an outsider. 'You're from the islands', he says as his rage begins to dissipate, 'of course, now I see that! . . . I'm from the islands too'. And instead of apologizing, he bids for reconciliation by dropping the name of his famous father. What follows is one of the most painful and moving acts of mercy in the book (and a subtle echo of Caliban's act of mercy on Shakespeare's island: 'I . . . showed thee . . . all the qualities o'th'isle') [1.2.336–7]). Undeceived by Kit's shift from extravagant abuse to patronizing familiarity, the Underground[16] worker takes pity on the stranded wayfarers and offers them tea in his cramped shelter. 'I myself come over recently', he says, 'in the *Windrush* – you maybe hear of it?' (*Indigo* 71).

An historical note: on the 22nd of June 1948 the ship *MV Empire Windrush* docked at Tilbury with 1,027 passengers, 802 of whom stated their last country of abode to be Jamaica, Trinidad and Tobago, or other parts of the British West Indies. Over the next two decades, they would be joined by nearly half a million fellow migrants from the Caribbean Commonwealth. They were the Windrush Generation, as it later came to be known, Britain's answer to a severe postwar labour shortage, and a textbook illustration of the mutually constitutive links between imperialism, racism and the extractive foundations of capitalism: the Windrush Generation came in response to an explicit British government recruitment campaign. '[Many] of us, so many, leaving home', as Kit's interlocutor tells him, and like this man, guarding the entrance to the Underground on a dark London night, many had earlier served in the British armed forces: 'so many . . . recruited for work, yes, again' (*Indigo* 71). Because they came from within the British Commonwealth, these migrants understood themselves to be British citizens and to possess the rights of British citizens. Later on, as their former homelands gained independence and Britain progressively tightened restrictions on immigration, their 'right to settle' was meant to be secured by a 1971 Act of Parliament.[17] Because they were provided with no documentation, however, and because landing cards had in many cases been destroyed, many in the Windrush Generation had no way to establish their date of arrival or continuous residence when, in the early decades of the twenty-first century, they began receiving deportation orders, denial of reentry and denial of benefits. In 2018, news media began to inform the British public of the extent to which the very people who had been so essential to postwar recovery had seen their lives turned upside down by legislative gaps, bureaucratic mismanagement and public indifference. In addition to those who were detained or forcibly removed from the UK, many lost jobs and livelihoods, lost medical care, lost the ability to rent or pay the mortgage on homes they had lived in for years, even decades. The longer sorry story of the Windrush Generation was yet to come when Marina Warner published *Indigo* in 1992, but as this early episode at a fog-bound London tube station makes clear, the seeds of betrayal were there from the beginning.

In Shakespeare's England also, immigrants faced a profoundly ambivalent reception. On the one hand, competition for international markets made skilled immigrants a valuable asset for developing industries, and they were welcomed, even recruited, by communities in Norwich, Maidstone, Halstead and Colchester.[18] On the other hand, London-based guilds routinely expressed concern and apprentices downright hostility towards the influx of foreign craftsmen. On the one hand, shared faith and Christian hospitality obliged the English to welcome fellow Protestants fleeing persecution in France, Italy, the Netherlands and elsewhere on the continent (as a number of English men and women had fled in the opposite direction during the reign of Queen Mary). On the other hand, these co-religionists arrived in such numbers as to constitute, to many minds, a threat: sixteenth-century London was the scene of repeated demonstrations and occasional riots against its resident 'strangers'. Internal migrants also – the poor, the disinherited, the unfortunate of every stripe – were omnipresent in Shakespeare's England and were subject to harsh regulation. Famously, the 1572 'Acte for the punishment of Vacabondes' played a significant role in the patronage structure of Elizabethan theatrical companies.[19] When plague deaths closed the London theatres, Shakespeare's company, like its competitors, was forced to adopt the itinerant mode that had dominated theatrical performance earlier in the century. Internal or external, licensed or prohibited, provisionally welcomed or disavowed, migrant populations were and are among the most vulnerable of human beings on earth. *The Tempest* is populated by characters made subject to the vicissitudes of betrayal and hospitality. As are the characters in Marina Warner's *Tempest* adaptation. The first voice we encounter in *Indigo* is that of Serafine, the Afro-Caribbean woman brought to England as a nursemaid to the present-day Kit Everard when he was a child. She cares now for Kit's young daughter, Miranda, and will become one of the presiding figures in the novel, as she is in Miranda's developing imagination. Serafine (Feeny) is a weaver of tales, whose haunting stories both echo and anticipate the narrative tropes we encounter elsewhere in the novel. Her stories are designed for the nursery, yes, to comfort and entertain a young child, but in their mythic synthesis of family and colonial histories they share a portion of the prognosticating magic attributed to Sycorax in the sixteenth- and seventeenth-century sections of *Indigo*. In the first of her narrations, for example, shadowy versions of Gulliver in Lilliput and Midas in his kingdom disclose a cautionary tale about empire and inheritance, a tale whose outlines the reader will later discern in the fate of Warner's characters. Feeny knows much. To a child and to the reader alike, she seems to tap the sources of knowing.

Warner herself is Serafine's secret sharer in the art and moral mystery of the fable. An early christening scene in *Indigo* reverberates with traces of the Sleeping Beauty tale: a golden child, an unwanted guest and a fateful curse. Ariel's failed effort to poison the first Kit Everard on the eve of an uprising is artfully repurposed by Kit himself and consolidated by family legend into a parable of love and rescue, a la Pocahontas. The uprising itself, in one of Warner's most wicked conceits, has been transmogrified into the sport of Empire: a bat-and-ball game (Flinders) unmistakably akin to cricket but exponentially complicated by an overlay of place names and strategies that commemorate the original Battle of Belmont Stockade. Warner is merciless on the British tendency towards self-mythologizing: the father of the present-day Kit Everard, Sir Anthony (Ant) Everard, 'is still a household name' (44) for his legendary feats on the Flinders field; metropolitan players, the great ones, are the 'fighter pilots of the ground' (40) in postwar England. On a more sombre note, though neither George Lamming nor the Haitian Ceremony of Souls is explicitly invoked in Warner's novel, the dead on the island and in the metropole alike are never really dead. From the seabed, from burial beneath an iconic tree, in the body of 'an ancient Indian hag' (224), in the voice of a ruined woman on an urban heath, in the dark complexions and 'light colored irises' (311) of a mixed race lineage, they speak to and with the living.

And what of Caliban's avatars in particular? The Windrush migrant whom Kit encounters at the London Underground is merely the first of these. The African child Dulé, whom Sycorax delivers from the grave of his mother's womb, grows up to become a hero of resistance: when English invaders break treaty after treaty and show no intention of leaving Liamuiga, Dulé gathers a rebel force of escaped slaves, maroons, redlegs (poor whites), impressed ship hands and pirates who have 'slipped the noose' (116) and leads them in an attack on the English settlement. They are defeated, many killed, the others captured: Dulé is maimed (his hamstrings slit) and made a bondsman, by way of warning to any who might think to follow his example. He is also renamed: as Caliban. 'He has already', writes the first Kit Everard to his patron Lord Clovelly, 'learned how to curse' (201).

In the novel's nineteen eighties, another would-be Caliban takes up the cause of insurrection. The oppressor this time is neocolonialism, the system Lamming's Teeton calls the 'swindle of treaties and concessions' (*WB* 39), the system Shakespeare's Trinculo unwittingly portends when he imagines Caliban as a commodified exhibit in early modern London.[20] In latter-day Liamuiga (now Enfant Béate), Abdul Malik (formerly Jimmy Dunn) acts in the name of the Shining Purity of the One God Liberation Movement (*Indigo* 349), seeking to cleanse the island of 'rum punches and mint juleps', 'Coca-Cola and Pepsi-Cola', 'the concession and the franchise, the deal and the dollar', all the accumulations he calls 'foreign putrefaction' (354–5). Warner is wont to treat the revolutionaries of her own era with a certain amount of wryness, and Malik is a very imperfect version of Dulé. But the corruptions he loathes are actual, and when 'the forces of civility and law' label him a terrorist and 'bl[o]w away half his skull' with a gunshot supposedly intended for his thigh, the reader is meant to feel the shock of historical recognition (which is all the keener, of course, for a reader in the era of Black Lives Matter).

The metropole has its revolutionaries as well, of course. In the nineteen-sixty-something section of *Indigo*, twenty-something Miranda is sent by her editor to interview a French film director on his London set. At the shoot, which is all Black Panthers and *Soul on Ice*, she is angrily confronted by George Felix, a Black actor, for taking photos without permission. 'Whitey', he calls her, though she has always been regarded ('couldn't he see it?') as a 'musty' (266). Years later, when Miranda encounters Felix again, he has changed his name to Shaka Ifetabe and is rehearsing the role of Caliban onstage. After a few defensive conversational gambits, they progress to tentative banter ('We're maroons together now', says

Shaka [*Indigo* 394]), and, as the narrator reports, '[t]hey had begun play' (395). It's a latterday reprise of the chess game in Prospero's cell: Miranda with her Caliban/Ferdinand.

Names too can carry the weight of fable. The child whose christening begins Warner's novel is Xanthe, Greek for golden-haired. She is the child of Anthony Everard's late middle age and her mother, unlike Kit's, is 'properly' English, which is to say, English and white. Like the golden daughter of Midas, she will live to fulfil a curse. The child born to Miranda and George/Shaka/Caliban at the end of the novel is Serafine, named to honour a Black household retainer. Though she is by no means a panacea for the long disease of racial and colonial oppression to which the novel testifies, the birth of this second child is meant to register as a blessing. Hovering over the novel as a whole is the irony of a thrice-named island: Liamuiga to its early inhabitants, Everhope to its chartered English settlers, Enfant Béate to the French who gained temporary title. 'And this was the name' – holy infant – 'that stuck' (47). 'Liamuiga', like 'Flinders', is one of Warner's liberal borrowings from the broader history of British empire: Liamuiga (fertile earth) is the name of a volcanic mountain on St. Kitt's (n.b.), a Caribbean island whose governance, like that of the fictional Liamuiga, alternated for a time between English and French control. Matthew Flinders (1774– 1818) was the English explorer who surveyed the coast of New South Wales and first suggested (in a letter to Joseph Banks) that the continent be called Australia. One other name bears mentioning here: though Malik's uprising on Enfante Béate fails, his attempted coup does lead to the advent of a new prime minister, whose policies bode a genuine increase of autonomy for the Béatois. Her name is Atala Seacole. Atala, from the Greek, like Xanthe, but divested of the ominous association with gold, crowned instead with a surname that links the bounties of the sea to blackness.[21] Atala, meaning 'young', which is the novel's way of looking forward. Atala, the granddaughter of Serafine Killebree, 'who went to England as a servant' (*Indigo* 375–6).

If *Indigo*'s varied glimpses of feminine empowerment suggest a substrate of mythic optimism, if reconciliation is easier to imagine in its pages than in Lamming's searing *Water with Berries*, this does not make Warner's vision blithely utopian. Her novel turns the same sardonic lens on the pieties of modern-day activism as on the self-aggrandizements of colonialism. The island restored to (partial) political autonomy still markets a sanitized version of itself to paying customers. In old age, the present-day Kit lives once again on the island where he was born, heir to the double lineage of Caliban and Prospero. Featured on the island's tourist brochure, he passes for one of its 'splendidly authentic natives' (*Indigo* 382). Native: 'that's what I've been all along', he says; 'As far as anyone can be said to be native at all' (*Indigo* 382). That rueful comment is as close as Kit ever comes to the binding premise of Warner's narrative. And it echoes the epigraph the author has drawn from William Empson: 'It is not human to feel safely placed . . . .' (*Indigo*, front matter).

* * *

In an earlier section of this chapter, I cited Rob Nixon's now classic article on *The Tempest* only to disagree with a portion of its argument. This was not to diminish its contribution to the subject of revisionary cultural appropriation but because the author's apparent premises in that early work[22] have helped me to think about and question my own. What is it we can ask of art in the context of sweeping social injustice? How ought we to think about the continuing aftermath of empire when its terrible logic is configured not only in a Dido or a Caliban or a latterday Miranda but also in the body of a three-year-old boy washed up on a Mediterranean beach, or teenager shot on the streets of Chicago, or a caravan of Central Americans making their way on foot to a border that will turn them away? Criticism and political theory have of course in recent decades powerfully articulated just such conundrums. The great advantage of literary or theatrical rendition – a playscript, a performance, a poem, a novel – is its status as *embodied thought*. Any medium, and above all language itself, is a vested inheritance of habits and momentums; therein lies its capacity for enlargement and resistance. Every word I use is freighted with the histories, colorations and occlusions of prior use. I can do my best to limit its connotations, but there will always be a residuum of possibility that escapes my control and subtly contributes to the shape of that which follows. This is true in analytical and polemical usage as in the work we choose to designate as 'art'. This is also why, and here the experience may be more particular to creative work, we sometimes say a work of art can 'think'. Warner's Sycorax turns blue from many years of processing indigo; Lamming's Caliban worships in the temple of language, which is once an imposition and an indelible gift; W. H. Auden turns to Shakespeare for the title of a book of essays on the craft of writing: *The Dyer's Hand,* 'subdued / To what it works in' (*Sonnet 111*).[23] Inseparable from the medium and indispensable to its resonance is also, and crucially, the constitutive response of reader, viewer and auditor. To speak about embodied thought is to acknowledge the irreducibly collaborative nature of making meaning. When George Lamming first asserted 'the positive value of . . . error', 'lived and deeply felt by men like me' (*PE* 13), he did so in the context of what we may loosely define as literary criticism. I have argued that the perceptual field he foregrounds here, what I call 'the *felt* legacy of oppression and displacement', has been more richly and effectively rendered in two creative adaptations, *Water with Berries* and *Indigo*, than in Lamming's own critical commentary on *The Tempest* or Nixon's assessments of 'urgent value' and diminution in postcolonial adaptations of the same. This is by no means to argue for the superiority of creative over critical inquiry *tout court*. Far less is it to deny the power of political polemic in any number of contexts. It is, however, to argue that polemical adaptation or polemically driven analysis is unlikely to capture the full critical and contestatory powers of novels, plays and other literary or performative modes of engagement. These powers are far suppler and more variable than the targeting of exemplary villains or liberatory role models would suggest. Literary and theatrical criticism is most trenchant when it remembers, and fully credits, the mediums it seeks to illuminate, when, in its own formulations, it manifests and acknowledges 'the status of value as an unstable social process rather than a static and . . . merely textual attribute' (Nixon 558). To that extent, this is an essay about method.[24]

Notes

1 Aimé Césaire, *A Tempest*, trans. Richard Miller (New York: Ubu Repertory Theater Company Publications, 1992); George Lamming, *Water with Berries* (Trinidad and Tobago: Longman Caribbean, 1971); Edward Kamau Brathwaite, 'Caliban', in *The Arrivants: A New World Trilogy* (Oxford: Oxford University Press, 1973); Lemuel Johnson, *Highlife for Caliban* (Ann Arbor: Ardis, 1974); Jimmie Durham, *The Caliban Codex* (Museum of Modern Art, 1992); Marina Warner, *Indigo or, Mapping the Waters* (London: Vintage, 1992). For a detailed discussion of Robert LePage's First Nations production of *The Tempest*, see Françoise Besson, 'L'île mouvante de Caliban: île théâtrale et île autochtone, deux mises en scène de *La Tempête* par Robert Lepage', *Caliban: French Journal of English Studies* 52 (2014): 53-74.

2 UNHCR, UN High Commissioner for Refugees.

3 https://www.unhcr.org/refugee-statistics/ and https://www.unhcr.org/globaltrends (accessed 28 September 2022). These figures, released on 22 June 2022, were based on data available as of December 2021.

4 Citations from *The Tempest* and other works by Shakespeare are taken from Richard Proudfoot, Ann Thompson, David Scott Kastan, and H. R. Woodhuysen, eds, *The Arden Shakespeare Complete Works, Third Series* (London and New York: The Arden Shakespeare, 2021).

5 Marcus Junianus Justinus (third century) describes Dido bargaining for a piece of land on the coast of North Africa, 'as much as could be covered with an ox-hide', and outwitting her trading partners by cutting the oxhide into thin strips (*Epitome of the Philippic History of Pompeius Trogus*, trans. Rev. John Selby Watson (London: Henry G. Bohn, 1853); https://www.forumromanum.org/literature/justin/english/trans18.html (accessed 10 September 2020). To a modern reader this might seem to anticipate the notorious trading practices of European adventurers in North America.

6 Her father, King of Tyre, had left the kingdom jointly to Dido and her brother Pygmalion.

7 Peter Hulme, *Colonial Encounters: Europe and the Native Caribbean 1492–1797* (London: Methuen, 1986), 112.

8 Barbara Fuchs, 'Conquering Islands: Contextualizing *The Tempest*', *Shakespeare Quarterly* 48 (1997): 45–62.

9 Michel de Montaigne, 'Of Cannibals', in *The Complete Essays of Montaigne*, trans. Donald. M. Frame (Stanford: Stanford University Press, 1958), 150–9. Scholars have long noted echoes of this essay in Gonzalo's project for a perfect commonwealth.

10 Rob Nixon, 'Caribbean and African Appropriations of *The Tempest*', *Critical Inquiry* 13 (1987): 557–78; passage cited 569.

11 On this subject, Nixon (577) cites Edward Said, 'In the Shadow of the West', *Wedge 7/8* (Winter/Spring 1985): 10.

12 Here and elsewhere, citations from *Water with Berries* are drawn from the Peepal Tree Press edition (Leeds: Peepal Tree Press, 2016) of the original 1971 publication by Longman Caribbean Ltd; new to the 2016 edition is an introduction by J. Dillon Brown.

13 'A Monster, A Child, A Slave', Chapter 6 in *The Pleasures of Exile* (London: Michael Joseph Ltd., 1960).

14 For the relationship of *Water with Berries* to Lamming's larger corpus, and for a less sceptical assessment of The Gathering, see Supriya Nair, *Caliban's Curse: George Lamming and the Revisioning of History* (Ann Arbor: University of Michigan Press, 1996).

15 Even after nominal independence, the history of San Cristobal, to Teeton's mind, 'had been a swindle of treaties and concessions. Its sovereignty was no more than an exchange of ownership' (*WB* 39).

16 And yes, the Underground to which this immigrant is relegated combines with the portrait of dystopian postwar London to suggest a pagan Underworld. On *Indigo*'s mythic structures more broadly, see below.

17 Although the 1971 Immigration Act (c77), like the earlier Acts of 1962 and 1968, served chiefly to restrict immigration, it also introduced the concept of *patriality* or *right of abode*, granted to citizens of the British Commonwealth who had settled or would settle in Britain prior to 1 January 1973, the date on which Britain was scheduled to join the European Commonwealth. https://www.legislation.gov.uk/ukpga/1971/77/contents (accessed 11 July 2020).

18 Scott Oldenburg, *Alien Albion: Literature and Immigration in Early Modern England* (Toronto: University of Toronto Press, 2014), 4. Rejecting broader generalizations about xenophobia in early modern England, Oldenberg traces a complex history of tension between hospitality and hostility towards strangers.

19 See inter alia Andrew Gurr, *The Shakespearean Stage 1574–1642*, 3rd edition (Cambridge: Cambridge University Press, 1992), 27–8.

20 'Were I in England now . . . and had but this fish painted, not a holiday fool there but would give a piece of silver. There would this monster make a man . . . .' (2.2.26–30).

21 As one of my editors has suggested, the surname also invokes another of the remarkable figures who feature in the longer history of British/Caribbean relations. Jamaican born Mary Seacole (1805–81) was a medical practitioner in Kingston and Panama before setting up a hospital for British soldiers in Crimea during the Crimean War. Her autobiography, *Wonderful Adventures of Mrs. Seacole in Many Lands*, was published in 1857 by James Blackwood.

22 'Caribbean and African Appropriations of *The Tempest*' was published when Nixon was still a graduate student at Columbia. He has gone on to publish a series of important and justly celebrated books, most recently *Slow Violence and the Environmentalism of the Poor* (Cambridge, MA: Harvard University Press, 2011).

23 *Shakespeare's Sonnets*, ed. Stephen Booth (New Haven: Yale University Press, 1977).

24 Warmest thanks to Valerie Traub and Steven Mullaney for penetrating comments on earlier versions of this chapter, and to Sandra Young and Christopher Thurman for organizing the conference (Shakespeare and Social Justice, Cape Town, 2019) that occasioned its first iteration.

3

What makes Global Shakespeares an exercise in ethics?

Alexa Alice Joubin

Stage and screen adaptations of Shakespeare's plays raise ethical questions – that is, questions about how human beings should act and treat one another. In which contexts might cross-cultural enterprises be naturalizing the values associated with Shakespeare to exploit unequal power relations among artists of different backgrounds? Conversely, to what end are artists using the brand of Shakespeare? How do festival organizers tap into the ideological purchase of being 'global' (which means being connected to several locations) by inviting productions that feature diverse casts and cultural references? These are just some of the questions driving critical engagements with Shakespearean adaptations from the past five decades.

Adaptations that specifically draw on global Shakespeare as a working concept range from Akira Kurosawa's film *Throne of Blood* (Toho, 1957), which appropriates Noh masks and stylized movements to interpret Lady Macbeth's psyche,[1] to Iqbal Khan's 2001 Royal Shakespeare Company stage production of *Much Ado about Nothing* (with Paul Bhattacharjee as Benedick and Meera Syal as Beatrice), which borrowed from Bollywood conventions to interpret rituals and gender roles.[2] In the latter case, Syal was the first woman of South Asian heritage to play Beatrice in England; the cast may have looked and sounded foreign, but they were part of the English local theatre scene. In Kenneth Branagh's Japanesque film *As You Like It* (BBC and HBO, 2006), Wakehurst Place is dressed up with a Zen garden, shrine gate and trappings of a nineteenth-century Japan torn between samurai and European merchants. During the sumo match between Orlando and Charles, Duke Frederick dons dark samurai armour and sits behind Rosalind and Celia who are in European dresses. A Bunraku puppet represented Ariel in Julie Taymor's 1986 Off-Broadway production of *The Tempest* for the Classic Stage Company in New York City.[3] The puppet's head floated above the stage, working its magic in various scenes.

Some of the abovementioned works are 'multi-ethnic' in terms of their mise-en-scène and casts, while others are created by white directors who found inspiration in non-Western aesthetics. White directors working in London and New York face different challenges than non-Anglophone directors touring their works to Edinburgh or distributing their films beyond Japan. Anglophone directors such as Taymor and Branagh appropriate elements of the non-Western world differently from, say, an Indian-British director (such as Khan) or a director based outside the Western metropoles (such as Kurosawa). Directors' perceived ethical responsibilities shift along with their places of origin. Likewise, artists' racial identities can sometimes incriminate them in either ethnic 'selling out' or cultural imperialism. Yukio Ninagawa's Kabuki-style *Macbeth* (Edinburgh, 1985; London, 1987), renowned for its cherry blossom motif, has drawn criticism for its self-Orientalizing selling out to festival audiences. Branagh, on the other hand, has been taken to task regarding his deployment of a 'dream of Japan' ornamentally in his signature visual romanticism. Both directors engage in some forms of Japonaiserie, but their racial identities became a dominant factor in critics' assessment of their artistic transgressions. In some contexts, artists' cultural origins and locations exonerate them from cultural appropriation – as if Ninagawa's appropriation of pre-modern Japanese sensibilities are by default more authentic than a white director's cross-cultural borrowing. Complicating matters further, directors of colour often give their adaptations an 'ethnic' flavour when these go on tour so as to make the works more palatable to international audiences.

The reception of touring productions reflects uneven power dynamics between governments and between companies. Some companies are compelled to produce works with references to their local cultures, while others have the privilege to simply tour the same production to different places around the world. For instance, Feng Gang, who wrote *The Revenge of Prince Zi Dan*, a Beijing opera adaptation of *Hamlet* that toured to the Edinburgh Festival in 2011, told the *Daily Telegraph* that he and his colleagues 'designed this play for foreign audiences'. While it would be ideal to take traditional *jingju* plays overseas, he added, they would be 'incomprehensible to foreigners' no matter how 'eye-catching' the performance might be.[4] This is an example of adaptations being shaped by the political expediency that I analyse in the next section. By contrast, occupying a more privileged position in terms of cultural prestige and finances, the Royal Shakespeare Company (RSC) does not usually localize its productions when it tours internationally; an example is Loveday Ingram's *The Merchant of Venice*, which toured in Beijing and Shanghai in 2002.[5]

On the one hand, the reception history of such works reveals the self-proclaimed and imposed ethical burden that cross-cultural works carry.[6] The appropriation of non-Western cultural elements can be fraught with problems if deployed carelessly and ornamentally. On the other hand, there are tensions between contemporary and early modern ethics. Gertrude's decision to marry Hamlet's uncle after the death of Old Hamlet has typically been interpreted from a Western perspective as 'unethical', but Laura Bohannan's anthropological account of the reception of *Hamlet* among the Tiv people of Nigeria points out the flaw in the presumed universal validity of moral codes in that play (this is one of the most prominent instances of Shakespearean cultural relativity; the performance history of *King Lear*, which reflects a perceived ethical burden to explain Lear's problems away or to legitimize the characters' suffering, is another).[7]

Pedagogical instrumentality

The dialogues between Shakespeare and his modern interlocutors are driven by ethical claims and the use of Shakespeare for social justice or political expediency. As Susan Bennett points out, global

Shakespeares have been appropriated for the purpose of enhancing diversity 'quotas' in scholarship and curricula in the United Kingdom, the United States and Canada.[8] It is problematic when a group of works are used to service academic advancement rather than serve marginalized communities. This pedagogical instrumentality of global Shakespeare adaptations can have a positive impact if the works are analysed in their own rights rather than using the artists' diverse identities as a means to the bureaucratic end of demonstrating (superficial) inclusiveness in the curriculum.

Here Gilles Deleuze and Félix Guattari's concept of *deterritorialization* is useful. This refers to a process that separates cultural practices from their 'native' habitats or points of origin. It sheds new light on cultural relations that are in flux. Shakespeare's texts and Japanese Noh style, for example, become available for appropriation by any artist of any background. Adaptations, however, to borrow again from Deleuze and Guattari, can reterritorialize plays or performance styles when they go on tour and take up space in new venues.[9] However, as I mentioned in the previous section, some companies, such as the RSC, do not seem to be interested in the process of reterritorialization either due to their imagined neutrality or privileged position. From 2014 to 2016, the London Globe toured Dominic Dromgoole's production of *Hamlet* through some 200 countries and territories with the same English script and cast, and little adjustment for local audiences.[10]

By asking what makes global Shakespeares an exercise in ethics, I am concerned with the often glossed-over deterritorializing effect of global arts, rather than with who is more entitled to appropriate a particular culture. In this light, we gain a better understanding of intercultural works through cultural locations that have been performatively constructed. Transnational networks of collaboration and funding make it more meaningful to speak of a work's set of reference points rather than singular points of geographical origin: a French-Japanese *Richard II* by Ariane Mnouchkine in Paris and on tour, for example, or Lin Zhaohua's *Richard III*, a production set in a no-place, made in Beijing and presented in Berlin.[11]

The ambitious Globe to Globe Festival in London in 2012 provided a taste not only of festive cosmopolitanism but also of what seems to be a common claiming of moral high ground in the language that festival organizers use to justify their efforts – a tacit narrative about how Shakespeare's universal moral values help artists in dire situations find meanings in life. Globe to Globe stories told by visiting companies helped to sell performances of war zones to audiences in a carnival zone, as evidenced in particular by the *Comedy of Errors* (Roy-e-Sabs Company) in Dari Persian from Afghanistan. The artists themselves also pointed to Shakespeare's timeliness. The production's director, Corinne Jaber, found the *Comedy* particularly relevant to Afghanistan with 'a father searching for his lost family' after decades of war. The Roy-e-Sabs Company had to rehearse their production in Delhi after narrowly escaping a Taliban attack on the British Council building in Kabul.[12] Performing the play helped the company take shelter from harsh Afghan politics. The marketing arm of Shakespeare's Globe capitalized on the media coverage of the difficulties faced by this small theatre company, whose name means 'path of hope'. Their journey to the World Shakespeare Festival was meant to inspire hope in humanity. One couldn't help but notice how metropolitan festival organizers – like collectors – cast a colonialist gaze towards productions located in the fraught category of 'global Shakespeares'. Performances originating from the Global South have continued to be co-opted for their inspirational merit.

In 2016, the Oregon Shakespeare Festival produced Desdemona Chiang's *Winter's Tale* with an Asian-American cast, an adaptation that set the romance in pre-modern China and America's Old West, combining both Asian and Asian-American perspectives. In this instance, Shakespeare served as a platform for minority performers to engage an increasingly diverse audience and to bring to the fore some questions regarding ethnic identities. In 2018, the independent film company Shanty Productions debuted their *Twelfth Night* with a multi-ethnic cast (directed by Adam Smethurst). In the film, Sheila Atim's Black Viola is one of several refugees washed ashore on a pebble beach. Smethurst drew on the idea of using Shakespeare as 'an Other within' during an interview: 'With the widespread rise of anti-immigrant populism and governments actively encouraging a hostile environment for refugees, telling the story of the outsider surviving in an alien world on her wit, charm and ingenuity became and remains compellingly urgent.'[13] These are examples of colour-conscious practices – choices made to counteract the erasure of minorities caused by the much-criticized notion of colourblindness.[14]

Global Shakespeare seems conveniently to offer answers to competing demands from both conservative and neoliberal societies, namely, the demands that educators and artists become more transnational in outlook while simultaneously sustaining traditional canons. For both conservatives and innovators, the genre of global Shakespeare is politically expedient in a neoliberal, free-market economy that tends to compartmentalize, privatize and commercialize individual suffering.

As a result, works by artists of colour engaging with Shakespeare are imagined to fix their intellectual content 'by way of a national, ethnic, or cultural location'.[15] Western, white examples are assumed to be more effective in their explanatory power, while African, Asian and Latin American materials are recruited to serve as the exceptional particular. Henry Louis Gates Jr. makes a similar observation in his call for developing a 'Black theory' specifically for the interpretation of African American literature to counter the tendency not to see aesthetic merit in Black literature. He writes that 'black literature and its criticism . . . have been put to uses that were not primarily aesthetic'; rather, they are part of the discourse about the role of African Americans in 'the order of things'.[16]

Uneven valuation

This chapter proposes that we theorize global Shakespeare through questions of ethics. Acts of appropriation carry with them strong ethical implications; a crucial component is one's willingness to listen to and be subjected to the demands of others. In the pull and tug of appropriating a work, the polyphony of voices – including voices once obscured by history – can regain moral agency. Appropriation as an act of quoting others can be an exercise of channelling, letting through and enabling feeble voices. These metaphorical citations create moments of self and mutual recognition.

I would like to note that while artists and critics alike gravitate towards inspirational narratives, there is the risk of selling out on art's potential impact in terms of social justice. Advertising trends – or cultural paratexts around performances – sometimes give false impressions of the works' inclusiveness. Marketing shortcuts can contradict artists' ethical claims in relation to the presentation of racial and gender diversity. In some cases, productions driven by inclusive casting choices may be aesthetically incoherent; in others, queerness, for instance, is framed as a defining feature when a production does not actively engage with gender diversity or employ queer actors.

With increased media attention to whiteness and gender identities, theatre companies from all-female and genderqueer groups to original practice troupes have led a new advertising trend, emphasizing a queer 'vibe'. As Sawyer Kemp points out, companies do this without actually employing trans-identifying performers or engaging substantively with the trans community, which is ethically problematic.[17] The gender-fluid paratext around a performance builds expectations or enhances a work's perceived social justice quotient. However, productions that engage in 'post-gender' casting practices, such as Michelle Terry's Globe productions in 2018, do not quite subvert the status quo other than not treating gender as a meaningful denominator in dramaturgical terms. Terry played Hamlet in her own production, which participated in a long tradition of women playing Hamlet.[18] Mark Rylance's all-male *Twelfth Night* at the Globe in 2012 (directed by Tim Carroll) focused more on its merit as proof of concept for original practice performances in modern times than on rethinking gender roles and identities.

As with gender, race is a key vector in embodied identities. Despite and because of artistic director Gregory Doran's defence of its 'non-culturally specific casting' practice, the RSC was criticized for its predominantly white cast in *The Orphan of Zhao* (2012).[19] Productions with racially diverse casts face their own problems, too. In 2017, the Shakespeare Theatre Company in Washington, DC, produced a pan-African *Macbeth*, directed by Liesl Tommy with a multi-ethnic cast. The production, set in a fictional African country, brought to mind Orson Welles's landmark 1936 *Macbeth*, which was set in Haiti and featured an all-Black cast. Tommy reimagined the Scottish play in a north African political landscape with visual references to Russian and CIA (or rather, UIA in the production) intervention in civil wars and regime change in an unnamed 'third-world' country. The production boasted non-traditional and gender-bending casting, featuring more women and actors of colour than in previous productions by the same company, with Jesse J. Perez (Macbeth) and Nikkole Salter (Lady Macbeth) in the lead roles. Not coincidentally, Hecate and the witches were the only white characters in this universe, which accentuated not only the clash between Western imperialism and the developing world but also the power imbalance between Black and white communities. The transposition strategy of adaptation reflected the life experience of Tommy, who was raised in Cape Town, South Africa, during the late apartheid era.

Contrary to expectations, however, this BIPOC (Black, Indigenous, and People of Colour)-led production addressing political oppression received a mixed response as a result of its lack of coherence in dramaturgical conceptualization. It was perceived that the multi-ethnic cast was used for ornamental value, even though Tommy's production engaged in two models of non-traditional casting outlined by the Alliance for Inclusion in the Arts and Ayanna Thompson: conceptual casting, a model 'in which actors of color are [self-consciously] cast in roles to enhance the play's social resonance', and cross-cultural casting, an approach that translates the universe of the play to a different culture and location.[20] As in Welles's *Macbeth*, the ethnicity and race of Tommy's cast matched those of the characters and cultures in the adaptation's universe.

Casting people of colour is an important step, but, as Philip J. Mazzocco's research points out, there is an important distinction between colour-conscious and colour-blind casting practices. The former brings actors' identities to bear on dramaturgical meanings. The latter 'perpetuates prejudices against minority rather than eradicating them', because it erroneously equates social justice with the absence of stereotyping in selection processes. Mazzocco points out that colour-blind practices can propagate 'harmful anti-minority prejudice'.[21]

Shakespeare to the rescue?

The cases I have discussed thus far demonstrate that adaptations have strong ethical implications whether or not the artists make claims about ethics – mutually accepted guidelines on what constitutes a good action. Since acting involves embodying and channelling the pathos of the characters, performances have become the primary area where beliefs in the remedial functions of art are manifested and contested.

To elucidate my theory of ethics, I work from a growing archive of recent instances of ethical claims about global Shakespeares. Behind global performances lie either ethical questions or efforts to link the classics to social justice. My research has shown that many screen and stage adaptations are informed by a philosophical investment in Shakespeare's reparative merit, a preconceived notion that performing the Shakespearean canon can improve not only local art forms (such as attracting a larger audience or securing invitations for international festivals or tours) but also personal and social circumstances (such as addressing issues that are otherwise difficult to discuss publicly).[22] Shakespeare is imagined to have a reparative effect on the artist's or society's outlooks on life when the time is 'out of joint' (*Hamlet*, 1.5.156) or during identity crises. Michael Dobson has used the term 'sentimental myths' to characterize the tendency, on the part of enthusiasts, to imagine socially remedial, politically effective Shakespeares.[23] Examples include the idea that 'all productions . . . in the former Eastern Bloc were urgently political' or the myth of Shakespeare's 'intercultural transparency' on account of successful translations of his oeuvre into multiple languages (which in turn is used as evidence that his work 'must somehow transcend all of them').[24]

Some artists and audiences see performing or reading Shakespeare as a strategy to set things right. Appropriations by both politicians and artists have tapped into Shakespeare's perceived remedial functions. Take, for example, the curious case of Nelson Mandela's reading of Shakespeare. A smuggled copy of *The Complete Works of Shakespeare* is said to have inspired Nelson Mandela while he was imprisoned on Robben Island off the coast of Cape Town. The South African political prisoners there signed their names next to passages that were important to them. The passage Mandela chose on 16 December 1977 was Caesar's stoic defiance before leaving for the senate on the Ides of March:

> Cowards die many times before their deaths;
> The valiant never taste of death but once.
> Of all the wonders that I yet have heard
> It seems to me most strange that men should fear;
> Seeing that death, a necessary end,
> Will come when it will come. (*Julius Caesar* 2.2.32–37)

In journalistic discourses, these lines supposedly taught Mandela how to dream and how to rise from the ashes. Interestingly, the story about the 'Robben Island Bible' has gained much more traction outside South Africa, particularly in London thanks to the British Museum's exhibition during the 2012 London Olympics (this was followed by an exhibition at the Folger Shakespeare Library in Washington, DC, in 2013). Many political prisoners who signed their names in that *Complete Works* could not recall their choice of passage or its significance during interviews. For the individuals directly involved, the political purchase of these citations was no longer relevant. South African scholars are more realistic in their assessment of the claims about Shakespeare's moral centrality to the liberation movement. David Schalkwyk has noted that 'Mandela pays little attention to the context of the speeches from which he draws his lessons or comforts'.[25] Ashwin Desai, in his book based on interviews with eight former inmates, cautions that 'Shakespeare is part of a Eurocentric canon that crowds out valuable and more relevant black and female voices'.[26]

Contradictory to the British media's celebration of Shakespeare's centrality in South African politics, prominent figures in the post-liberation African National Congress disavowed the Robben Island Bible's significance in political reform. Jackson Mthembu (former African National Congress [ANC] spokesman and parliamentarian) said it is not an inspiration and only iconic 'to those who want to make it iconic'.[27] Likewise, Ahmed Kathrada (former advisor to Mandela and parliamentarian), who was among those who put their names in the *Complete Works*, dismissed the idea that Shakespeare has politically reparative functions. This is an instance of 'ethical impact' in the eyes of beholders. In fact, it is not the South African politicians but British cultural institutions, such as the British Museum, that are deeply invested in the notion of Shakespeare setting things right – both within and outside the UK.

The political agency that comes with appropriation can lead to political advocacy or a false impression of ethical agency. Take *The Merchant of Venice*, for example. Shylock's 'Hath not a Jew eyes?' speech is one of the most often appropriated and cited passages. Al Pacino's superb performance in the Michael Radford film (MGM, 2004) brought humanity to the character and highlighted the difficulty of wrestling with a complex speech that is simultaneously a human rights declaration and a demonstration of vindictiveness.

The speech is featured in Roman Polanski's *The Pianist* (Canal+, 2002) and is particularly prominent in the film's trailer. As the Polish pianist Wladyslaw Szpilman (Adrian Brody) and his family wait in a yard to be shipped off to a concentration camp, he asks his brother what he is reading. His brother reads begrudgingly from the volume in his hand: 'If you prick us, do we not bleed? If you tickle us, do we not laugh? If you poison us, do we not die?', pausing right before the passage turns vindictive ('And if you wrong us, shall we not revenge?'). Szpilman's brother hands the book to him; he endorses it as a very appropriate choice for the occasion. The camera lingers just enough to show the play's title on the book cover. *Merchant* has become an iconic work when it comes to critiquing anti-Semitism. The citation of multi-layered histories and Shakespeare together is powerful and moving. However, as a form of deterritorialization, such reductive citations gloss over anti-Semitism within the play by amplifying the de-contextualized humanist message.

These instances point to a larger phenomenon that might be called remedial interpretations of Shakespeare. In a different context, Douglas Lanier has raised questions about 'reparative Shakespeare', the performance of socially conscious, inspirational narratives that use Shakespeare as their centrepiece.[28] Fictional and documentary works in this genre, such as *A Midwinter's Tale* (dir. Kenneth Branagh, 1995), *A Dream in Hanoi* (dir. Tom Weidlinger, 2002), *Mickey B* (dir. Tom Magill, 2007), *The Last Lear* (dir. Rituparno Ghosh, 2007), *The Road to the Globe* (dir. Mike Jonathan, 2012), *The Hobart Shakespeareans* (dir. Mel Stuart, 2005) and *Cesare deve morire* (*Caesar Must Die*, dir. Paolo Taviani and Vittorio Taviani, 2012), often feature a foolhardy troupe or director working with unlikely Shakespearean actors for a high-stakes performance. Despite seemingly insurmountable obstacles and setbacks, the narratives end with a triumphant performance. Lanier theorizes that such works 'invest Shakespeare with magical reformational power', and the socially marginalized – refugees, women of colour, inmates – can be empowered accordingly.

Popular culture shares this impulse to put literature, and Shakespeare in particular, to socially enlightened uses. In *Shakespeare in Love* (dir. John Madden, 1998), the stuttering tailor and aspiring thespian, Wabash, plays the chorus in the premiere of *Romeo and Juliet*. As he delivers the prologue, his stammer gradually disappears; eventually he is able to finish reciting the speech. Even though reparative performances come with their own affective rewards, the universalist moralization of the classics can be problematic. Shakespeare is believed to be a catalyst for social change and source material for 'feel good' narratives. For these reasons, earnest performances of Shakespeare's reparative efficacy sometimes align themselves with conservative interpretations of the plays. They assume that, if one tunes in carefully, one could receive moral lessons contained in the dramatic situations and thereby improve one's personal and social circumstances.

Among Shakespeare's plays, *King Lear* has been used frequently for reparative purposes. Anglophone pop culture gravitated towards *King Lear* through memes and quotes during the global Covid-19 pandemic, especially in early 2020. On Shakespeare's birthday, 23 April, at the height of the pandemic, Canada's Stratford Festival kicked off their online film festival with artistic director Antoni Cimolino's 2014 *King Lear*; this became their most watched video, with 85,000 viewers. One reason for this popularity is that *Lear* is widely but erroneously thought to be written during an outbreak of the bubonic plague. Despite its bleak outlook, the play was appropriated to reassure audiences of their pre-existing beliefs about humanity during a global crisis.

There were pop cultural references to Lear and ageing as an undignified process before the pandemic, too. In Christopher Nolan's film *The Dark Knight* (2008), Gotham City's district attorney Harvey Dent says, in a foreshadowing scene, that one either 'dies a hero [in a timely manner]' or 'live[s] long enough to see yourself become a villain', implying that longevity simply brings more opportunities to embarrass oneself. Passages from *King Lear* have been used to play a healing role in narratives about ageing and dying with dignity. Iconic scenes have also been used to comment on situations outside the play's world and its fictional logic. Kristian Levring's film *The King Is Alive* (Newmarket Capital Group, 2000), shot in the avant-garde style of Dogme 95, features performances of various scenes of *King Lear* as a desperate diversion by a group of tourists stranded in the Namibian desert.

Other adaptations deploy speeches from the tragedy as therapy for both characters and audiences. In Rituparno Ghosh's 2007 film *The Last Lear*, which is inspired by Utpal Dutt's play *Aajker Shahjahan*, an eccentric, ageing Shakespearean stage actor in Kolkata, Harish 'Harry' Mishra (Amitabh Bachchan), reenacts scenes of plays he used to perform. In the final scene, Shabnam (Preity Zinta) comes to visit Harry and wakes him from a coma by reading lines from the reconciliation scene (*King Lear* 4.7). An actress herself and an admirer of Harry, Shabnam slips into the role of Cordelia, while Harry dies reciting the lines he knows by heart: 'You are a spirit, I know . . . Where have I been? . . . I know not what to say . . . I am a very foolish, fond old man.' It is a scene of reconciliation and self-recognition because in his career, Harry was ill-suited for the transition from stage to screen.

Similar to *The Last Lear,* John Kani's two-hander *Kunene and the King* depicts how characters come to terms with racialized biases and their mortality through situations that parallel those in *Lear*. Jack, a white South African actor coping with terminal liver cancer, and his Black male nurse, Lunga, end up reenacting and reciting scenes from the play. Through *Lear*, Jack and Lunga expose each other's cultural biases and eventually reconcile their differences. This co-production by the RSC and the Fugard Theatre was mounted in Stratford-upon-Avon and Cape Town in 2019 and performed by Kani and Antony Sher, a British actor of South African origin who has written at length about his diasporic experience.[29] A decade prior to their collaboration on *Kunene and the King*, Kani and Sher starred in Janice Honeyman's *The Tempest* (RSC and Baxter Theatre, 2009), where Kani played Caliban to Sher's Prospero, addressing, in Sandra Young's words, 'a post-apartheid hermeneutic heaving with anger at decades of racial injustice'.[30]

In a similar but more sombre vein, the independent film *Lear's Shadow* (dir. Brian Elerding, 2019) follows two friends as they use *Lear* to prove their points in an argument. Jack (Fred Cross) takes on the role of Lear, while Stephen (David Blue) plays all three of Lear's daughters. They act out scenes from *Lear* while attempting to rebuild their friendship and deal with grief. *Lear* becomes both a pretext for the film and a therapeutic source for the characters.

The myths of Shakespeare in modern culture are partially responsible for the artistic and critical predilection for reparative performances. When Shakespeare is evoked, the play or passages are given an ethical burden and sometimes a curative quality. In our contemporary context, ethics are often interpreted specifically in terms of a responsibility towards people who have been treated unfairly. We owe it to the artist who created the works that we study. We owe it to ourselves to listen intently to what they have to say.

Two relevant concepts here are Rita Charon's 'radical listening' and Emmanuel Levinas's theory of ethics in knowledge production. Radical listening, a communication strategy, is attuned to the roots of stories in a manner that allows for 'an egality between teller and listener that gives voice to the tale'.[31] Ethics takes precedence over organized forms of knowledge about a subject, and we should be on the lookout for unconscious and discriminatory biases in the production and dissemination of knowledge. The British Museum, for instance, suggested one particular way to 'know' the cultural significance of the Robben Island Bible within the UK's understanding of international affairs, while South African political prisoners had their own pathway to alternative knowledge about their experience and political reform. There is an ethical imperative in the formulation of ideas about a given topic after facts have been compiled. We are also responsible for the preservation of the alterity of the Other, even as we make the obscure known by 'freeing it of its otherness' – in other words, we are constantly striving against 'the imperialism of the same', an assertive move of acquisition that maps unfamiliar things onto what we think we know.[32]

If knowledge production is an acquisitive move, it has also given rise to 'knowledgeable ignorance', which, according to Norman Daniel, is the tendency to insist on 'knowing' something as one's own ideological construct. It is a form of laziness and irresponsible action to know 'people as something they are not, and could not possibly be, and [to maintain] these ideas even when the means exist to know differently'.[33] Equally problematic is the tendency to regard the global and the local as politically expedient, diametrically opposed categories of difference in an often-unarticulated agenda to preserve a literary elite. The global is imagined to be whatever the United States and the United Kingdom are not.[34] Since 1940, the United States and the United Kingdom have been close military allies, though their governments may diverge on foreign policy and worldviews. Notwithstanding their political and cultural differences (captured aptly by Oscar Wilde: 'We have really everything in common with America nowadays, except, of course, language'), these two countries – with a combined population of 400 million – have collectively maintained the dominant role of the English language and Anglophone cultural production in the modern world.³⁵ This phenomenon has contributed to the tendency, in English-language scholarship, to assume that the global refers to cultural realms beyond the United States and the United Kingdom.

Site-specific ethics

To address the blind spots of misguided 'ethical' questions, we can develop site-specific knowledge. Location-specific narratives in Shakespeare adaptations unfold alongside their intricately crafted mise-en-scène with ethnographic details, revealing the physical, fictional and geocultural dimensions of the cultural work being carried out under the name of Shakespeare. Films and theatre productions accrue site-specific meanings as they are toured or viewed in different locations. Site-specific epistemologies consist of the production and dissemination of location-based meanings, as 'epistemic evaluation' depends on 'practical concerns' such as the cultural backgrounds of the artists and audiences.³⁶ The setting and venue of a performance is key to location-specific narratives and ethics. The site-specific epistemologies that audiences can, or choose to, access depends on their theatre-going habits and cultural backgrounds.

Understanding that the meanings of any adaptation are relational can lead to a deeper appreciation of how multiple localities are brought together to craft a new narrative. Take John Kani's work, for example. His landmark performance of Othello in a 1987 production (dir. Janet Suzman) at the Market Theatre in Johannesburg received critical acclaim. Known internationally for his performance of King T'Chaka in *Black Panther* (dir. Ryan Coogler, Marvel, 2018) and *Captain America: Civil War* (dir. the Russo Brothers, Marvel, 2016), Kani is one of the most prominent South African actors today. As a Black Othello under apartheid, Kani's presence alone was a milestone in self-representation and equality, similar to Ira Aldridge's first Black Othello in London in 1825 when exclusively white casts were the norm. The significance of Kani's and Aldridge's performances, obviously, is diametrically opposed to that of Laurence Olivier's blackface Othello in Stuart Burge's 1965 film version, which, in turn, inspired Ma Yong'an's performance in *Aosailuo* (Beijing Experimental *Jingju* Theatre, 1983), the first blackface Othello in Beijing opera and the first

Chinese operatic adaptation of a Western play after the Cultural Revolution (1966–76). Blackface performances signified differently in South Africa, the UK and China due to variances in social discourses about race.

By contrast, Kani's Caliban in the 2009 *Tempest* accrued divergent meanings in Cape Town and London, leading to uneven reception. Sher's younger Prospero kept Kani's elderly Caliban on a tether and delivered the epilogue as an apology to Caliban rather than to the audience. The production received favourable reviews when it toured Britain, where the postcolonial allegory helped white audiences justify enjoyment of the African carnival. The production's global reception is at odds with the reaction within South Africa. Noting Kani's stature as 'the master of the (post-) apartheid stage', Sandra Young has pointed out that to cast Kani as 'the supposed monster ... is to invite outrage before he has spoken a word in Caliban's voice'.[37] Within South Africa, the production was not as successful as the 1987 *Othello* because, by 2009, the idea of decolonization was no longer politically revolutionary. Audiences were also divided over the staging's humour, which offended some but for others helped to bring a welcome light-heartedness.

Conclusion

Theatre and film artists continue to challenge fixed notions of tradition and a narrow definition of cultural authenticity. As Shakespeare performances enter a postnational space, where identities are blurred by the presence of international performers and tourist audiences, transnational corporate sponsors and the logics of international festivals, ethical concerns and claims continue to be articulated through site-specific epistemologies and location-specific cultural meanings. Since the postnational space, like many liminal spaces, is discursively formed, global Shakespeare becomes an exercise in ethics when dramaturgical meanings are produced across cultural and social contexts. An adaptation accrues meanings through its touring activities or the locations where it is viewed. When actors embody various characters, they draw attention to their skin colour, accents and (un)intentionally highlighted or concealed traces of cultural inscriptions in their life. Deterritorialization and reterritorialization – processes that unmark or conceal a work's point of 'origin' – have important implications for how the field of global Shakespeare conceives of itself. A work may have a self-proclaimed social justice quotient in one location but suffer from an imposed ethical burden in another context. An exercise in ethics attends to these meanings that are in flux and supports site-specific epistemologies.

Notes

1 See Alexa Alice Joubin, *Shakespeare and East Asia* (Oxford: Oxford University Press, 2021), 30.
2 See Iqbal Kahn, '1960s Birmingham to 2012 Stratford-upon-Avon', in *Shakespeare, Race and Performance: The Diverse Bard*, ed. Delia Jarrett-Macauley (New York: Routledge, 2017), 137–45.
3 See D. J. R. Bruckner, '*The Tempest* at New Audience', *New York Times*, 27 March 1986: 15. Available online: https://www.nytimes.com/1986/03/27/theater/stage-the-tempest-at-new-audience.html.
4 Malcolm Moore, 'Edinburgh Festival 2011: *The Revenge of Prince Zi Dan* – The Secret of Hamlet in Chinese', *Daily Telegraph,* 15 August 2011. Available online: https://www.telegraph.co.uk/culture/theatre/edinburgh-festival/8701649/Edinburgh-Festival-2011-The-Revenge-of-Prince-Zi-Dan-The-secret-of-Hamlet-in-Chinese.html.
5 For a general assessment of the RSC's tours to China, see Alfred Hickling, 'Sit Down and Shut Up', *The Guardian*, 11 June 2002. Available online: https://www.theguardian.com/stage/2002/jun/12/rsc.artsfeatures.
6 Alexa Alice Joubin and Elizabeth Rivlin, Introduction, *Shakespeare and the Ethics of Appropriation,* ed. Alexa Alice Joubin and Elizabeth Rivlin (New York: Palgrave Macmillan, 2014), 2–3.
7 A man may not marry his brother's wife, as specified by item 18 of 'A Table of Kindred and Affinity, Wherein Whosoever Are Related Are Forbidden in Scripture and Our Law as to Marry Together', *The Anglican Book of Common Prayer* (1559), ed. John E. Booty (Charlottesville: University of Virginia Press, 2005). See Laura Bohannan's 'Shakespeare in the Bush: An American anthropologist set out to study the Tiv of West Africa and was taught the true meaning of *Hamlet*', *Natural History* 75 (1966): 28–33.
8 See Susan Bennett's chapter in this volume, 'Re-thinking "Global Shakespeare" for Social Justice'.

9   Gilles Deleuze and Félix Guattari's approach is parallel to the concept of economic deterritorialization, as discussed in their two-volume *Capitalism and Schizophrenia: Anti-Oedipus* [vol. 1, 1972], trans. Robert Hurley, Mark Seem, and Helen R. Lane (London: Continuum, 2004), and *A Thousand Plateaus* [vol. 2, 1980], trans. Brian Massumi (London: Continuum, 2004).

10 See Dominic Dromgoole, Hamlet *Globe to Globe: Two Years, 193,000 Miles, 197 Countries, One Play* (New York: Grove Press, 2017).

11 For an extract from Mnouchkine's *Richard II*, see https://www.youtube.com/watch?v=XquydfFTvos&ab_channel=artlabchicago. For a video recording of Lin's *Richard III*, see https://globalshakespeares.mit.edu/li-cha-san-shi-lin-zhaohua-2001/.

12 See 'Afghan Actors Gear Up for Shakespeare at London Olympics', *Firstpost*, 27 February 2012. Available online: https://www.firstpost.com/world/afghan-actors-gear-up-for-shakespeare-at-london-olympics-226044.html.

13 Quoted in 'Olivier Award-Winner Sheila Atim Stars as Shipwrecked Twins Viola and Sebastian in a New and Timely Screen Adaptation of Shakespeare's Much-Loved Comedy *Twelfth Night*', *Shakespeare Magazine* (2018). Available online: http://www.shakespearemagazine.com/2018/10/olivier-award-winner-sheila-atim-stars-as-shipwrecked-twins-viola-and-sebastian-in-a-new-and-timely-screen-adaptation-of-shakespeares-much-loved-comedy-twelfth-night-released-on-25-october/.

14 See Philip J. Mazzocco, *The Psychology of Racial Colorblindness: A Critical Review* (New York: Palgrave Macmillan, 2017), 11 and 39.

15 Rey Chow, 'Introduction: On Chineseness as a Theoretical Problem', *boundary 2* 25, no. 3 (1998): 3. Chow continues: 'Hence, whereas it would be acceptable for authors dealing with specific cultures, such as those of Britain, France, the United States . . . to use generic titles . . . authors dealing with non-Western cultures are often expected to mark their subject matter with words such as *Chinese, Japanese, Indian, Korean, Vietnamese*, and their like.' See also Adele Lee, *The English Renaissance and the Far East: Cross-Cultural Encounters* (Madison, NJ: Fairleigh Dickinson University Press, 2018), 150.

16 Henry Louis Gates Jr., 'Talking Black: Critical Signs of the Times', in *The Norton Anthology of Theory and Criticism*, ed. Vincent B. Leitch et al. (New York: Norton, 2001), 2428.

17 Sawyer K. Kemp, 'Transgender Shakespeare Performance: A Holistic Dramaturgy', *The Journal for Early Modern Cultural Studies* 19, no. 4 (Fall 2019): 265–83.

18 Tony Howard, *Women as Hamlet: Performance and Interpretation in Theatre, Film and Fiction* (Cambridge: Cambridge University Press, 2007).

19 Quoted in Matt Trueman, 'Royal Shakespeare Company Under Fire for Not Casting Enough Asian Actors', *The Guardian*, 19 October 2012. Available online: https://www.theguardian.com/stage/2012/oct/19/royal-shakespeare-company-asian-actors.

20 Ayanna Thompson, *Passing Strange: Shakespeare, Race, and Contemporary America* (Oxford: Oxford University Press, 2011), 76. See Alexa Alice Joubin, 'Shakespeare Theatre Company's Macbeth and the Limits of Multiculturalism', *Early Modern Culture* 13 (2018): 240–6.

21 Mazzocco, *The Psychology of Racial Colorblindness*, 4.

22 See Alexa Alice Joubin, 'Screening Social Justice: Performing Reparative Shakespeare against Vocal Disability', *Adaptation: The Journal of Literature on Screen Studies*, October 2020: 1–19.

23 Citations from Shakespeare's plays are taken from Richard Proudfoot, Ann Thompson, David Scott Kastan and H. R. Woodhuysen, eds, *The Arden Shakespeare Complete Works, Third Series* (London and New York: The Arden Shakespeare, 2021).

24 Michael Dobson, 'Afterword: Shakespeare and Myth', in *Local and Global Myths in Shakespearean Performance*, ed. Aneta Mancewicz and Alexa Alice Joubin (London: Palgrave, 2018), 262–3.

25 David Schalkwyk, *Hamlet's Dreams: The Robben Island Shakespeare* (London: Bloomsbury, 2013), 65. See also Schalkwyk, 'Mandela, the Emotions, and the Lessons of Prison', in *The Cambridge Companion to Nelson Mandela*, ed. Rita Barnard (Cambridge: Cambridge University Press, 2014), 59.

26 Ashwin Desai, *Reading Revolution: Shakespeare on Robben Island* (Chicago: Haymrket Books, 2014), ix.

27 Quoted in Anita Li, 'African National Congress Disputes Iconic Status of Robben Island Bible Displayed in British Museum', *Toronto Star*, 19 July 2012. Available online: https://www.thestar.com/news/world/2012/07/19/african_national_congress_disputes_iconic_status_of_robben_island_bible_displayed_in_british_museum.html.

28 Douglas Lanier, 'Shakespeare and the Reparative Turn', La Société Française Shakespeare Annual Conference, Paris, 18–20 January 2018.

29 See Gregory Doran and Antony Sher, *Woza Shakespeare*: Titus Andronicus *in South Africa* (London: Bloomsbury, 2006).

30 Sandra Young, *Shakespeare in the Global South: Stories of Oceans Crossed in Contemporary Adaptation* (London: Bloomsbury, 2019), 88.

31 Rita Charon, *Narrative Medicine: Honoring the Stories of Illness* (Oxford: Oxford University Press, 2006), 66 and 77; see also Charon in Portland Helmich, 'Interview: How Radical Listening Can Heal Division – And Why It Matters Now More Than Ever', *Kripalu*, 1 June 2021. Available online: https://kripalu.org/resources/how-radical-listening-can-heal-division-and-why-it-matters-now-more-ever.

32 Emmanuel Levinas, *Otherwise Than Being or Beyond Essence*, trans. Alphonso Lingis (London: Kluwer Academic Publishers, 1991), 114 and 117.

33 Norman Daniel, *Islam and the West* (Edinburgh: Edinburgh University Press, 1964), 12.

34 See Siddhartha Deb, 'The Rise of the Global Novelist', *New Republic*, 25 April 2017. Available online: https://newrepublic.com/article/141676/rise-global-novelist-adam-kirsch-review.

35 Oscar Wilde, *The Canterville Ghost* (Seattle: Prime Classics, 2005), 7.

36 Alan Millar, Adrian Haddock, and Duncan Pritchard, 'Introduction', in *Epistemic Value*, ed. Haddock, Millar and Duncan Pritchard (Oxford: Oxford University Press, 2009), 9.

37 Young, *Shakespeare in the Global South*, 88.

PART II

Resisting racial logics

4

Making whiteness out of 'nothing'

The recurring comedic torture of (pregnant) Black women from medieval to modern

Dyese Elliott-Newton

On 16 January 2015, Charlena Michelle Cooks, a Black woman, was violently arrested in an elementary school parking lot after bringing her second grader to school. After interviewing the white woman who called the police and acknowledging that he did not see any crime in the women's initial altercation, the officer at the scene asked for Cooks's version of events. Cooks shared her account of events and proceeded to call her partner. Because Cooks declined to give her full name, the officer forced her to the ground with her hands behind her back to place her in handcuffs. Cooks was eight months pregnant.[1]

As I reflected on Cooks's story, I was both enraged and heartbroken. It fit the 'normal' narrative of police brutality targeting Black bodies, and yet, it still felt distinct.[2] There was something additionally painful about seeing a *pregnant* Black woman, a woman who looked like my own mother, being thrown down to the ground stomach first. This image has since lived in my memory, and it is only recently that I have been able to understand the totality of its violence. As the officer becomes physical, Cooks states, 'Please don't touch me. I'm pregnant.' The officer continues to grab at her and eventually calls for back-up. If you listen closely to the recording, you can hear Cooks scream, 'Please, I'm pregnant! I'm pregnant!', and you can hear the officer say, 'Please ma'am. Why are you resisting?' During an interview, just a few months later, Cooks explains that the officer made her feel 'like an animal, like a monster, like [she] didn't exist, like [she] was not human'. Still traumatized, she says, 'it's like [the officer] looked at me and said "oh she must be this way" and I'm not that way'. The city's response to the bodycam footage was only that 'it is apparent that Ms. Cook [sic] actively resisted arrest. The Barstow Police Department continues to be proactive in training its officers to assess and handle interactions with emotionally charged individuals. . . . The incident was in no way racially motivated as implied by the ACLU' (American Civil Liberties Union).[3]

The violence begins before Cooks's pregnant stomach hits the concrete, and it will have a long afterlife. In reviewing the footage, it is clear that the officer is wilfully choosing not to recognize Cooks's condition. In doing so, he makes her screams and resistance seem unwarranted and ultimately criminal, since Cooks is only charged with resisting arrest. The injury is furthered by the city's decision to label Cooks as 'emotionally charged', highlight the officer's training, and spell Cooks's name wrong in the official statement. We are told to perceive Cooks as irrational, but what happens if we take her seriously? What happens if we acknowledge her as 'monstrous' and 'non-existent' in this moment? It is only through Cooks's narrative that the officer's actions make sense. It is only her version of events that allows her pregnancy to be invisible and her actions to become hysterical.

Since Cooks's version of events is necessary for the social order in the United States to be maintained, it is imperative to investigate the source(s) of this narrative. How did she become monstrous? How did she come to exist as non-existent? It would be all too easy to mark

American chattel slavery as the source of this violence, and I would argue that the plantation only points us to the physical violence, which would be equivalent to beginning the story when Cooks's stomach hit the ground. We must instead ask ourselves about the mechanisms that made it possible for Cooks to be a threat in the first place, the stories that made it necessary for the police to be called. We must ask ourselves about the narratives that made it necessary for Cooks to repeatedly state her condition, even though it is one that is highly visible, and her assertions and cries were clearly ignored. To these questions, I am offering the medieval period as the birthplace of these stories and the early modern stage as the vehicle for their propagation.[4] To illustrate my points, I will juxtapose readings of *Morkinskinna* (1220), *The Merchant of Venice* (c.1595) and *The Masque of Blackness* (1605). As you will see, the Black woman, never the focus, but consistently the object of choice, functions as a safe and useful space to bury the various social anxieties that challenge the 'perfection' and 'supremacy' of whiteness. I argue that laughter is the antidote for white anxiety and that comedic violence, through storytelling, particularly on the space of the early modern stage, provides the necessary instruction for which bodies should regularly provide this culturally necessary comic relief. Since the Black woman's body still exists as a site for relief of these social anxieties, as in the case of Cooks, it is important to name comedic violence, and the resulting laughter, as not only forms of instruction but also forms of torture.

Morkinskinna is the longest account depicting the mental illness of the Norwegian king Sigurðr Magnússon (1090–1130).[5] The account details many of the king's major episodes, but there is one that particularly stands out. It takes place at Christmastime:

> It happened one evening during Christmas that King Sigurðr was sitting in the hall, where the tables were set up. The king said: 'Bring me meat.' They answered: 'It is not customary in Norway, sire, to eat meat at Christmas.' The king said: 'That is the custom I desire.' They came in with porpoise on the platters. The king stuck his knife in but did not eat. Then the king said: 'Bring me a woman.'

Here the episode takes a disturbing turn:

> They brought a woman into the hall. She had her face covered. The king put a hand to her head and said: 'You are an uncomely

woman, but not beyond endurance.' Then he looked at her hand and said: 'Not a handsome hand and misshapen, but not intolerable.' Then he told her to stretch out her foot. He looked at it and said: 'A big and monstrous foot, but let it pass.' Then he told her to lift her tunic, and he looked at her legs. 'What legs! They are both thick and black. You must be some kind of a whore.' He said that he wanted nothing to do with her and told them to take her out.[6]

The first peculiarity in this scene is the king's violation of the Christmas tradition by requesting meat at his table; however, it would seem that his request for a woman does not interfere with the customs since he is not challenged for this request. When the woman is brought in, he proceeds to inspect her features meticulously. He uses the terms 'uncomely,' 'misshapen' and 'monstrous' to describe her, yet each of these is tolerable. It is not until he sees her thick black legs that he dismisses her on the basis that her blackness indicates that she must be a 'whore'. In terms of her features, these three terms respectively correlate to ugliness, physical abnormality or disability, and monstrosity, which is unhuman. It is interesting that each of these is visible and excusable until it is revealed that she is Black. It could be that her blackness is meant to be understood as the reason for the deformities, but the text also requires us to consider whether any of these abnormalities would have been noticeable had her black visage been visible upon her arrival. Based on his repulsion at the sight of her black legs, it is evident that the king would not have taken the time to evaluate her head, hands or feet had her complexion been noticeable from the start.

In her article, 'Recovering Shakespeare's Racial Genealogies', Katherine Gillen uses *Hamlet*'s source texts, *The Revenge of Amleth* (1150?) and François de Belleforest's *Histoires Tragiques* (1572), to examine the ways in which blackness is mobilized to express white melancholia.[7] Gillen writes:

> Hamlet largely aligns the English with the Danes and works to recuperate members of both groups by cleansing them of northern barbarism, a quality attributed to them in classical paradigms. Hamlet draws select Northerners into a vision of pan-European whiteness, a subject position bolstered in the play through the racist denigration of Moors and Turks.[8]

It is this positioning of white melancholia beside blackness that assists my reading of the *Morkinskinna*, which portrays a Northern king's mental illness. One could argue that the king's Northern barbarism reveals itself when he requests meat despite the Christian custom, a gesture which is heightened by the stabbing of the meat, which he ultimately does not consume. Instead, he consumes the humanity of this Black woman. Gillen reminds us of Hamlet's being continuously 'shrouded in black' due to this melancholia which oddly resonates with this scene within the Norwegian court. When the Black woman emerges, 'her face [is] covered', and this veiling no doubt bears significance in terms of faith and chastity. Désirée Koslin writes that dating back to Syro-Mesopotamian cultures, the veil served as both metaphorical and literal 'protective covers for [women's] honor'.[9] However, this woman's covering has no power here, as she is still forced to lift her tunic publicly before the king. At this moment, she is humiliated as she is shamed for her colour. It is important to recognize that, at this moment, the king's illness is shrouded, and this woman's alleged monstrosity and misshapenness are reconfigured as belonging to her blackness. The king is cleansed of his Northern barbarism and melancholia, because at this moment, the Black woman's body absorbs his own displaced difference. Thus, the hypervisibility of her blackness distracts the court from his melancholia.

This violation of the veil and public humiliation of the Black woman serve as a prime example of Carissa Harris's theorization of obscene pedagogy and its implications in perpetuating rape culture.[10] Harris argues that the obscene is a highly effective method of (sexual) instruction because its shock value garners listeners' attention and forces us to consider our views on 'violence, power, and desire'.[11] I am particularly invested in Harris's argument that one strength of the obscene is its ability to provoke laughter. When the Black woman is dismissed, it appears that this is a moment where we are encouraged to laugh at her and her multiple 'deformities' instead of gazing at the unstable white king.

The use of the obscene to make blackness a marker of sexual deviance and monstrosity certainly holds as effective pedagogy, as roughly 400 years later, a seemingly identical scene emerges on the Elizabethan stage within Act 3 of *The Merchant of Venice*:

JESSICA   Nay, you need not fear us, Lorenzo: Lancelot
           and I are out. He tells me flatly, there is no

	mercy for me in heaven, because I am a Jew's daughter: and he says, you are no good member of the commonwealth, for in converting Jews to Christians, you raise the price of pork.
Lorenzo	I shall answer that better to the commonwealth than you can the getting up of the Negro's belly: the Moor is with child by you, Lancelot.
Lancelot	It is much that the Moor should be more than reason: but if she be less than an honest woman, she is indeed more than I took her for.

(3.5.29–40)[12]

In this scene, blackness and sexual deviance are juxtaposed so that the spectator looks away from Lancelot's own barbarism, that is the sexual violation of this woman, which resulted in the pregnancy, as well as Lancelot's own lowly status as a servant. Furthermore, the 'Negro's belly' becomes the target for Lorenzo's fury resulting from his chosen partner, Jessica, being abused for her Jewish identity, which she has already vowed to forsake through a valid Christian union. Therefore, this move, in effect, also serves to whiten Jessica by contrast.[13] The difference in the Black woman's pregnancy in this scene, however, is significant, as it resituates the disability onto the, already racialized, Black woman's body, and instead of acknowledging her disability as an additional reason to protect her, the pregnancy is used to spark a discussion concerning her 'sexual deviance'. Regarding Lancelot's reaction to the pregnancy, David Bevington's footnotes indicate that Lancelot is surprised by the woman's condition. This surprise is unsurprising given the circulation of the Black women's inherent monstrosity that had already gained traction during the Middle Ages, as evidenced in King Sigurðr's court. Additionally, the depth of this surprise is further illuminated when read alongside *Measure for Measure,* as the play offers us a moment to think about chastity in the context of whiteness, a moment that speaks directly to the crux of the insult in both *Morkinskinna* and *Merchant*.

In Act 5.1 of *Measure*, Mariana explains that she is neither 'maid,' 'widow' nor 'wife' (170–5). In response, Duke Vincentio claims that she is 'nothing' (176) if she is not able to neatly fit into one of these categories, while Lucio concludes that she may be a 'punk' (178). Megan Matchinske explains that this line of interrogation is meant to label her as a sex worker (which in the period would be an attempt to humiliate and marginalize her).[14] This reading of *Measure* highlights the rhetorical violence directed at sex workers, in that the language of 'nothingness' is used to characterize their existence. And, when juxtaposed with *Morkinskinna* and *Merchant*, it is evident that Black women are automatically assumed to be in sex work. Sex work is simultaneously dehumanized and racialized, which is important given the ongoing criminalization of sex work. Using critical fabulation, Saidiya Hartman retells the stories of Black girls and women in early-twentieth-century Philadelphia and New York, who were targeted and exploited by the state for leading lives that similarly avoided these lingering constructions of 'maid, wife and widow'. Hartman finds these women in archives about the 'slums' as well as police records, as they were labelled 'vagrants' and 'wayward'.[15] Hartman rightly traces this issue of vagrancy status to late-fourteenth-century England, where vagrancy statutes were implemented to revive the working population following the 'Black Death'.[16] These laws, developed in response to the Black Death, catalyzed a new phase of Black death within the United States. As Hartman writes, the vagrancy statutes were transferred to the North American colonies, and more importantly they supplanted the Black Codes post-Emancipation.[17] And since 'vagrancy was a status, not a crime', Hartman adds that these 'status offenses were critical to the remaking of the racist order in the aftermath of Emancipation and they accelerated the growing disparity between black and white rates of incarceration in northern cities at the beginning of the twentieth century', and ultimately, 'status criminality was tethered irradicably to blackness'.[18] Additionally, these vagrancy laws forced Black women into domestic labour, which Hartman identifies as the project of transferring Black women into a domestic space ordered by white, patriarchal authority, as Black domestic space was viewed and treated as the 'locus of prostitution and criminality'.[19] Hartman once again illuminates the violence of the archives, showing that even in trying to recover these stories, Black women are historically presented as criminal, licentious and violent, while the histories of their being systemically exploited, abused and violated are intentionally erased and/or ignored.

Hartman clearly emphasizes how deviant sexuality and waywardness are attached to Black being, something that is readily unfolding via Lancelot's multiple attacks upon the pregnant Black woman. Borrowing this language of 'nothingness', which he effectively invokes through his accusation that in being 'less than honest' the Black woman is still 'more than [he] took her for', Lancelot marks this woman as 'wayward' and 'deviant' (*Merchant of Venice*, 3.5.38–40). Due to his determination that this woman is then, inherently 'nothing', and his ability to label her being as 'criminal' and 'other', Lancelot is absolved of any crime against her, which is likely sexual violence, and, moreover, he has forced her into labour, which is the carrying of this child, of which Lancelot feigns ignorance. This all occurs before this quick moment of rhetorical violence in Act 3. And, of course, this is the only moment that the audience sees and hears. This is the moment that is constructed for laughter and the moment that contributes to the construction of routine sexual, physical and rhetorical violence towards (pregnant) Black women.

To this point, even as obscene pedagogies are used to teach social norms, they double as language pedagogy. This is exemplified in *The Art of English Poesie,* as George Puttenham makes use of blackness to explain the mechanism of antiphrasis: 'Or when we deride by plaine and flat contradiction, as he that saw a dwarfe go in the streete said to his companion that walked with him: See yonder gyant: and to a Negro or woman blackemoore, in good sooth ye are a faire one, we may call it the broad floute.'[20] Kim Hall reads this passage as signifying the ways in which the binary of dark and light, or fair, is used in reference not only to beauty and morality but to distinguish between the 'self' and social 'others'.[21] To this, I would add that one of the key elements of defining self in this passage relies on the juxtaposition of white disability and blackness. Puttenham identifies what he sees as a deformity in an individual that we can assume to be white for a lack of racial markers.[22] To parallel the relationship between the individuals that he classifies as 'dwarf' and 'gyant', Puttenham identifies the pairing of a Black person and a 'faire' one. Both the 'dwarf' and the 'gyant' are meant to signify some difference from an unnamed standard, but both conditions are put in relationship to each other. Neither is put in opposition to fairness because blackness is left to do that work. In this moment, as in the previous scenes, blackness is reconfigured as a deformity, and attempting to name blackness, as 'faire', or beautiful and/or good, is, rhetorically speaking, a 'broad floute', or mockery. The passage, even as it is rhetorically violent, additionally models the manner through which the violence injures. The individual that is identified as 'dwarf' is observed, while the Black individual is addressed. The speaker says 'ye are a faire one', which means that the Black individual's person is also marked as being both vulnerable and available to such harmful addresses.

In her poetry book, *Citizen: An American Lyric*, Claudia Rankine narrates a moment where Judith Butler explains that language is made hurtful by addressability – that is the idea that one's being renders them 'exposed to the address of another'.[23] Reflecting on this answer, Rankine writes that 'you begin to understand yourself as rendered hypervisible in the face of such language acts. Language that feels hurtful is intended to exploit all the ways that you are present'.[24] Julie Phillips Brown argues that *Citizen*'s motif of chronic addressability effectively recreates the chronic exhaustion that Black and Brown people endure, while also situating this chronic addressability as the mechanism facilitating systemic police brutality, as these fatal interactions are initiated when Black people are profiled and targeted by white civilians and police officers.[25] This idea of chronic addressability further emphasizes the harm in Puttenham's rhetoric, as it demonstrates the relationship between this dehumanizing rhetoric and the physical violence that often follows, or accompanies it, while also emphasizing the fact that it is chronic. Additionally, Brown's reading echoes Charlena Michelle Cooks's account of her arrest where Cooks, being a Black woman, was addressable by both a white civilian and a white police officer, and being perceived as 'animal', 'monster' and 'not human', she became a target for physical violence despite being pregnant.

Considering *Morkinskinna*, *Merchant* and Puttenham's example in conversation encourages us to think about disability and race separately and then to consider what differences, if any, surface when disability exists for the Black individual. Lancelot's surprise is useful in this context because pregnancy is not a subjective condition in the way that 'uncomliness' and 'misshapenness' might be; rather, it is a highly visible physical condition, albeit a temporary one. Still, it is the presence of the pregnancy in this moment that enables us to think about what is happening with disability in the figure of the Black woman. *Morkinskinna* places white disability beside blackness, which is then used to cure the white subject of his illness (or at least divert the court's attention from it). Puttenham similarly uses blackness to supplant disability by solely positioning this blackness in opposition to whiteness, goodness and beauty. In doing so, what happens to the disabled Black subject? In this scene, Lancelot does not register the woman's condition because of her blackness. She is 'Negro' and 'Moor' rather than pregnant. Does this then mean that blackness makes disability illegible on the Black subject?

Therí Alyce Pickens examines this relationship between race and disability in *Black Madness :: Mad Blackness*, outlining the manifold ways that discussions of disability erase blackness and discussions of blackness erase disability.[26] She begins her discussion by assessing the tendency of those who identify as disabled, as well as the discipline of disability studies, to use the language of race to better understand disability and make it legible. In a reading of Leonard Kriegel's, 'Uncle Tom and Tiny Tim', Pickens criticizes Kriegel's use of Franz Fanon's discourse on race to meditate on his own experience as a disabled white man living within a rehabilitation facility during the 1960s.[27] Pickens writes that 'despite the fact that Kriegel's rehabilitation facility is in Harlem, he does not think through the life of the Black disabled person, nor does he speculate about the interiority of those around him. They are merely sullen'.[28] Even within a Black neighbourhood, in a facility where everyone bears the identity of 'disabled', Kriegel actively denies the existence of the Black patients' disabilities. I appreciate Pickens's use of the term 'sullen' in this moment. The idea that the same disability that is very present for this white man is regarded as moodiness for the Black person is telling, and it is useful for thinking about what is happening with the Black women in *Morkinskinna, Merchant* and even *Poesie*. Pickens outlines the various readings of Black madness – that is, Black anger, Black excess and Black people with any mental illness – and she explains how the preoccupation with Black anger and excess effectively eliminates the visibility of legitimate illnesses on Black bodies. While Pickens is specifically drawing our attention to non-visible disabilities such as neurodivergence and mental illness, her point is augmented by the fact that this violent erasure can be, and is applied to, highly visible conditions, such as pregnancy, for the purposes of my argument.[29] The scene that plays out within the *Morkinskinna*, that is the marking of blackness as distorted, sets the stage for Lancelot's surprise and Puttenham's rhetoric. If the visible can be made invisible, then will the non-visible (disabilities) always be seen as the natural defect of blackness?

This rendering of Black disabilities and illnesses as invisible is a prime example of what Calvin Warren identifies as ontological terror. Warren argues that blackness is essentially equipment, in which Black people serve as the embodiment of the 'nothing' that the white world desires to rule, understand and dominate.[30] As a result, he writes that 'Blacks, then, have function but not being'.[31] Moreover, Warren adds that '[m]etaphysics uses blacks to maintain a sense of security and to sustain the fantasy of triumph – the triumph over the nothing that limits human freedom' and because of this, the full liberation of Black people 'would constitute a form of world destruction'.[32] If Black freedom is world destruction, then it is fair to say that Black subjugation provides structure for the world. If this is the case, then *Morkinskinna* and *Merchant* present us with formulas for worldbuilding. The weight of Warren's argument urges us to examine the function of blackness and Black people in both texts. I have argued that the Black women provide comic relief in both scenes and that this comedic violence serves to protect white supremacy by normalizing the mad king, whitening the Jewish convert, and shrouding the white man's sexual violence, respectively.

In the *Morkinskinna*, the violation of the Black woman is one that King Sigurðr does not have to make amends for. The moment in which the Black woman is discarded is a moment in which the king's 'normalcy' is visible. We shift our gaze from his instability and the resulting implications for his throne, and we, instead, begin to ask ourselves why or how is it that the Black woman is so 'uncomely' and 'misshapen'. The treatment of her body reveals a hierarchy that does not allow blackness to occupy beauty, morality, normalcy, femininity and/or humanity. In *Merchant*, Lancelot uses this rhetoric of Black nothingness to direct our gaze away from himself. Lancelot, Lorenzo and Jessica each benefit from the Black woman's presence. Her blackness shrouds all three: the spectator is made to ignore Jessica's religious difference, Lorenzo's miscegenation (due to the racialization of Jews in the period) and Lancelot's barbarism (the violation of this Black woman). Hearkening back to Gillen, the barbarism is displaced onto the Black woman. And, in referring to her as both 'Negro' and 'Moor' she becomes the physical marker for both racial and religious otherness. Once again, her body is used to rewrite the social code, and the seemingly stable nature of blackness makes this white, Christian social code more useful. As

Lancelot, Lorenzo and Jessica are each able to point to someone else, the Black woman stands silent, and so spectators may finally laugh without the labour of looking elsewhere. Given the significant distraction that she provides, we are forced to unpack comic relief. We must ask ourselves, what does comedy relieve? In both cases, I would argue that it relieves white anxiety.

White anxiety stems from the need to maintain whiteness as perfection, as existing without blemish. The effort to reinforce the superiority of English whiteness is all too apparent in Ben Jonson's *Masque of Blackness*.[33] Within Jonson's masque, the daughters of Niger make the decision to leave their father (Father Niger) in pursuit of romance in 'Brittania'. In the prologue, Jonson explains that the pregnant Queen Anne desired to cast 'blackamoors', and he accommodated her wishes by casting white women in blackface. Queen Anne is, of course, among the women cast as the daughters of Niger. Joyce Green MacDonald writes that the figure of the African woman is employed to 'reinscribe her disappearance within a narrative more securely closed through the resources of royal patriarchy and of racial rivalry between men', referencing both Ben Jonson and Inigo Jones.[34] MacDonald adds, 'Niger's daughters voluntarily transfer themselves to the "Britain men," initiating an exchange of women which effectively removes one male party – their father – from the transaction. Niger's fatherly authority disappears as much as his daughters' blackness is intended to do.'[35] Within the script, Jonson effectively makes white patriarchalism both seductive and triumphant: it is significant that the daughters of Niger choose to leave their father despite the beauty of their homeland. In doing so, they subject themselves to this new authority, which initiates the erasure of their blackness within the text. Additionally, Jonson authenticates the superiority of English whiteness by retelling stories of whiteness and the origins of blackness through a detailed recitation of Greek and Roman mythology. Ian Smith argues that the story of Phaeton, which is heavily employed within the masque, draws the conclusion that

> Error is the sign under which the black Ethiopian race is born, and the accidental nature of its beginnings makes a strong case for blackness being the unintended and unexpected result of a wayward undertaking. As an accident, the result of a young man's overreaching, blackness is the distortion of the original

course of human nature. The correlate to blackness, whiteness is construed as the Ethiopians' former, natural state that has been completely undone. An entire race of people is represented as a mistake or a flaw that stands out against the chiaroscuro of an emergent racialized humanity.[36]

Once again, the idea of blackness as inherently distorted emerges upon the stage and it is validated using ancient mythology. Smith's reading of 'flawed blackness' underscores the gravity of having mythologies of accidental blackness read aloud as a prosthetic Black pregnant woman dances through the court. The figure of the Black woman re-emerges. However, the production is intentionally structured to replicate this 'error', that is, distorting the queen's whiteness using blackface.[37]

These 'comedic' moments effectively avert our gaze from breaks in this white ideal, and when repeated they do the work of informing and protecting whiteness. White monarchy, white patriarchy, white Christianity and white femininity each emerge unscathed when we laugh at the Black woman, who is effectively named 'Negro', 'Moor', 'whore' and 'error'. This black function is of great service to whiteness, but what does it do to the figure of the Black woman? What does white laughter and disregard cost her? Since comedy, and its resulting laughter, is the tool, or pedagogy, that cements her identity as monstrous and/or 'nothing', it would be useful to classify this comedy as a form of torture.

In her work *Performing Race and Torture on the Early Modern Stage*, Ayanna Thompson argues that torture was one of the mechanisms for constructing race.[38] Thompson challenges the idea that torture was solely invested in revealing one's interiority, as the performance of torture often emerges beside performances of race. In early modern England, 'torture was used to detect secrecy within its own population', based on the fear that traitors, also being English, were indistinguishable.[39] However, 'when representations of torture were staged . . . the victims' and torturers' roles were rewritten. No longer representing the threat within, the theatrical victims of torture were primarily constructed as racialized figures.' These moments signal a shift that made exteriority and interiority equally important. As depicted in *Morkinskinna* and *Merchant*, this external difference is recoded and read as a signifier of internal depravity, and, as such, makes the racialized figure an automatic threat to whiteness. This narrative, of course, creates room for the normalization of violence towards certain racialized bodies, while simultaneously justifying the actions of the (white) torturers, by reframing these torturers as protecting themselves from the inherent monstrosity of blackness and other iterations of otherness. Once again, white anxiety provokes, justifies and perpetuates the torture of non-white bodies. Comedy is weaponized to facilitate this torture as it encourages narratives about one's inward qualities to be attached to the exterior. Through the very act of laughing, each of the deformities propagated as inherent to blackness is reinforced as truth. As a result, a highly visible condition such as pregnancy can be wilfully disregarded. Comedic violence reconfigures uncomeliness, misshapenness and monstrosity as constants for the Black body.

White anxiety does, however, eventually shift to white rage, and the verbally tortured Black body then becomes the site for targeted physical violence and brutality.[40] The use of the pregnant Black woman certainly evolves beyond the early modern stage. Lancelot's violence, once meant to provoke laughter, now plays out on the 'stage' of the American plantation. This 'unheard, unnamed, and unseen' Black woman, as Kim Hall calls her, that once 'expose[d] an intricately wrought nexus of anxieties over gender, race, religion, and economics' is now the foundation of the white economy and the target for normalized repeated sexual violence.[41] Beyond the use of her womb, she is ungendered flesh.[42] This modern barbarism denies Black femininity while being fully reliant on it for the production of additional slave labour through the birth of children who are also viewed as property, or nothing, by the state.

The narratives that made it possible and acceptable for Charlena Michelle Cooks to be thrown onto the concrete, stomach first, are the same narratives that left the officer perplexed by her screams, and it is evident that these narratives emerged long ago. This long history of laughing at Black bodies has made it so that disability is not seen in blackness; rather, it is perpetuated as inherent to blackness while simultaneously weaponized against blackness to make whiteness feel secure. This normalized way of reading disability poses grave implications for the disabled white person as well. If disability is constructed as inherent to blackness in order to preserve the narrative of white 'perfection', then the disabled white person remains a liability to whiteness. The disabled white person (without the presence of the Black person) is made an outcast, and the disabled Black person, deemed invisible and non-existent, is made a liability to efforts for Black liberation and denied care. This denial of care often makes disabled Black people more vulnerable to criminalization and abuse. While the scope of my work focuses on the sufferings of women that stand at the intersection of blackness and disability within the United States, this work also requires us to open ourselves to the stories of Black disabled women throughout the diaspora. Not only is this targeted violence prevalent throughout, but it is regularly overlooked, as movements within Western Europe and the United States are often centred in the discussion. This is a global issue, and I wish to engage it as such, as there is much at stake. The work of integrating discussions concerning disability and race still has a long way to go, but it is necessary to continue for the increased visibility and normalization of the experiences and existence of those who are both Black and disabled. In doing so, these conversations may enable a push for the recognition, protection and honouring of the sanctity and inherent worthiness of Black motherhood, and, with that, Black womanhood and girlhood globally and in their entirety.

Notes

1 By Michael Martinez and Kyung Lah CNN, 'Police Video Shows "horrifying" Arrest of Pregnant Woman, ACLU Says', *CNN*, 29 May 2015. Throughout this chapter I will address various forms of violence that are directed towards Black women. Following Saidiya Hartman, I would like to stress that my purpose here is not to recreate this violence and retraumatize Black women. I am not using Black women's bodies and traumas as a means to reduce my own academic labour. Instead, I, as a Black woman, am centring Cooks's own language from her interview to prioritize Black women's interpretation of their own stories. This chapter centres Cooks's account of her attack and seeks to validate her experience by reinforcing the truth of her narrative, emphasizing the ways in which this violence is carefully constructed. Leaning also on the language of Gayatri Gopinath, I wish to curate this project regarding violence towards pregnant (disabled) Black women with care. See Saidiya V. Hartman, *Scenes of Subjection: Terror, Slavery, and Self-Making in Nineteenth-Century America* (Oxford: Oxford University Press on Demand, 1997). See also Gayatri Gopinath, *Unruly Visions: The*

Aesthetic Practices of Queer Diaspora (Durham: Duke University Press, 2018).

2 I would simply like to stress the fact that Cooks's story *felt* distinct. The United States has a long history of abusing pregnant Black women. Even as I searched for Cooks's story, I came across footage of another young pregnant Black woman by the name of Deja Stallings being violently arrested in a similar fashion. Konstantin Toropin and Lauren M. Johnson CNN, 'Footage of a Kansas City Officer Kneeling on the Back of a Pregnant Black Woman Sparks Ongoing Protest', CNN. See also LaKisha Michelle Simmons, 'Black Feminist Theories of Motherhood and Generation: Histories of Black Infant and Child Loss in the United States', *Signs: Journal of Women in Culture and Society* 46, no. 2 (2021): 311–35. Simmons curates a collection of oral histories from previously enslaved Black women regarding child loss within their ancestral lineages. Many of the accounts contain vivid details of violence. For example, it was commonplace that pregnant women were lowered into a hole and tied down to 'protect' the womb, and still beaten with cowhide. It is this practice that served as one of the primary motifs in Toni Morrison's classic novel, *Beloved*, as the 'tree' on Sethe's back was the direct result of punishment in this exact manner; see Toni Morrison, *Beloved* (New York: Vintage Books of Penguin Random House LLC, 1987).

3 CNN, 'Police Video Shows "horrifying" Arrest of Pregnant Woman, ACLU Says'.

4 For more extensive histories on the construction of race and use of racialized language during the Middle Ages, see Cord J. Whitaker, *Black Metaphors: How Modern Racism Emerged from Medieval Race-Thinking* (Philadephia: University of Pennsylvania Press, 2019); See also Geraldine Heng, *The Invention of Race in the European Middle Ages* (Cambridge: Cambridge University Press, 2018).

5 Ármann Jakobsson, 'Morkinskinna', in *Medieval Disability Sourcebook: Western Europe*, ed. Cameron Hunt McNabb (Santa Barbara: Punctum Books, 2020), 379–92.

6 Ibid., 386–7.

7 Katherine Gillen, 'Recovering Shakespeare's Racial Genealogies: Slavery, Barbarism, and Whiteness in *Hamlet* and Its Sources', *Shakespeare Quarterly* 73, no. 1-2 (2022): 1–23.

8 Ibid., 2.

9 Désirée G. Koslin, '"He Hath Couerd My Soule Inwarde": Veiling in Medieval Europe and the Early Church', in *The Veil: Women Writers*

on Its History, Lore, and Politics (Berkeley: University of California Press, 2008), 160.

10 Carissa M. Harris, *Obscene Pedagogies: Transgressive Talk and Sexual Education in Late Medieval Britain* (Ithaca: Cornell University Press, 2018).

11 Ibid., 4.

12 Citations from works by Shakespeare are taken from Richard Proudfoot, Ann Thompson, David Scott Kastan and H. R. Woodhuysen, eds, *The Arden Shakespeare Complete Works, Third Series* (London and New York: The Arden Shakespeare, 2021).

13 Though this play seeks to 'whiten' Jessica, it is important to still consider the racialization of Jews that the play is more generally committed to as we see through the simultaneous villanization of Shylock. See Lindsay Kaplan, *Figuring Racism in Medieval Christianity* (Oxford: Oxford University Press, 2018). Kaplan analyses medieval visual culture as well as Christian theology to demonstrate how they work together during the period in an attempt to physically mark Jewishness.

14 Megan Matchinske, 'Legislating "Middle-Class" Morality in the Marriage Market: Ester Sowernam's Ester Hath Hang'd Haman', *English Literary Renaissance* 24, no. 1 (1994): 154–83.

15 Saidiya Hartman, *Wayward Lives, Beautiful Experiments: Intimate Histories of Social Upheaval* (New York: WW Norton & Company, 2019), 7–8.

16 Hartman, *Scenes of Subjection*, 215. For more on vagrancy statutes in fourteenth-century England, see Judith M. Bennett, 'Compulsory Service in Late Medieval England', *Past & Present* 209, no. 1 (November 1, 2010): 7–51.

17 Hartman, *Scenes of Subjection*, 215.

18 Ibid., 216.

19 Ibid., 217.

20 George Puttenham, *The Arte of English Poesie Contriued into Three Bookes: The First of Poets and Poesie, the Second of Proportion, the Third of Ornament* (London, 1589), 159.

21 Kim F. Hall, *Things of Darkness: Economies of Race and Gender in Early Modern England* (Ithaca: Cornell University Press, 1995), 2, 22.

22 See Richard Dyer, *White: Essays on Race and Culture* (London: Routledge, 2013). White argues that individuals must possess the appropriate features to be identified as white, but the power and

privileges associated with whiteness thrive in the 'invisibility' of whiteness. That is, not needing to name whiteness. As such, whiteness becomes a 'universal standard' through which humanity is assessed and understood, and non-white groups are racialized and othered. Dyer's project is invested in deconstructing this framework and naming whiteness. This moment in Puttenham's argument is a prime example of whiteness being unnamed. The first individual is identified by his disability, and they are placed beside an individual that is identified by racial markers. See also Kandice Chuh, *The Difference Aesthetics Makes: On the Humanities 'After Man'* (Durham: Duke University Press, 2019). Chuh argues that this unnamed whiteness is the foundation of what she has coined the 'illiberal humanities'. That is, the humanities rests on holding Western European liberalism tradition as the standard, which in turn reinforces the marginalization and/or erasure of alternate forms of knowing and educating. Chuh pushes for a reimagining of the humanities because to uphold this system as it is, is to disguise this violence as a means to liberation, as implied by the name 'liberal arts'.

23 Claudia Rankine, *Citizen: An American Lyric* (Minneapolis: Graywolf Press, 2014), 49. In this book of poetry, Rankine makes use of the second person to enable her readers to experience, first-hand, the microaggressions that Black and Brown people endure daily. It is only after the reader experiences these personal injuries that Rankine offers Buter's explanation as to why language hurts.

24 Rankine, *Citizen*, 49.

25 Julie Phillips Brown, 'Otherbreath: Bare Life and the Limits of Self in Claudia Rankine's Citizen', *Jacket2*, 20 June 2019. Available online: https://hcommons.org/deposits/objects/hc:28190/datastreams/CONTENT/content. For more on Butler's construction of addressability and its relationship to power, see Judith Butler, *The Psychic Life of Power: Theories in Subjection* (Redwood City: Stanford University Press, 1997).

26 Therí Alyce Pickens, *Black Madness: Mad Blackness* (Durham: Duke University Press, 2019).

27 Leonard Kriegel, 'Uncle Tom and Tiny Tim: Some Reflections on the Cripple as Negro', *The American Scholar*, 1969, 412–30 (as cited in Pickens, *Black Madness*).

28 Pickens, *Black Madness*, 1–3.

29 See Renee Mehra et al., 'Black Pregnant Women "Get the Most Judgment": A Qualitative Study of the Experiences of Black Women at the Intersection of Race, Gender, and Pregnancy', *Women's Health*

Issues 30, no. 6 (1 November 2020): 484–92. This violent erasure has real implications as Mehra et al. demonstrate in their study. The gendered racism directed towards pregnant Black women impacts health outcomes for both mother and child. Mortality rates have climbed for both mothers and infants in the United States, with Black women being three times as likely to die from complications during their pregnancies, and Black infants' mortality rate being 2.5 times higher than that of white infants. Additionally, Black infants are almost twice as likely to be born prematurely. Even in such cases, much of the scholarship addressing these disparities is wrong and racist, as many seek to attribute these disparities to race instead of racism.

30 Calvin Warren, *Ontological Terror: Blackness, Nihilism and Emancipation* (Durham: Duke University Press, 2018), 18.
31 Ibid.
32 Ibid., 19.
33 Ben Jonson, *Masque of Blackness*, 1605.
34 Joyce Green MacDonald, *Women and Race in Early Modern Texts* (Cambridge: Cambridge University Press, 2002).
35 MacDonald's commentary on the rupture of Father Niger's patriarchal authority presents us with a stark contrast to the way that patriarchal authority is treated in Merchant. See R. W. Desai, 'Mislike Me Not For My Complexion', in *The Merchant of Venice: New Critical Essays*, ed. John W. Mahon and Ellen Macleod Mahon (London: Routledge, 2002), 305–23. Desai writes that 'though [Portia] dismisses each of her European suitors disdainfully while discussing with Nerissa their national traits, ironically they have already rejected her, not regarding either her beauty or her wealth as sufficient inducements to offset the risk of being doomed to celibacy should their choice of the right casket miscarry'. Desai further comments on this distinction arguing that while the Northern European princes dismiss the refuse to subject themselves to authority of Portia's father, Morocco and Aragon readily do the opposite: subject themselves to this father's authority, risking their romantic futures for a chance at Portia's hand. The masque augments this point by showing us that Northern European men not only dismiss the patriarchal authority of social 'Others', but, as we see in the case of Father Niger, render it null and void, and replace it. In fact, though the use of blackface, the masque undermines, distorts and disinherits both Black fatherhood and Black motherhood, by objectifying them for the purpose of white storytelling.

36 Ian Smith, *Race and Rhetoric in the Renaissance: Barbarian Errors* (New York: Springer, 2009), 54.

37 Ian Smith, 'The Textile Black Body', in *The Oxford Handbook of Shakespeare and Embodiment: Gender, Sexuality, and Race*, ed. Valerie Traub (New York: Oxford University Press, 2016), 170–1. Smith refers to the usage of blackface as the making of the 'prosthetic black body'. He describes this process as violating Black bodies and identities, while additionally, serving as a precursor for 'colonial objectification'. Smith stresses the idea that this use of expensive paints, dyes and textiles in order to 'invent' Black bodies for the stage adds yet another layer to this colonial project of making blackness analogous to economy; see also Sara B. T. Thiel, 'Wielding the Maternal Body: Queen Anna of Denmark Performs Blackface Pregnancy', *Shakespeare Studies* 46 (2018): 156–61. Theil writes that Queen Anne's decision to use blackface was motivated by her desire to make her pregnancy visible, following her long custody battle and the politics surrounding her womb. Here, we have a white woman making use of blackness to make a statement about her fertility. Once again, the Black woman is rendered nothing, and the queen's efforts fail, as the production still prioritizes her 'blackness' over her womb.

38 Ayanna Thompson, *Performing Race and Torture on the Early Modern Stage* (London: Routledge, 2013).

39 Ibid., 5.

40 Carol Anderson, *White Rage: The Unspoken Truth of Our Racial Divide* (London: Bloomsbury Publishing, 2016). Anderson writes that continued Black resilience and advancement, despite systemic marginalization, is the trigger for this White rage that seeks to displace itself onto the Black body.

41 Kim F. Hall, 'Guess Who's Coming to Dinner? Colonization and Miscegenation in *The Merchant of Venice*', *Renaissance Drama* 23 (1992): 89.

42 See Hortense J. Spillers, 'Mama's Baby, Papa's Maybe: An American Grammar Book', *Diacritics* 17, no. 2 (1987): 65–81. What Thompson reveals concerning the performance of torture is realized as Hortense Spillers writes: 'that the African female subject, under these historic conditions, is not only the target of rape – in one sense, an interiorized violation of body and mind – but also the topic of specifically externalized acts of torture and prostration that we imagine as the peculiar province of male brutality and torture inflicted by other males. A female body strung from a tree limb, or bleeding from the breast on any given day of field work because the "overseer", standing

the length of a whip, has popped her flesh open, adds a lexical and living dimension to the narratives of women in culture and society ... This materialized scene of unprotected female flesh – of female flesh "ungendered" – offers a praxis and a theory, a text for living and for dying, and a method for reading both through their diverse mediations.' The very act of directing violence towards Black women ungenders the flesh, certainly augmenting the violence because it is precisely Black womanhood that keeps the institution of slavery alive – that is, through the use of their wombs.

5

Feeling in justice

Racecraft and *The Merchant of Venice*

Derrick Higginbotham

The Merchant of Venice is a comedy of turbulent feelings, with characters professing love and venting anger, forming bonds between each other and painfully excluding others – sometimes at the very same time. In the courtroom, for instance, Portia appears to deal with Shylock earnestly, even though she suggests that he should be merciful and take the monetary offer of three times the bond's value. Yet, when Shylock demands the bond's terms, Portia concurs with him. The play frames what happens next as her master stroke since she outwits Shylock by appropriating his own legal strategy: just as Shylock demands the terms of the bond to the letter, so too does she. Because the bond does not denominate 'blood' as part of Shylock's penalty for Antonio's forfeiture, Shylock can only obtain the flesh without spilling blood, something that the other characters in the courtroom and the audience in the theatre know is impossible. As she turns the tables on Shylock, Portia also informs him that he will have 'justice *more* than thou desir'st' (4.1.312; emphasis mine), indicating the aggravation that motivates her legal manoeuvres.[1] By adding the determiner 'more', Portia betrays her aim to overwhelm Shylock. Portia not only imposes a religious and racial exclusion by insisting Shylock cannot spill 'Christian blood' (306) when he takes Antonio's flesh, but she also indicates what she is about to do, which is to use the law to grab hold of Shylock in another way. Her emotions spur and express this aim, exposing the politics of feelings within a supposedly austere institution like the Venetian legal system.

Portia's crafty approach to closing Shylock's case and then punishing him legally crackles with 'white rage' as Carol Anderson defines it, a rage that is typically subtle in its expression.[2] This anger appears 'almost imperceptibly' since it is conducted, for instance, via laws already on the books, drawing on, in Shylock's case, the knowledge that he can never be fully Venetian, that he is legally an 'alien', not a 'citizen' of Venice (4.1.346–8). Importantly, Anderson does not claim that this racially motivated anger is invisible, only that it is 'almost' imperceptible. It is a distinctive type of 'white incivility' that frequently appears understated, which differentiates it from more spectacular forms of racism, although white rage can be blunt in its effects.[3] My argument will examine the range of ways that such expressions of white anger work in *The Merchant of Venice*, with emotions functioning not as a by-product of the recognition of racial difference but as a means to create this difference and reinforce a racist hierarchy that produces injustice.[4]

While Christine Varnado and Ruben Espinosa focus on Portia and Bassanio in their examinations of whiteness in this comedy, I turn attention to Antonio and Gratiano in this chapter for two reasons.[5] First, the play associates the whiteness of these two men with a ferocity and wildness that receives scant critical attention. This ferocity and wildness, which exist on a spectrum of behaviour from fierce to fragile and wild to calm, disclose how whiteness induces a forgetfulness that enables those who are deemed white – and those around them who accede to that whiteness – to disregard the violence they execute to preserve their authority. Second, this whiteness requires perpetual maintenance since it is constituted by a set of beliefs that establish a specific racial order, and those beliefs must be renewed to affirm the exclusions that strengthen its power. As Kim F. Hall has convincingly argued, the resolution of *The Merchant of Venice* requires the 'redistribution of wealth from women and other strangers to Venice's Christian males', an outcome that demonstrates the imbrication of male domination and racialized whiteness as well as their triumph.[6] Before effecting this ending, though, this play dramatizes mutability in social dynamics because it imagines people struggling to fix differences between groups; instability often appears in the contradictions such efforts generate. More than once, for instance, Shylock expresses the ways in which he, as a Jewish person, is like the white Christian Venetians, such as the well-known 'If you prick us, do we not bleed?' speech (3.1.49–66), and his claim that he and they are equivalent because they share a willingness to purchase human flesh (4.1.89–99). Regarding the former, though, Shylock claims that if he learns to seek revenge from white Christian Venetians, he will 'better the instruction', outdoing them on the grounds of their sameness (3.1.66). He will not only be the same as them but more than the same, which destabilizes his claim to sameness, a destabilization that evinces the contingency of such categories.

Shylock's claims to sameness contradict the efforts of white Christian Venetians to imagine him as racially and radically different, signalling the political struggle that inheres in endeavours to delineate such distinctions. When arguing with Salanio and Salarino over Jessica's elopement with Lorenzo, Shylock maintains that she is his own 'flesh and blood', yet Salarino immediately denies Shylock's assertion, declaring that there is more difference between Shylock and Jessica's flesh than is between 'jet and ivory' (3.1.33–5). In contesting Shylock's claim, Salarino constructs Shylock's flesh as blackened, effectively inventing a somatic difference, given the repeated emphasis in the play on Jessica's fairness, as Dennis Britton documents.[7] Thus, Salarino draws a cultural boundary separating Shylock from those who are a part of the white Christian Venetian world, yet that line is, as Patricia Akhimie puts it, 'the imposition of a natural mark'.[8] Its provisional status means this boundary must be drawn and redrawn in acts of racecraft that are 'nested in mundane routine', quotidian acts of interpersonal speech and behaviour.[9] Even though the comedy's resolution affirms the enclosed world of white Christian Venetians, its plot dramatizes the 'visibly labored efforts' to preserve that religiously based racial homogeneity.[10]

My argument about *The Merchant of Venice* centres individual and collective emotions and their role in struggles for what different people and groups categorize as justice. It draws upon a globalized politics of feeling that transitional justice studies make visible. Over a decade after the Rwandan genocide, for instance, President Paul

Kagame and his government established a law in 2004 against 'genocide ideology', a law that the government renewed in 2008; this law sweepingly curtails speech and writing since it prohibits, among other possibilities, mocking others or stirring up 'ill feelings' when representing either individuals or groups.[11] Because of its broadness, the governing Rwandan Patriotic Front has used this law to marginalize opponents and to produce an official narrative of the past that inhibits a fulsome account of the genocide, which hinders rebuilding civil society. As David Mwambari demonstrates, vernacular forms of memory-making by Rwandan individuals, families and communities that counter the government's version enable people to reclaim *agaciro*, a homegrown notion of dignity.[12] Comparatively, in 2015, Ukraine embarked upon another phase of de-communization when then president Petro Poroshanko signed laws that banned communist iconography, inaugurating a new wave of Leninopad – the destruction of statues of Lenin – in the country, and barred communist parties from participating in elections. While these laws generated heated debate about representing the past and the practice of democracy, they aligned with the interests of those Ukrainians who supported the Revolution of Dignity in 2014 that sought closer economic and political ties with the European Union.[13] These admittedly brief examples dramatize that feelings of hatred and dignity, although expressed variously in different locales, energize political engagements, inspiring people to act justly and unjustly in little and big ways.

Reading with a globalized politics of feeling in mind proves fruitful when interpreting a play like *The Merchant of Venice*, with its attention to tempestuous emotions and the formation of collective identities, particularly the intertwining of religious and racial identities. This global frame focused on emotions reveals one reason why *Merchant* continues to resonate with audiences across time and within different national and cultural contexts, rather than the hoary belief that Shakespeare, as a playwright and institution, speaks a universal idiom that transcends time and place.

Fragile and fierce

The contradiction between Antonio's fragility and his fierceness shows how emotions facilitate the stability of race, casting it as firmly in place; as well, this contradiction renders perceptible the potency of obliviousness in the practice of white power. Antonio emphatically dramatizes the legal precarity of his position by creating a contrast between his fortitude and Shylock's violence near the beginning of the trial. The scene begins with the Duke expressing his sympathy to Antonio because Shylock appears intransigent. He will not drop the lawsuit. Recognizing the Duke's efforts to change Shylock's mind, Antonio agrees that there appears no legal remedy to his predicament. Antonio then clarifies that he stands as an example of 'patience' when compared to Shylock's 'fury', elaborating that he must 'suffer with a quietness of spirit' Shylock's 'tyranny and rage' (4.1.10–12). Such a moment sharply frames the legal contest between the two men as a scene of injustice, and, from Antonio's perspective, it is he who endures this wrong. Antonio only underscores his sense of victimization later when Shylock insists that the judge hear his suit. During a brief lull in the trial scene, Bassanio attempts to fortify Antonio's spirits by telling him that he will protect Antonio. In reply, Antonio paints a pathetic picture of himself since he imagines himself as the 'weakest fruit' of a tree, the fruit that drops first to the ground (4.1.113). His construction of himself as weak underlines the supposed brutality of Shylock's pursuit of legal resolution since Shylock harms someone who seems unusually vulnerable.

As readers and audiences well know, this specific conflict is not the first one between these two men; the play also represents them at odds at its start when they establish the bond that finances Bassanio's pursuit of Portia, although in that conflict the roles are reversed. We hear initially about Antonio's victimization of Shylock. In an aside, Shylock reveals Antonio's contempt for Jewish people since he 'hates our sacred nation', but Antonio has also critiqued Shylock specifically, objecting to Shylock's work providing interest-bearing loans to others, for example (1.3.44–6). During the men's business negotiations, Shylock does not hesitate to enumerate the ways that Antonio has harassed him: in the past, Antonio has called Shylock a 'misbeliever' and a 'cut-throat dog', even spitting on him (1.3.107–8). Just as Antonio displays patience during the trial, Shylock insists that he takes this harassment with 'a patient shrug' (1.3.105). On one level, then, the trial scene echoes this moment, reversing the power dynamics between the two men and suggesting a similarity between them. I want to highlight that in this earlier scene, Antonio does not contest Shylock's claims of abuse. Seething with anger, Antonio instead informs him that 'I am as like to call thee so again, / To spit on thee again, to spurn thee too' (1.3.125–6). Shylock takes note of Antonio's anger: 'Why, look you, how you storm!' (1.3.133). Antonio's relentlessness and the fierceness of his hatred for Shylock diverge acutely from his later claims about his weakness, pointing to the play's construction of Antonio as a more contradictory figure than we usually appreciate.[14]

Antonio later reveals no sense that Shylock's animosity towards him is at least partially a response to Antonio's abuse, which suggests that Antonio envisions himself as filled more with love than with hatred. In the play's opening scene, Antonio's inability to know why he feels sadness could indicate why he forgets his own role in fostering Shylock's enmity, a lack of discernment in Antonio that restricts his capacity to act justly. This obliviousness appears especially after Shylock has Antonio arrested. When Antonio is taken into custody by a jailor, he pleads to speak with Shylock, presumably to try to change his mind. In witnessing Shylock's refusal to hear Antonio out, Salanio begins to denounce Shylock, but Antonio orders him to desist. Antonio then offers this explanation for what he perceives as Shylock's ruthlessness:

> His reason well I know:
> I oft delivered from his forfeitures
> Many that have at times made moan to me;
> Therefore he hates me. (3.3.21–4)

In this account, Shylock's hatred for Antonio appears solely economic; it is Shylock's reaction to Antonio's generosity towards those facing penalties for violating their contracts. Such a rationale undoubtedly underscores the stereotype of Jews as greedy, since Antonio contends that the sole basis for Shylock's animosity is his loss of wealth. This statement, however, also allows Antonio to ennoble himself: he charitably saves those who make 'moan' to him. His statement signals a type of forgetfulness vital to the working of whiteness, with Antonio overlooking his own hatred and reinforcing the purported difference between him (and others who, like him, have forfeited their bond) and Shylock. Maybe Antonio can do this because his anger is impulsive and unpremeditated, but that makes this feeling no less socially efficacious.

Antonio's charity intertwines with his later claims of weakness, generating a vision of him as goodhearted, and he aims to make this vision of himself public. Importantly, as the jailor arrests Antonio, Shylock speaks to this officer, wondering 'that thou are so fond / To come abroad with him at his request' (3.3.9–10). He insinuates not only that this officer favours Antonio but that Antonio wants his arrest to be seen by others, implying that Antonio seeks to display his own downfall to fellow Venetians like Salanio. Moreover, in response to Salanio's insistence that the Duke will not let this lawsuit go forward, Antonio explains that the Duke cannot 'deny the course of law' and must protect the city (3.3.26–31). He then declares that 'these griefs and losses have so bated me / That I shall hardly spare a pound of flesh / Tomorrow to my bloody creditor' (3.3.32–4). His vision of his love for others whom he protects thus combines with this image of his diminishment, evoking the defencelessness that he will display in the trial scene. His claim literalizes his condition since he asserts that his economic and legal losses have depleted his body, making him appear littler than he is, potentially overwriting any sense of his rage against Shylock individually and against Jews collectively. That Antonio thinks of himself as insubstantial echoes Portia's earlier claim in Act 1 when she enters with Nerissa, asserting that her 'little body' is weary of the world (1.2.1). This claim to smallness belies the power that she can and will exercise throughout the play, intimating that both Portia and Antonio imagine themselves as less powerful than they are, a distinctive sense of white Christian fragility.[15]

Even as the play increasingly presents Antonio as emotionally and economically reduced, it seeks to demonstrate his capacity to love, ranging from those indebted to Shylock to, of course, Bassanio. All this love is the glue that sticks white Christian Venetians together. When Salarino reports on Antonio and Bassanio's final meeting before Bassanio travels to Belmont, he highlights Antonio's 'kindness', claiming that no one else on earth is as humane as he (2.8.35). Then, he describes the way these two men say goodbye. Antonio, first, demands that Bassanio not worry about his bond with Shylock and attend only to his business in Belmont, hinting at his willingness to sacrifice himself for Bassanio. Secondly, in a choreographically complex fashion, Antonio turns away from his friend, his eyes big with tears, only to reach back behind himself to shake Bassanio's hand (2.8.46–9). It is a moment, as Salarino claims, when Antonio's affection for Bassanio was 'wondrous sensible' (2.8.48). This account of the two men departing one another and the intensity of the emotion Antonio feels emphasizes the bond between them, a bond felt by others like Salarino. Furthermore, this bond is mutual. After Bassanio chooses the correct casket, a messenger appears with the bad news about Antonio. Portia notices the immediate impact of this message on her soon-to-be husband. In his reply to her query about the letter, he outlines that Antonio is 'the dearest friend to me, the kindest man, / The best-conditioned and unwearied spirit / In doing courtesies' (2.8.291–3). The repetition of Antonio's kindness as well as the image of him as even tempered ('best-conditioned') and tireless in doing good deeds ('courtesies') does not cohere with his capacity to harass others like Shylock; it again signals a distinctive type of forgetting, one that substitutes images of Antonio's ferocity against Jews with images of his love and kindness.

It is not just that Bassanio and the other Christian Venetians do not grasp Antonio's penchant for harassing Jews. Rather, their mutual love, sealed by the kindnesses that they do for one another, constitutes a boundary that casts others as outsiders. *The Merchant of Venice* thus works hard to demonstrate, via Antonio, the intensity of the love between the white Christian Venetians. As Sara Ahmed observes when thinking about the cultural, and thus the racial, politics of emotions, '*because we love, we hate, and this hate is what brings us together*'.[16] In other words, Antonio loves Bassanio, and Bassanio loves Antonio. Because Gratiano loves Bassanio, he also loves Antonio; because Portia loves Bassanio, she loves Antonio. Their love interlinks these white Christian Venetians; it binds them together and produces an experience of cohesion grounded in their shared feeling (if not their similar interest in protecting that love) that appears to require hedging others out.

To justify this exclusion, Antonio and the other Venetians require an explanation as to why others do not receive their love and regard, and it is the imposition of this rationale that excites racist thinking. An example of this racism occurs near the start of the trial, when Bassanio begins arguing with Shylock about his insistence on the bond and Antonio demands that Bassanio stop, in a rhetorically rich reply:

I pray you, think you question with the Jew.
You may as well go stand upon the beach

> And bid the main flood bate his usual height;
> You may as well use question with the wolf
> Why he hath made the ewe bleat for the lamb;
> You may as well forbid the mountain pines
> To wag their high tops, and to make no noise
> When they are fretted with the gusts of heaven;
> You may as well do anything most hard
> As seek to soften that, than which what's harder –
> His Jewish heart! (4.1.69–79)

Antonio's use of anaphora ('You may as well') underscores Shylock's obstinance, highlighting the impossibility of changing his mind via examples drawn from nature. Bassanio, for instance, might as well stand on the beach and tell the tide not to come in, which is futile. Antonio finishes by insisting that softening Shylock's heart would be harder than doing any of these impossible tasks, which constructs Shylock as inherently unyielding. Besides rhetorically dramatizing Shylock's refusal, Antonio also links this insistence to a somatic feature, Shylock's heart; to Antonio, it seems like Shylock's hardness is an immutable, potentially biologically grounded, difference that is distinctive not just to him but to all Jews.[17] Yet the hardness that Antonio ascribes to Shylock also appears in Antonio's fixed and reductive perception of Jews. He seems wholly unaware of this hardness, which again indicates the ways that this group's identity as white Christian Venetians inhibits what they know – or can admit – about themselves, an ignorance that the play repeatedly displays.

Calm and wild

Moving from the spectrum of fragility and fierceness to the spectrum of calm and wild, and from a focus on Antonio to one on Gratiano, unearths another aspect of the work of whiteness – specifically, the strenuous effort it takes to create and animate particular racial distinctions that order the social world. *The Merchant of Venice* makes this effort palpable via the contradictions it creates when representing the white Christian Venetians' responses to those they cast as other. In this light, Gratiano becomes especially compelling as a character since he not only has a distinctive investment in

Bassanio's success, given that his marriage to Nerissa depends on Bassanio's capacity to win Portia, but he also embodies a wildness – an instinct for anger and unpredictable behaviour – that the play seeks to distinguish from Shylock's wildness. This comedy strives to create such a distinction because Shylock's wildness can appear all too like the risk-taking of Antonio, Bassanio and Gratiano, a likeness that threatens to collapse the conceptual grid of racial distinctions that suffuses the worldview of the white Venetian Christians.

Gratiano's investment in wildness appears in the play's first scene when he chastises Antonio for his sadness, warning Antonio that the potential benefits of appearing melancholic should not outweigh the expression of one's impetuosity. In this longer speech, Gratiano insists upon the value of vitality: 'Why should a man whose blood is warm within / Sit like his grandsire cut in alabaster?' (1.1.83–4). From Gratiano's perspective, those who sit as still as an alabaster statue do so as a posture, a performance that tries to create an image of 'wisdom' and 'gravity' (1.1.92). Gratiano's focus on bodily conduct ultimately points to the play's metatheatrical qualities, especially the various ways that it employs dramatic irony, highlighting the conceptual instability characteristic of this play: such ironies pluralize meaning, rather than stabilize it. The speech also underscores that the image of stillness, linked via the alabaster statue to whiteness, is manufactured. Once invented, this posture requires work to preserve. Gratiano yet again becomes the vehicle to articulate this distinction between calmness and wildness and its concomitant instability once he joins Bassanio in the quest for Portia. When Bassanio agrees to let Gratiano travel with him to Belmont, he cautions Gratiano, telling him that he is 'too wild, too rude and bold of voice' (2.8.173). Gratiano must temper his 'skipping spirit' with 'cold drops of modesty' because if he does not, he and (by implication) Bassanio will be misunderstood by everyone in Belmont (2.8.178–9). To reassure Bassanio, Gratiano emphasizes that he will use 'all the observance of civility' when in Belmont (2.8.187). Not only does Gratiano articulate that calmness and wildness exist on a spectrum, with people having the capacity to transform one response into the other, but he also accentuates his ability to deploy both civility and incivility selectively to generate social effects.

This propensity for wildness that Gratiano voices is part of the deeper logic of *The Merchant of Venice*; it reappears in the finale when Lorenzo reminds audiences of the spectrum between calmness and wildness in a long disquisition on music. In the final act, Jessica and Lorenzo sit outside of Portia's home in Belmont, looking at the stars, when Jessica asserts that she is never merry when she hears music. Lorenzo replies by contending that it is a sign of her attentiveness. He notes that if a 'wild and wanton herd' of colts who follow the heat of their blood hear any kind of music, then their 'savage eyes' will turn to a 'modest gaze' (5.1.71–8). He then explains that there is

> naught so stockish, hard and full of rage
> But music for the time doth change his nature.
> The man that hath no music in himself,
> Nor is not moved with concord of sweet sounds
> Is fit for treasons, stratagems and spoils;
> The motions of his spirit are dull as night
> And his affections dark as Erebus.
> Let no such man be trusted. (5.1.81–8)

Music has the capacity to modify the inborn savagery – the 'rage' – not just of colts but also of humans, altering their 'nature' enough to make them modest, if only temporarily. Lorenzo makes a significant qualification here, however. Any person not moved by music is especially fit for 'treasons, stratagems and spoils', which, in turn, signifies that such a person's affections are 'dark', suggesting a darkness that points to the pattern of anti-Black racism that recurs throughout this comedy. Someone who cannot be moved by music alarmingly appears outside the order of creation itself since music can sway even animals. Furthermore, that person also lacks the competence to control their deployment of wildness and calmness, especially compared to the skilful conduct that Gratiano has previously endorsed.

Lorenzo's speech, read in conjunction with an earlier moment when Shylock shares his views on music, reinforces the racialization of Shylock, even after he disappears from the play at the end of Act 4. In the second act, Lancelet announces that Shylock might be entertained by a masque at Bassanio's dinner, which startles Shylock. He then orders Jessica to keep the doors to the house locked, and should she hear 'the vile squeaking of the wry-necked fife', she must not climb to the rooftop to watch and hear the Christians as they perform (2.5.29). He does not want the 'sound of shallow foppery' to enter into his 'sober house' (2.5.34–5). Shylock's apparent distaste for music – at least the 'vile squeaking' of masques – could signal that it does not move him to feel harmony, that such sounds are jarring to him.[18] His sobriety then is not the same as the Christian Venetians' sense of civility. At this moment, he seems oblivious to the appeal of music, and retrospectively when audiences watch the final act, this obliviousness recalls his inner darkness, emphasizing his racialized and radical otherness, especially if his distaste for music means that his senses are dulled to an appeal that even animals can hear.

The Merchant of Venice further expresses the different quality of Shylock's wildness by either mocking his anger, making it seem more unreasonable than that of other characters, or by imagining it as baseless. A well-known instance of this ridicule is Salanio's report of Shylock's response to discovering that his daughter, Jessica, has not only eloped with Lorenzo but has also stolen money from her father. As a witness to Shylock's response, Salanio reports that he never heard 'a passion so confused, / So strange, outrageous and so variable' because Shylock apparently runs screaming in the street (2.8.12–13). In his fit, Shylock conflates his daughter with his ducats, indicating once again his stereotypical greediness, even as he declaims that she has stolen 'two rich and precious stones' (2.8.20). Salarino builds on this final image, noting that a group of boys follow Shylock, teasing him as they cry out, 'His stones, his daughter, and his ducats' (2.8.24). It is hard not to imagine that Salanio and Salarino rehash these events in a way that belittles Shylock's anger, particularly as they recycle the boys' pun about Shylock losing his two stones, an image of castration meant to demonstrate that Jessica's actions have depleted Shylock economically and sterilized him reproductively, rendering him weak and unmanly.

Because the play fashions Shylock as exceptionally uncontrolled, it can make Gratiano's wildness seem less pronounced, yet his anger should not be forgotten. It erupts visibly in the trial scene, creating a distinctive parallel between him and Antonio in relation to Shylock. Gratiano asks Shylock if any prayers might change his mind. Shylock flatly states no, at which point, Gratiano begins his outburst by declaring, 'O, be thou damned, inexecrable dog, / And for thy life let justice be accused' (4.1.127–8). His apostrophe at the start of this speech registers his fury, at the same time as he degrades Shylock verbally. He continues to do this throughout his response, telling Shylock that his very presence almost undermines Gratiano's faith in Christianity and proclaiming that Shylock is a 'bloody, starved, and ravenous' wolf that preys on others (4.1.137). While Lorenzo's speech in the next act will intimate that Shylock's unresponsiveness to music locates him outside the human/animal distinction altogether, Gratiano in this instance labels Shylock a wolf to categorize him as subhuman, an 'untamed and unwelcome outsider', so that animal metaphors can articulate social exclusion in the play.[19] Shylock also marks the intensity of Gratiano's rage, replying: 'Till thou canst rail the seal from off my bond / Thou but offend'st thy lungs to speak so loud' (4.1.138–9). Here, 'to rail' means to rant so much that this fury peals the seal off the bond, suggesting that Gratiano's anger, while heated, is not scorching enough. Needling Gratiano, Shylock asserts that Gratiano's rage will only harm his lungs.

This dynamic between Gratiano and Shylock appears to reiterate the one that occurs between Antonio and Shylock in the play's first act, when Antonio reacts to Shylock's enumeration of the different ways Antonio has harassed him over the years. Like Gratiano, Antonio succumbs to heated anger in this earlier interaction with Shylock, with Shylock also calling attention to how Antonio storms. This parallel points to another way that the Venetians are aligned with one another in the presentation of their rage. To a degree, Gratiano and Antonio's potential for wild behaviour invites a comparison with Shylock's own storminess. The play, however, sanctions the anger of the white Christian Venetians via this comparative gesture. Their anger can appear more palatable, especially as a response to what they construe as unjust, and it can be productive in its capacity to underscore behaviour that they deem beyond the pale. By contrast, Shylock's 'darkness' characterizes his wildness as being of a different magnitude; this demonstrates the ways that racist thinking instantiates an exclusion that orders the world, determining who can and cannot be justly angry as well as who can and cannot belong.

Early in the play, Portia articulates her understanding that the world can be ordered in such a manner, which indicates her readiness to play the role that she fulfils in the trial scene of securing the boundary between white Christian Venetians, as a group, and others. After the Prince of Morocco pledges his worth to Portia, she complains that her father 'scanted me / And hedged me' with the casket game (2.1.17–18). Her father confined her via this lottery, such that the game is like a hedge that divides land and people, creating exclusions.[20] Still, she intimates that she can evade her father's hedging. Later, she tells Nerissa that she should put a glass of wine on the wrong casket when the Duke of Saxony's nephew makes his choice, indicating that this act will influence the outcome of the 'lottery'.[21] Portia never appears truly subject to the order that her father created, signalling her capacity to step outside the boundaries he established. Her evasion of the rules and her anger also never appear as wrongdoing in the play's logic, nor does Gratiano's or Antonio's fury, especially as compared to the censure of Shylock's anger. This white rage marks the presence of racecraft, the 'mental terrain' that secures a racist order; that is, *The Merchant of Venice* reminds us of the 'pervasive beliefs' that catalyze emotions, which index the interplay of the psychic and the social, when the former impinges on the latter and vice versa.[22]

Highlighting the ways in which everyday interactions reinforce racial thinking and racism, this comedy dramatizes the role of feeling in the creation of (in)justice, an important insight since cruelties of all types emerge from commonplace interactions and the emotional states they generate. The efforts of state legislatures in the United States to enact memory laws when regulating education – such bills have passed in Oklahoma and Texas, and have been submitted to state governments in Tennessee, Rhode Island and Florida, among others – reveal the emotional and thus political backlash forming in response to recent challenges to white supremacy, specifically those inspired by the Black Lives Matter movement and the 1619 Project. Legislators often frame these bills as ensuring that public school teachers do not create social studies courses that make students 'feel discomfort, guilt, anguish, or any other form of psychological distress on account of [their] race or sex'.[23] By legally insisting that 'American history', as a body of knowledge, not address the complexities of race, racism and enslavement, as well as those of sexism, homophobia and transphobia – and the violence that all these generate – such regulations enforce an ignorance that will translate socially into expressions of innocence and/or anger, especially by white students, when they do confront these issues outside of the classroom. Such claims of innocence or anger will emotionally exacerbate social conflicts. As with the memory laws in places like Rwanda and Ukraine, this US legislation can create roadblocks to social change because people find themselves in polarized dynamics that make finding solutions so inconceivable as to leave individuals and communities politically stymied. *The Merchant of Venice* ends with the white Christian Venetians having closed their ranks and having redistributed their wealth to the men, signalling its efforts to create the kind of comfort that memory laws aspire to: a comfort that can only be a dangerous illusion.

Acknowledgement

I want to thank Dennis Britton and Ruben Espinosa for generously sharing with me their work in progress; I also want to thank Vin Nardizzi and Valerie Wayne for their thoughtful feedback on this chapter.

Notes

1. All quotations from *Merchant of Venice* are taken from Richard Proudfoot, Ann Thompson, David Scott Kastan and H. R. Woodhuysen, eds, *The Arden Shakespeare Complete Works, Third Series* (London and New York: The Arden Shakespeare, 2021).

2. Carol Anderson, *White Rage: The Unspoken Truth of Our Racial Divide* (New York: Bloomsbury, 2017), 3; see also Ruben Espinosa's essay, 'White Anger: Shakespeare's My Meat' in *White People in Shakespeare*, ed. Arthur Little Jr. (New York: Palgrave Macmillan, forthcoming), 3.

3. For the phrase 'white incivility', see Espinosa, 'White Anger', 2.

4. Sara Ahmed makes the case that emotions carve out racial differences, rather than existing as a response to racial difference. See *The Cultural Politics of Emotion* (New York: Routledge, 2005), 52–5.

5. See Christine Varnado, 'The Quality of Whiteness: *The Thief of Bagdad* and *The Merchant of Venice*', *Exemplaria* 31, no. 4 (2020): 245–69, and Espinosa, 'White Anger', *passim*.

6. Kim F. Hall, 'Guess Who's Coming to Dinner? Colonization and Miscegenation in *The Merchant of Venice*', *Renaissance Drama* 23

(1992): 99. As Urvashi Chakravarty deftly puts it, the play ensures that 'the future . . . will not be foreign'; Chakravarty, '"I had Peopled Else": Shakespeare's Queer Natalities and the Reproduction of Race' in *Queering Childhood in Early Modern English Drama and Culture*, ed. J. Higginbotham and M. A. Johnston (New York: Palgrave Macmillan, 2018), 65.

7 Dennis Britton examines the detailed way that the play represents white flesh in his 'Flesh and Blood: Race and Religion in *The Merchant of Venice*', in *Shakespeare and Race*, ed. Ayanna Thompson (Oxford: Oxford University Press, 2021), 117. On the effort to imagine Jessica as white and possibly Christian via her marriage to Lorenzo, see also Mary Janell Metzger, '"Now by my Hood, a Gentle and No Jew": *The Merchant of Venice* and the Discourse of Early Modern English Identity', *PMLA* 113, no. 1 (1998): 57–8; Janet Adelman, 'Her Father's Blood: Race, Conversion, and Nation in *The Merchant of Venice*', *Representations* 81, no. 1 (2003): 14; and Lara Bovilsky, *Barbarous Play: Race on the English Renaissance Stage* (Minneapolis: University of Minnesota Press, 2008), 86.

8 Patricia Akhimie, *Shakespeare and the Cultivation of Difference: Race and Conduct in the Early Modern World* (New York: Routledge, 2018), 22.

9 Karen E. Fields and Barbara J. Fields, *Racecraft: The Soul of Inequality in American Life* (New York: Verso, 2012), 18–19 and 25.

10 Akhimie, *Shakespeare and the Cultivation of Difference*, 19.

11 See specifically chapter 1, article 2, number 2 in Rwanda: Law No. 18/2008 of 2008 Relating to the Punishment of the Crime of Genocide Ideology, 23 July 2008. Available online: https://www.refworld.org/docid/4acc9a4e2.html (accessed 18 April 2022).

12 See David Mwambari, '*Agaciro*, Vernacular Memory, and the Politics of Memory in Post-Genocide Rwanda', *African Affairs* 120, no. 481 (2021): 619–22.

13 See Alina Cherviatsova, 'On the Frontline of European Memory Wars: Memory Laws and Policy in Ukraine', *European Papers* 5, no. 1 (2020): 123–5.

14 It is surprising how many critics downplay Antonio's viciousness, often framing him in ways that exculpate him from responsibility for racism, possibly because certain lines of inquiry are not as compelling if they are complicated by his bigotry. Beginning with Auden, the argument about Antonio's homoerotic interest in Bassanio and his queerness more generally can sometimes lead critics to overstress his almost sacrificial character, at the expense of his aggression.

See W. H. Auden, *The Dyer's Hand and Other Essays* (New York: Vintage, 1968), 230–2; Alan Sinfield, 'How to Read *The Merchant of Venice* Without Being Heterosexist', in *Alternative Shakespeares*, ed. Terence Hawkes (London: Routledge, 1996), 138–40; and Steve Patterson, 'The Bankruptcy of Homoerotic Amity in Shakespeare's *The Merchant of Venice*', *Shakespeare Quarterly* 50, no. 1 (1999): 13–16 and 20. A sense of the threat of violence to Antonio's body and Antonio's generosity can also make Antonio immune to critique. See, for instance, Adelman, 'Her Father's Blood', 21–3 and Henry Turner, 'The Problem of the More-Than-One: Friendship, Calculation and Political Association in *The Merchant of Venice*', *Shakespeare Quarterly* 57, no. 4 (2006): 430–6. More recently, Christine Varnado stresses Antonio's 'thankless love' and his distinctive economic vulnerability to contrast him with Bassanio and Portia, whom she understands as the characters that demonstrate white supremacy. This framing of Antonio can cover over his racism and his violence. See Varnado, 'The Quality of Whiteness', 259.

15 This notion of white Christian fragility in the play resonates with Robin DiAngelo's theorizing about contemporary forms of white fragility. For instance, DiAngelo defines white fragility as 'a state in which even a minimum amount of racial stress becomes intolerable, triggering a range of defensive moves'. The fragility of many white people presumes that they perceive themselves as incapable of handling stress or conflict, a perception of incapacity that seems like Portia's and Antonio's perception of themselves as insubstantial. See DiAngelo's 'White Fragility', *International Journal of Critical Pedagogy* 2 (2011): 57–8 and her book, *White Fragility: Why It's So Hard for White People to Talk about Racism* (Boston: Beacon Press, 2018), 115–30.

16 Ahmed, *The Cultural Politics of Emotion*, 43; emphasis in the original.

17 Antonio's bigotry in this speech draws upon a longstanding racial fantasy about the differences between Christians and Jews that locates the difference(s) between these two groups of people in their bodies. While Antonio's reference to the hardness of Shylock's heart can be read as primarily a metaphor – one's heart as one's inner life – it still retains the capacity to signify Shylock's fleshly heart, marking a biological difference. On this longstanding form of race thinking that construes Jewish people as biologically different, see Geraldine Heng's *The Invention of Race in the European Middle Ages* (Cambridge: Cambridge University Press, 2018), 27–31 and 75–81.

18 Britton makes a similar point. See 'Flesh and Blood', 120.
19 Bruce Boehrer, 'Shylock and the Rise of the Household Pet: Thinking Social Exclusion in *The Merchant of Venice*', *Shakespeare Quarterly* 50, no. 2 (1999): 163.
20 Portia's use of this metaphor captures both the exclusion that hedges establish and their generative aspect since they can continue to grow, which signals the expansiveness of her father's (and by extension her own) power; on hedges and the cultural work they do, see Frances E. Dolan, *Digging the Past: How and Why to Imagine Seventeenth-Century Agriculture* (Philadelphia: University of Pennsylvania Press, 2020), 156–8.
21 For this point, see Espinosa, 'White Anger', 3.
22 Fields and Fields, *Racecraft*, 18.
23 For a copy of Texas Bill HB3979, see https://capitol.texas.gov/BillLookup/Text.aspx?LegSess=87R&Bill=HB3979, and for this quotation specifically, see Section 1, subsection h-3, part 4.b.vii. HB1775 passed in Oklahoma in 2021.

6

Marking Muslims

The Prince of Morocco and the racialization of Islam in *The Merchant of Venice*

Hassana Moosa

> SERVINGMAN The four strangers seek for you, madam, to take their leave; and there is a forerunner come from a fifth, the Prince of Morocco, who brings word the Prince his master will be here tonight.
>
> PORTIA If I could bid the fifth welcome with so good heart as I can bid the other four farewell, I should be glad of his approach. If he have the condition of a saint and the complexion of a devil, I had rather he should shrive me than wive me.
> (*The Merchant of Venice*, 1.2.120–9)[1]

Before the Prince of Morocco appears in Act Two of Shakespeare's *The Merchant of Venice* (1596–8), Portia presents the audience with her expectations about this character. In doing so, she establishes links between his racial and religious differences. In considering whether this 'stranger' might have the combined aspects of a holy 'saint' and an evil 'devil', Portia draws attention to the Prince's religious identity. At the same time, by anticipating his 'complexion', Portia also references his racial identity. Since evil was associated with darkness in early modern English religious discourses, and devils were typically imagined as black, Portia's statement seems to imply that the Prince of Morocco is dark-skinned.[2] By using the religious image of the 'devil' to racially colour the Prince, Portia asserts a close relationship between racial and religious identity – a relationship that persists throughout the play.

The particulars of this relationship between the Prince's religious and racial identity are not easy to discern since, as Nabil Matar has observed, Shakespeare makes no specific reference to the religious identity of the 'Moor' on stage, who 'projects neither Christian nor Islamic zeal'.[3] Despite the absence of any explicit indicators of his religion, critics like Kim F. Hall, Ania Loomba and Jonathan Burton have identified this character as a Muslim, particularly because of the cultural aspects in the play that imply his Muslim identity.[4] By thinking closely about the relationship between the Prince's race and religion, which Portia highlights in her initial remarks about him, we can see that Shakespeare's use of cultural signifiers rather than religious ones to indicate the Prince's Muslim identity demonstrates how Islam is racialized on the early modern stage. As I will show in this chapter, the Prince of Morocco's attempts to mitigate his differences by illustrating his racial and religious sameness to Portia counterproductively work to draw our attention back to his perceived differences in the white, Christian world of Belmont. While the Prince's religious otherness is not clearly marked in religious terms, Shakespeare uses cultural symbols that are connotative of Islam in the period to 'profile' the Prince as Muslim. This, I argue, demonstrates how Islam is racialized on the early modern stage, as Shakespeare replaces Islam's theological essence with a series of cultural, non-religious characteristics to produce the image of a 'Muslim'.

In exploring Shakespeare's racialization of Islam in *The Merchant of Venice*, I draw on the definitions of race outlined by pre-modern critical race scholars. Kim Hall and Peter Erickson describe race as an 'ideology that organizes human difference and power' through a range of 'narratives' and 'vocabularies'.[5] This definition implies that while race holds a consistent relationship to power, the organizing mechanisms of race are not always fixed. For example, the word 'race' in early modern English discourse connoted ideas of 'family, class or lineage'.[6] Yet the term was also used to describe groups of people with other inherited or shared characteristics such as nation, gender and religion.[7] Similarly, as Ania Loomba and Jonathan Burton have observed, even in contemporary discourses where race is commonly used in reference to people with common 'physical traits', the term 'race does not carry a precise set of meanings, but becomes shorthand for various combinations of ethnic, geographic, cultural, class, and religious differences'.[8] Nevertheless, while race is articulated in various ways in different contexts, its effects and structures are often similar across space and time. Thus in exploring the racialization of Islam, via racialized Muslims, on the early modern stage, it is necessary to rely on both contemporary and early modern vocabularies and understandings of race.

The study of pre-modern race, in turn, allows us to trace the development of racial and racist paradigms that were prevalent in the past, and to place these paradigms into conversation with contemporary modes of problematic discrimination. This chapter will attempt to do so by serving as a starting point for bringing Shakespeare into contemporary, global, critical conversations about the racialization of Islam and studies of Islamophobia or anti-Muslim sentiment as forms of racism. Many of these conversations on race and Islam have their roots in critiques of orientalism dating back to the early twentieth century, and were developed further following the publication of Edward Said's pivotal study *Orientalism* (1978), which showed how Europeans imagined and represented Muslims and Arabs as 'other' and socially inferior to themselves during periods of imperialism and later colonialism.[9] The topic has become increasingly prevalent in the past few decades, especially in the years following global-impact events that implicated Muslims in significant ways, including 9/11 and the 'War on Terror'.[10] Critics who assess the racialization of Islam in contemporary contexts – such as Saher Selod, Tariq Modood, Mahmood Mamdani, Louise Canker, Zareena Grewal, Naser Meer, Steve Garner and Junaid Rana – have done significant work to shed light on global tendencies of discriminating against Muslims and their faith based on non-religious aspects of identity, including physical appearance, ethnicity, clothing, language and nationality.[11] This occurs especially prominently in American and European contexts but also in other parts of the world.[12] The way that cultural modes of characterization are employed to profile and discriminate against Muslims, while (authentic) aspects of Islamic faith are simultaneously erased and ignored, makes this practice racial in nature. As Steve Garner and Saher Selod have shown, 'racialisation is a concept that helps capture and understand how this [practice] works, in different ways at different times, and in different places'.[13]

While critics have compellingly used racial frameworks to show how Muslims have been demonized in a range of different ways, times and places, this field of study has yet to meaningfully consider the racialization of Islam in the context of sixteenth- and seventeenth-century English culture, and specifically in the profoundly influential works of Shakespeare.[14] *The Merchant of Venice* is perhaps the most fitting text to begin thinking about the racialization of Islam in Shakespeare's oeuvre as the play already demonstrates intersections of race and religion in early modern representations of Jewishness. Contemporary scholarship on the racialization of Islam frequently connects the historical racialization of Muslims and Jews, by tracing the racial discrimination of these religious groups to the Christian reconquest of Islamic Spain in 1492. The Castilian preoccupation with the 'purity' of Muslim and Jewish blood in the dynasty's management of these groups represented an early practice of racializing religious subjects.[15] Moreover, as critics such as James Shapiro, Mary Jannell Metzger, M. Lindsay Kaplan and Lara Bovilsky have shown, Jews and their perceived differences were often racialized in early modern English discourses – especially through tropes such as blackness and blood – and such racializing mechanisms are at work in Shakespeare's representation of Shylock and Jessica in *The Merchant of Venice*.[16] My essay complements this scholarship by demonstrating how Islam, as a religious category, is also pushed into the realm of racial identity in Shakespeare's play. Moreover, as I will show in the final section, exploring how Islam is racialized in early modern English drama can offer significant insights into the way Muslims are racially demonized in present-day contexts.[17] Through this analysis, I hope to demonstrate how logics of social injustice were bred in early modern dramatic representations of Muslims; and, further, I hope to bring Shakespeare – the playwright and the cultural institution – to task for establishing racial modes of defining and then discriminating against Muslim subjects.

Concealing and confirming differences

To prove his sameness to the white, Christian Portia, the Prince of Morocco employs two strategies to counteract his identity as a 'stranger' and the effect he expects this might have on his desirability. In the first instance, the Prince addresses the issue of his physical differences by pointing to the primacy of his skin colour as a site of difference, before turning to the biological feature of blood in order to make claims to sameness. He does this immediately on entering the play, when he acknowledges skin colour as a barrier to his courtship of Portia:

> Mislike me not for my complexion,
> The shadowed livery of the burnished sun,
> To whom I am a neighbor and near bred.
> Bring me the fairest creature northward born,
> Where Phoebus' fire scarce thaws the icicles,
> And let us make incision for your love
> To prove whose blood is reddest, his or mine. (2.1.1–7)

By attempting to account for his complexion through his geographic origins, 'the burnished sun' which he is a 'neighbor' to, the Prince draws on early modern racial principles of climatology and humoralism which held that geographical regions and their respective climates could determine a person's 'complexion', where complexion referred to both their skin colour and their 'temperament'. Such theories were prevalent in the period and discussed by writers such as Jean Bodin, who in his *Methods for the Easy Comprehension of History* asserts that 'fire and sun color men black' and that such colouring is contingent on an individual or nation's position relative to the 'Tropics' and 'equator'.[18] The Prince accordingly attempts to draw attention away from this sign of his difference by turning inward towards the less visible, less variable, physical aspect of blood. As Janet Adelman notes, the Prince 'gestures powerfully toward the common blood just beneath the skin of difference' to evoke ideas of sameness.[19] He confronts his difference by linking the superlative 'reddest' to its earlier counterpart 'fairest', suggesting that it is not possible for either him or his competitor to have the 'reddest' blood in the same way that it is possible for one of them to be the 'fairest'. Blood is intrinsic to humanity, monochromatic, and inside of the body, making its variations more difficult to detect, unlike outward differences of fair and dark skin.

However, blood was not an unequivocal site for sameness in early modern Europe but was, instead, deeply embroiled in the organization of social differences. It was used as a means of creating and organizing hierarchies of race, class and gender, especially through descent, since bloodlines were 'passed' through lineage.[20] Thus the claim that the Prince of Morocco makes to his 'reddest' blood could also translate as a gendered claim towards having the most superior form of blood. As Elizabeth A. Spiller has observed, in early modern romantic narratives blood was 'a mark of reproductive potency' as well as a 'sign of valour' and therefore having the 'reddest' blood would be a competitive advantage for the Prince, framing him as chivalrous and fertile.[21] Spiller contends that Morocco evidently 'understands "red" blood according to romantic codes as a mark of bravery and nobility' and uses this to his advantage.[22] His allusion to 'reddest' blood might therefore be a claim that his blood is the 'best' in comparison to suitors of different (lighter) complexions, thus presenting a convincing case for his courtship.[23] This claim would be especially useful for the Prince to make given that in the context of climatic-humoral theory his skin colour could also be interpreted as a sign of his sexual incapacity. As Mary Floyd-Wilson argues, to convince Portia of his desirability and sexual stamina, the Prince must remove himself from the 'humoral corollary', which sees Africans as having less blood and therefore being less sexually driven because of their 'southern origins'.[24] Thus, by diverting attention away from his skin and towards his blood the Prince draws on systems of difference which hold currency in Belmont, in order to assert that his own blood marks him as either equal or superior to his 'northward' competitors in his masculinity, and to prove that his blood makes him equal or superior to Portia in nobility. Moreover, since 'race' in early modern English discourse was defined by notions of lineage that were inherently related to blood, by identifying that his blood makes him the same as Portia, the Prince evidently makes a claim for racial sameness. The Prince proposes that while his outward appearances mark him as racially different to Portia, his inside shows that he is racially the same.

The second strategy that the Prince employs to prove his sameness to Portia in Belmont mirrors the first. He uses religious rhetoric in a way that allows him to make an outward show of how well versed he is in Christian discourse, and therefore to oppose any ideas Portia might have about his religious identity. The Prince consistently uses Christian imagery and vocabulary to express his desire for Portia, beginning with his final lines in Act 2 Scene 1, in which he asserts that his trial in the casket challenge will make him either 'blest or cursed'st among men' (2.1.46). The Prince continues to use this language in his soliloquy during the casket scene, where he attempts to locate Portia's image in one of the three caskets by judging the value of the casket materials in relation to his understanding of Portia's worth. He begins his search for Portia's 'heavenly picture' (2.7.48) by proclaiming '[s]ome god direct my judgement' (2.7.13). The word 'some' in the sixteenth century did not only refer to an undetermined 'one or other' but could also be used as an adjective alongside a noun to indicate something 'certain', a specific 'one'.[25] Thus, '[s]ome god' could imply the Prince's belief in the specific God of monotheistic traditions, as much as it may reflect his pagan belief in multiple deities. Proceeding to consider the caskets, the Prince immediately dismisses the lead one and briefly considers the 'silver' because of its 'virgin hue' (2.7.22).[26] But the Prince is ultimately convinced that because of her desirability (2.7.37), Portia must be embedded in the gold casket since she is a 'mortal, breathing saint' for whom men undertake great journeys (2.7.40). As Hall notes, the Prince produces the image of a pilgrimage here as he observes chivalric journeys through the 'Hyrcanian deserts and the vasty wilds' in 'Arabia' that 'foreign spirits' undertake in pursuit of the 'fair Portia'(2.7.41–6).[27] In denouncing the lead and silver caskets in favour of the gold one, the Prince describes the prospect of undervaluing Portia as a 'damnation' (2.7.49), as 'sinful' (2.7.54), and thus equivalent to a religious evil. He concludes his description of Portia as 'gold' by comparing her to the 'figure of an angel' that is 'stamped' into a gold English coin (2.7.55–7). Through his references to chaste 'virgins', damnable sins, religious journeys and beautiful 'angels', the Prince proves his ability to wield Christian terminology and thus his capacity to be effectively integrated into the world of Belmont.

While both of the Prince's strategies seem, at first, to be effective ways of representing his sameness in the play, they both prove to have adverse results as they ultimately reveal his racial and religious differences from Portia. In his argument for racial sameness, the Prince's turn to blood to prove his nobility relies on a framework of social difference which also reminds the early modern audience that the Prince may have impure bloodlines because of his identity as a Black or Brown man, and is thus a racial other. That his racial difference prevails over his features of sameness is evidenced by Portia's lasting impressions of the Prince, which are characterized by his skin colour. When his 'labour [is] lost' (2.7.73) and the Prince takes his 'tedious leave' (2.7.77) of Portia, she closes the scene conveying relief at the 'gentle riddance' (2.7.78) of the Moroccan Prince and proclaims her hopes that 'all of his complexion choose me so' (2.7.79), shunning this suitor and all others that share his physical darkness.

Similarly, the Prince's use of religious language has a detrimental effect for his pursuit of Portia, as it demonstrates his lack of understanding of Christian principles. The Prince's blasphemous rendering of Portia as an idol to be worshipped demonstrates his transgression of pivotal tenets of the monotheistic Christian faith. Moreover, in imagining Portia as an 'angel' on a coin, the Prince indicates that he has derived his knowledge of Belmont's religious discourses through encounter and commercial exchange rather than theology. Accordingly, when the scroll chastises the Prince for his decision, its assertion that the Prince should have been 'as wise as bold' (2.7.70) refers to not only his misjudgement of the caskets but also his misuse of the Christian discourses he tries to wield. His failure to convince Portia of his religious sameness is further proven by Portia's request that 'all of his complexion [should] choose me so' (2.7.79). As Dennis Britton has argued, 'in light of [Shakespeare's] other uses of "complexion"', Portia's reference to 'complexion' in the play 'asks the audience to think about the connection between Morocco's outside and inside, between his skin colour and his religious condition'.[28] Thus, in expressing her final disdain for the Prince of Morocco, Portia's reference to his 'complexion' implies that it is not only the Prince's outward, physical, 'devilish' appearance that she is relieved to have avoided but also his inward, supposedly devilish, spiritual state.

Ania Loomba has observed that given the logic of the casket challenge, in which a suitor must correctly read the external appearances of the caskets to deduce their inward realities, 'only an insider [to the white, Christian world of Belmont] can win Portia, because only an insider can recognize the difference between inner and outer selves'.[29] Accordingly, the Prince's differences are ultimately confirmed by his inability to win Portia in the casket challenge, for which the character leaves the play 'cursed' rather than 'blessed'. The strategy of turning inward (to blood) that the Prince uses to demonstrate his racial sameness works adversely to highlight his external differences. Similarly, the strategy of turning outward (to apparent religiosity) that the Prince uses to make a show of his religious sameness counterproductively highlights his internal differences. Thus, by the time the Prince exits the play he has shown himself to be conclusively different to the white, Christian Portia, both inside and out.

Moroccan and Muslim

While *Merchant of Venice* is very clear in terms of the Prince's outward racial difference as marked by his dark skin, to a modern reader or audience member, the play is less specific about his religious differences. The only statement in the play that might offer some indication of the Prince's religious affinities is his invocation of '[s]ome god' (2.7.13), where the Prince replaces his earlier invocation of Greco-Roman deities and demigods like 'Phoebus' (2.1.5) and 'Hercules' (2.1.32) with the ambiguous reference to 'God' in the singular. The line does not offer any conclusive reading of the Prince's religion. Yet his failed attempt at proving his religious sameness implies that the Prince is necessarily a religious other.

Critics often suppose that the Prince is a Muslim and would have been imagined as such by early modern English audiences. He is described in the stage directions as a 'tawny Moor', and 'Moorish' identity in early modern English discourses typically referred to persons who were Muslim and/or Black and/or North African.[30] The term 'Moor' thus functioned as a synonym for Muslims in the period in ways similar to the term 'Turk'. However, 'Moor' was not always coterminous with Muslims and could mean simply Black. It was also variously used by English writers as a designation for Indians from the sub-continent, and Native Americans from the so-called new world.[31] Moreover, in the case of the Prince, Moorish identity is not a wholly useful sign of religious identity since Shakespeare never uses this label in the dialogue of the play to categorize this figure. The playwright does use the word 'Moor' later in Act 3 in his description of the 'Moor [who] is with child by' (3.5.36) Lancelot, which indicates that Shakespeare had this racial/religious vocabulary in mind when writing the play. However, he elects not to describe the Moroccan Prince through this label, and so the audience is never told to recognize the Prince as a Muslim by virtue of his being a Moor.

Nonetheless, I too would argue that the Prince is a Muslim. Specifically, this is because of his geopolitical identity – Moroccans were unambiguously presented in early modern English discourses as Muslims, whereas the term 'Moor' held variable meanings. The Muslim identity of the Moroccan royal family in particular was explicitly represented in many texts printed in the period. For instance, in *The Second Part of the Booke of Battailes* (1587), the anonymous writer provides a description of the well-known Battle of Alcácer Quibir or 'The Battaile of Alcazar, fought in Barbarie, betwene Sebastian King of Portugall, and Abdelmelec the King of Marocco, the fourth of August 1578' (R3r).[32] The writer prefaces the description of the battle with an overview of the 'foundation and familie of these mightie Kings that reigne now at Marocco' (R3r). Here the writer describes '*Muley Mahamet Xeque*' as the 'founder of that familie' – referring here to the Saadī dynasty of Morocco who ruled over the Kingdom from the early sixteenth to the mid-seventeenth century – as a '*Moore* of the *Mahometicall* superstitiō[n]' whose father '*Muley Xarif*' was 'the chiefe man of the Moores (as he that was descended of the bloud & line of the damned and cursed false Prophet *Mahomet*)' (R3r–R3v). Thus, the writer characterizes the Moroccan royals as Muslim in their subscription to the '*Mahometicall* superstitiō[n]' or beliefs, and demonstrates further how this religious identity is entrenched by the Moroccan dynasty's familial, and thus racial, connection to Islam by describing the Saadī dynasty as descendants of the 'Prophet *Mahomet*'.[33]

Similar associations between Moroccans and Islam also appeared in fictional English writing that was circulating in sixteenth-century England. One text from which Shakespeare himself may have derived some knowledge of the religious identity of Moroccans is William Painter's *The Second Tome of the Palace of Pleasure* (1567). This second volume of Painter's popular and influential collection of short-prose narratives includes as its thirty-fourth tale a narrative entitled *The King of Marocco*, about a Moroccan ruler 'in BARBARIE', which Painter notes that he has taken from the Italian writer '*Nicholoso Baciadonne*' (5n2v).[34] Painter names the royal figure in 'thys discourse and facte' as 'Kyng Mansor of Marocco' whose 'children (by subtile and fained religion) Cherif succéeded, the sonne of whome at this day inioyeth the kingdoms of Su, Marocco' (5n2v). The King, Painter observes, 'was not onely the temporall Lord of the Countrey of *Oran* and *Moracco*, but also [. . .] Bishop of his law and the Mahomet priest' (5n3v). Painter also references the King's religious practices in detail, including the 'thousand Mahomet mowes, and Apish mocks' (5O1r) he makes in prayer and a 'pilgrimage to the Idolatrous Temple of Mosqua' (5n4v). Collectively, these descriptions of the Moroccan ruler distinctly frame Islam as a 'religion', albeit one that would be seen as heretical in Protestant English eyes, and the King as a Muslim. Given the wide readership of Painter's influential collections, especially among dramatists, and the fact that Shakespeare himself is believed to have consulted *The Palace* for source material, it is tempting to argue that the playwright may have taken inspiration for his Moroccan character from this volume.[35] At the very least, the explicitly Islamic references in Painter's tale, like those in *The Booke of Battaile*, illustrate how inextricably Moroccans were associated with Islamic faith in English literary culture.

The English were also able to make such connections between Moroccans and Islam through their own interactions with Moroccans, which, as critics such as Nabil Matar, Jerry Brotton, Jack D'Amico and Imtiaz Habib have shown, were extensive throughout the late-sixteenth and early seventeenth centuries.[36] During periods of significant diplomatic engagement between Elizabeth I and the Moroccan Sultan Ahmed Al-Mansur, several English delegations were sent to Morocco, and Moroccan ambassadors were similarly received in England on behalf of the Sultan.[37] News of the Muslim guests not only circulated among courtiers but also entered into spheres of public culture, including the theatres.[38] The similarities between Shakespeare's depiction of the Prince of Morocco and a portrait of one Moroccan ambassador, Abd al-Wahid bin Masoud bin Muhammad al-Annuri, who spent six months in England in 1600, suggests that the playwright too may have been informed by the presence of Moroccans in England. In the portrait, bin Muhammed al-Annuri has a pink-brown complexion; he is dressed in a white *thawb* or tunic and a white turban; and at his waist he has a decorated scimitar or curved sword with a gold hilt. Thus, appearing as what the English would have recognized as a 'tawny Moor, [dressed] all in white' (2.1.*s.d.*) with a 'scimitar' (2.1.24), and with a distinctive attachment to 'gold', the portrait of the Moroccan correlates with Shakespeare's description of his Moroccan Prince. Though bin Muhammed al-Annuri arrived in England after Shakespeare wrote *The Merchant of Venice*, the resonances between the real and imagined figures suggest that Shakespeare may have been influenced by other Muslim Moroccans like the ambassador who had visited England in earlier years.

Given the explicit associations between Morocco and Islam in England in the period, it would have been near impossible for Shakespeare and his audiences not to have been aware of the religious identity of Moroccans.[39] Thus I would assert that Shakespeare's reference to the Prince as a Moroccan (particularly in the dialogue at Belmont quoted at the start of this chapter) and not as a Moor is telling of the fact that the playwright was conscious of the religious connotations of the Prince's geopolitical identity. This is also significant in light of Shakespeare's other uses of the term 'Moor' on stage, most famously in *Othello*. Although 'Othello the Moor' is sometime demonized through anti-Islamic English tropes, this explicitly labelled Moorish character is notably ascribed with a non-Muslim identity. As Nabil Matar has observed, Othello's Christian character is highlighted when Iago describes the Moor's 'baptism' (*Othello*, 2.3.332).[40] As such, I would argue that in creating a Moroccan character, Shakespeare would have been aware that he was also necessarily creating a Muslim character.

Profiling Morocco as a Muslim

Shakespeare signals the Prince of Morocco's religion in the play by using cultural markers of identity rather than religious ones. The playwright draws on existing cultural tropes that the early modern English associated with Islamic identity in the period and uses them to 'read Muslim-ness onto' the Prince without ever stating that this figure is a Muslim.[41] I argue that in doing so, the playwright racializes Islam by establishing certain signifiers as indicators of Muslim identity without positioning these signifiers alongside any explicit religious references to Islam that were widely used to categorize Muslims both on and off the stage in the period.

There are two related signifiers which Shakespeare uses to 'profile' the Prince as a Muslim. The one that critics most often take as an indication of the Prince's Muslim identity are the references he makes to the Muslim world. In attempting to prove his valour and strength to Portia, the Prince asserts that with his 'scimitar' he has 'slew[n] the Sophy and a Persian prince' and 'won three fields of Sultan Solyman' (2.1.24–6). The Prince's description of his triumphs over the 'Persian prince', the Egyptian 'Sophy' and the Ottoman 'Sultan Solyman' certainly position this character in the geopolitical terrain of the early modern Islamic world. These allusions are complemented by the Prince's later reference to 'Arabia' which is another region notably associated with Muslims in the period, as the site of Islam's religious origins (2.7.42). The diplomatic engagements and encounters between England and the Ottoman Empire, and the Safavid Empire in Persia, meant that many of the early modern English were familiar with the religious identity of these geopolitical powers. Additionally, theatregoers would have recognized the Islamic identity of these rulers from an earlier well-known play that grouped analogous figures together alongside distinctly Islamic symbols: Christopher Marlowe's *Tamburlaine*. Marlowe's popular two-part play features a Persian Prince, an Ottoman Emperor, an Egyptian Soldan, the King of Morocco and the King of Arabia. The Muslim rulers in *Tamburlaine* highlight their own Islamic identities throughout the dialogue, such as the Ottoman Bajazet who 'swears' by 'the holy Alcaron' (C7r) and the Egyptian Souldan who declares to Tamburlaine, '[m]ighty hath God & Mahomet made thy hand' (F1r).[42] Moreover, Marlowe's inclusion of Muslim symbols such as the 'Alchoran' (the Qur'an), which Tamburlaine famously burns in a gesture of religious defiance (K5r), explicitly connects the narrative and its primary themes to Islam. Shakespeare does not make similar religious allusions in *The Merchant of Venice*. Instead, by aligning the Moroccan Prince to these rulers and regions Shakespeare invites the early modern audience to link the Prince with Islam via geopolitical associations.

Shakespeare's references to the Muslim Mediterranean Basin have two racializing effects. On the one hand, through this representation of the Prince, the playwright collapses religion into geography by suggesting that proximity to powerful Muslim empires specifically in the Mediterranean region is what constitutes and thus implies Muslim identity. On the other hand, the grouping together of these Muslim powers has a homogenizing effect. As Garner and Selod argue, 'racialisation draws a line around all the members of the group; instigates "group-ness", and ascribes characteristics' based on various factors such as work, ideologies, beliefs and social/cultural organization.[43] The basis of such racialization is not rooted in groups 'all looking vaguely the same', but it is 'the unity of the "gaze" itself' that groups them together.[44] As these critics contend, 'those who produce, absorb and reproduce representations' of Muslims 'can transform the clearly culturally and phenotypically dissimilar individuals . . . into a homogenous bloc'.[45] Although Shakespeare alludes to military conflicts in this world, as the Moroccan Prince claims to have killed a 'Persian Prince' and conquered Ottoman 'fields', by grouping together Ottomans, Persians and Egyptians in a way that situates the Prince in a 'Muslim world', Shakespeare invites the English audience to see those who inhabit these regions as 'homogenous' and thus a racialized group, implicitly joined together by their relationship to Islam.

The second signifier that Shakespeare uses to mark the Prince of Morocco as a Muslim is his 'scimitar' which the character implicitly shows to Portia in attempts to prove his valour. A scimitar was typically associated with Turks and other Muslim figures in early modern England. On the English stage, curved blades were weapons closely aligned with Muslim identity. For example, in the performance of the 'Solyman and Perseda' playlet in Thomas Kyd's *The Spanish Tragedy* (1592), Hieronimo insists that the Portuguese Prince Balthazar transform into a stage Turk by using 'a turkish cappe', 'black mustacio' and 'a fauchion' – another sword with a curved blade.[46] As Matthew Dimmock has shown, the inclusion of the Turk in Kyd's play reflects early modern English Protestants' views about the analogous evils of Islam and Catholicism.[47] The word 'Turk' was synonymous with 'Muslim' in England and parts of Europe during this period. The 'fauchion' therefore helps to turn Balthazar not only into a Turk but specifically a Muslim, and the sword becomes a visual symbol of Islamic identity in much the same way as the 'cappe' and 'mustacio'. The Prince of Morocco's wielding of the 'scimitar' alongside his reference to the Turkish 'Sultan Solyman' would have recalled this image of the Turk from the earlier performance of the Muslim Solyman in Kyd's popular play.

English understandings of curved swords as symbols of Islamic identity were sustained into the early seventeenth century, and the extent of this association becomes apparent in the performance of plays like Robert Daborne's *A Christian Turn'd Turk* (1612), in which a sword is imagined as having a significant role in a Christian's religious conversion to Islam or 'turning Turk'. In the conversion of the English Captain John Ward, which is staged in the play as a dumbshow, the sword is incorporated into the ritual of conversion. Before the Mufti '*swears*' Ward as a Muslim on the '*Mahomet's head*' stage prop, the naked Ward is first dressed in his '*turban*', '*robe*' and '*sword*' (8 s.d). This act of dressing suggests that marking the Englishman's new religious identity on his body is a pivotal part of the process of his religious transformation. Accordingly, when the Mufti '*girds*' the '*sword*' on Ward's body, his act characterizes this weapon as a visual symbol that marks Muslim identity (8 s.d). Although swords, turbans and robes are props that can be removed and therefore do not represent permanent or essential markers of physical difference, as Garner and Selod observe, 'people (physical bodies) are the ultimate site of racism, even if the path toward those bodies lies through cultural terrain'.[48] As such, the attachment of the sword to Ward's person indicates that this accessory has a racializing function as it helps to map religious difference onto the Muslim body. The Prince of Morocco's sword, I would argue, works to the same effect as it operates as an item of clothing that connects the Prince to early modern ideas of militant Turkish, and therefore militant Muslim, identity.

Thus, race and religion for the Prince of Morocco prove to be inextricably linked. The Prince's parallel attempts to prove his racial and religious sameness are ineffective as they ultimately highlight both his outward and inward differences from the white, Christian world of Belmont. However, the Prince's failed pursuit of Portia confirms for the audience that the Prince is necessarily a religious 'other' and given his specifically Moroccan character it is difficult to argue that Shakespeare and his audiences would have imagined this character as anything other than a Muslim. Thus, by marking the Prince's Muslim identity through cultural signifiers rather than religious ones, Shakespeare produces a version of Islam that is stripped of its theological essence and is racialized.

Marking Muslims, then and now

Shakespeare's portrayal of the Prince's Muslim identity reflects the early development of a problematic pattern of racializing Islam. Assessing the playwright's strategies of representation sheds new light on the origins of contemporary practices of profiling Muslims. Specifically, these are practices that set up channels for racists and Islamophobes to mark Muslims and to correspondingly enact forms of political and physical violence against them. Shakespeare's use of cultural symbols to classify the Prince as Muslim, for example, resonates with the racial profiling of Muslims that became prevalent in the aftermath of 9/11 and during the growing emphasis in the United States on the War on Terror. As Zareena Grewal recalls, 'Muslim Americans became the mass targets of surveillance' and were constrained by the introduction of 'a wide range of punitive US government policies that systematically criminalize Muslims and "Muslim-looking" people through a body of legislation that is race-neutral in its language but targets and racializes these special populations in its effects'.[49] Post 9/11, air travel globally became (and remains) one area where the racial aspects of these practices are tangible as crew members and airport security around the world started to '"read" Muslim bodies, to learn how to recognize and antagonize those who appear to be Arab, Muslim, or Middle Eastern'.[50] As Grewal notes, 'signs that make a person appear threatening' to travel staff include 'Muslim names', 'Sikh turbans and ceremonial knives', 'a T-shirt with Arabic writing across the chest' and 'olive-skinned bodies'.[51] These signs are strikingly similar to those Muslim-like characteristics Shakespeare gives to his Prince to invite us to read the character as a threatening Muslim foreigner, an undesirable stranger, in the world of *The Merchant of Venice*. These include his name ('Morocco'), clothing and accessories ('scimitar'), national/geographic associations ('Arabia' and the Mediterranean) and complexion ('tawny', 'shadowed livery').

Similarly, Shakespeare's problematic racialization of the Prince is echoed in contemporary representations of Muslims in popular media. This has been made apparent in studies on Hollywood's racialization of Islam. Film industries, like early modern theatres, represent key arenas of knowledge production and dissemination. Considering the racialization of Muslim bodies and spaces in films, Maheen Haider has shown that one strategy contemporary filmmakers typically use to identify Muslim men is the use of 'traditional dress of men of the Arab world', namely 'white clothing' or 'white robes' and 'turban[s]'.[52] In using this garb, Haider argues that filmmakers illustrate Muslim identity in a homogenizing way that deliberately masks 'ethnic differences' and allows Muslim characters to be easily identified as 'perpetrators of jihadist Islam'.[53] At the same time, Haider argues, racializing clothing also helps to single out Muslim figures in Western contexts such as in Kathryn Bigelow's *Zero Dark Thirty*.[54] Bigelow's film includes an unnamed Sheik who first appears dressed in white Arab traditional clothing in a club – a 'liberal setting' that 'ensures his alliance to the West' – where he is approached by the film's white protagonist.[55] Yet despite the Sheik's allegiance to the 'West' and his centrality to the narrative, Haider notes that the character is consistently presented as a 'suspicious Arab Muslim in contrast to the superior and intelligent white American character'.[56] The characterization of Bigelow's Sheik correlates interestingly with Shakespeare's Prince of Morocco. With both the Prince of Morocco and the Sheik, we are invited to read their differences as religious by interpreting their names and white, traditional clothing as signs of Muslim identity. However, while their titles and white clothing are meant to mark them both as recognizably Muslim, these superficial features offer no real indication of their inward, religious sensibilities. Moreover, while both characters seem to harbour outward qualities that allow them entry into the worlds of their white, European/American, Christian/secular counterparts, they are ultimately constructed as too different to be meaningfully accepted in those worlds.

Analysing Shakespeare's representation of the Prince of Morocco therefore helps to explain why Islamophobia is such a prevalent form of social injustice in our contemporary world. As I have tried to show here, tracing the paradigms of Islamophobia to Shakespeare's stage invites us to think closely about the exchanges between past and present modes of demonizing Muslims. Making such trans-historical connections forces us to think carefully about the authority that has long been given to the Shakespeare canon and other global institutions that continue to perpetuate ideas of Islamophobia alongside other forms of social injustice. At the same time, such studies provide us with an opportunity to confront social injustice, by allowing us to deconstruct and unlearn the logics of Islamophobia and discrimination that are deeply embedded in many cultural and political discourses around the world.

Notes

1 For all quotations from *The Merchant of Venice* and other Shakespeare plays, see Richard Proudfoot, Ann Thompson, David Scott Kastan and H.R Woodhuysen, eds, *The Arden Shakespeare Complete Works, Third Series* (London and New York: The Arden Shakespeare, 2021).

2 On the association between evil and darkness/blackness in early modern English religious and cultural discourses, see Kim F. Hall, *Things of Darkness: Economies of Race and Gender in Early Modern England* (New York: Cornell University Press, 1995). On the blackness of devils on the early modern stage, see Virginia Mason Vaughan, *Performing Blackness on English Stages, 1500–1800* (Cambridge: Cambridge University Press, 2005), 19–23.

3 Nabil Matar, *Britain and Barbary, 1589–1569* (Gainesville, FL: University Press of Florida, 2005), 23.

4 See Kim F. Hall, '"Guess Who's Coming to Dinner?": Colonialism and Miscegenation in *The Merchant of Venice*', *Renaissance Drama* 23 (1992): 97; Ania Loomba, *Shakespeare, Race, and Colonialism* (New York: Oxford University Press, 2002), 137; and Jonathan Burton, *Traffic and Turning: Islam and English Drama, 1579–1624* (Newark: University of Delaware Press, 2005), 207.

5 Peter Erickson and Kim F. Hall. '"A New Scholarly Song": Rereading Early Modern Race', *Shakespeare Quarterly*, 67 (2016): 12.

6 Ania Loomba and Jonathan Burton, eds, *Race in Early Modern England: A Documentary Companion* (Basingstoke: Palgrave Macmillan, 2007), 2.

7 Loomba, *Shakespeare, Race, and Colonialism*, 22–44.

8 Loomba and Burton, *Race in Early Modern England*, 2.

9 I refer here specifically to Edward W. Said's *Orientalism* (London: Penguin, 2003). Regarding early uses of the term 'Islamophobia' and

its historical origins, see Fernando Bravo López, 'Towards a definition of Islamophobia: Approximations of the Early Twentieth Century', *Ethnic and Racial Studies* 34 (2011): 556–73.

10 For a survey of the history of studies on the racialization of Islam and a recent mapping of the field, see Louise Canker and Saher Selod, 'Review on Race Scholarship and the War on Terror', *Sociology of Race and Ethnicity* 4 (2018): 165–77.

11 Junaid Rana, 'The Story of Islamophobia', *Souls: A Critical Journal of Black Politics, Culture, and Society* 9 (2007): 149; and Steve Garner and Saher Selod, 'The Racialization of Muslims: Empirical Studies of Islamophobia', *Critical Sociology* 41 (2015): 12.

12 For example, scholars have widely documented notable incidences of Islamophobia and the racialization of Muslims in countries in Africa and Asia. On the racialization of Muslims in Southern Africa, for instance, see Gabeba Baderoon, 'Shooting the East/veils and Masks: Uncovering Orientalism in South African Media', *African and Asian Studies* 1 (2002): 367–84; and Samadia Sadouni, *Muslims in Southern Africa: Johannesburg's Somali Diaspora* (London: Palgrave Macmillan, 2019), 95–138. For studies of racism towards Muslims in Asia, see Mohamed Nawab Bin Mohamed Osman, 'Understanding Islamophobia in Asia: The cases of Myanmar and Malaysia', *Islamophobia Studies Journal* 4 (2017): 17–36, on the case of Rohingya Muslims in Myanmar; Luwei Rose Luqiu and Fan Yang, 'Islamophobia in China: News Coverage, Stereotypes, and Chinese Muslims' Perceptions of Themselves and Islam', *Asian Journal of Communication* 28 (2018): 598–619, on the racialization of Muslims in China; and Ali Çaksu, 'Islamophobia, Chinese Style: Total Internment of Uyghur Muslims by the People's Republic of China', *Islamophobia Studies Journal* 5 (2020): 175–98, on Chinese racism towards Uyghur Muslims.

13 Garner and Selod, 'The Racialization of Muslims', 12.

14 Junaid Rana briefly references the important work of Nabil Matar in considering the stereotypical figures of 'Turks' and 'Moors' in 'The Story of Islamophobia', 153–5.

15 Ramon Grosfoguel and Eric Mielants, 'The Long-Durée Entanglement between Islamophobia and Racism in the Modern/Colonial Capitalist/Patriarchal World-system: An Introduction', *Human Architecture* 5 (2006): 2–3.

16 James Shapiro, *Shakespeare and the Jews* (New York: Columbia University Press, 1992); Mary Jenell Metzger, '"Now by My Hood, a Gentle and No Jew": Jessica, *The Merchant of Venice*, and the Discourse of Early Modern English Identity', *PMLA* 113 (1998): 52–

63; Lara Bovilsky, *Barbarous Play: Race on the English Renaissance Stage* (Minneapolis: University of Minnesota Press, 2008); and Lindsay M. Kaplan, 'Jessica's Mother: Medieval Constructions of Race and Gender in *The Merchant of Venice*', *Shakespeare Quarterly* 58 (2007): 4–10.

17 On the cross-historical links between Shakespeare's representations of Islam and blackness, and these discourses of identity in the context of the 'War on Terror', see also Ambereen Dadabhoy, 'The Moor of America: Approaching the Crisis of Race and Religion in the Renaissance and the Twenty-First Century', in *Teaching Medieval and Early Modern Cross-Cultural Encounters*, ed. Karina F. Attar and Lynn Shutters (New York: Palgrave Macmillan, 2014).

18 Quoted in Loomba and Burton, *Race in Early Modern England*, 94.

19 Janet Adelman, 'Her Father's Blood: Race, Conversion, and Nation in *The Merchant of Venice*', *Representations* 81 (2003): 15.

20 Loomba, *Shakespeare, Race, and Colonialism*, 23 and 32.

21 Elizabeth A. Spiller, 'From Imagination to Miscegenation: Race and Romance in Shakespeare's *The Merchant of Venice*', *Renaissance Drama* 29 (1998): 152.

22 Ibid.

23 On the Prince's 'reddest' blood, see also Adelman, 'Her Father's Blood', 18–19.

24 Mary Floyd-Wilson, *English Ethnicity and Race in Early Modern Drama* (Cambridge: Cambridge University Press, 2003), 42.

25 OED B. *adj* I.1.a; OED B. *adj* I.2.a.

26 Here the Prince alludes to the notion of 'fairness', which in early modern English culture was a complex, gendered term used to denote a woman's shining, silver-like, white beauty as well as their moral virtues and religious chastity. On the silver colour of fairness, see Farah Karim-Cooper, *Cosmetics in Shakespearean and Renaissance Drama* (Edinburgh: Edinburgh University Press, 2006), 11.

27 Hall, 'Guess Who's Coming', 97.

28 Dennis A. Britton, 'Flesh and Blood: Race and Religion in *The Merchant of Venice*', in *The Cambridge Companion to Shakespeare and Race*, ed. Ayanna Thompson (Cambridge: Cambridge University Press, 2021), 113.

29 Loomba, *Shakespeare, Race, and Colonialism*, 136.

30 William Shakespeare, *The Most Excellent Historie of the Merchant of Venice* (London, 1600), Qto. C1r.

31 Hall, *Things of Darkness*, 7.
32 *The Second Part of the Booke of Battailes*, trans. John Polemon (London, 1587). This battle was dramatized in George Peele's play *The Battle of Alcazar,* and Peele is thought to have derived his own source material for the play from this text. See Matar, *Britain and Barbary*, 16.
33 Matthew Dimmock describes 'Mahomet' as a pre-modern, fabricated 'Christian construction' of the Islamic figure Prophet Muhammed (PBUH). See *Mythologies of the Prophet Muhammed in Early Modern English Culture* (New York: Cambridge University Press, 2013), xiii.
34 William Painter, *The Second Tome of the Palace of Pleasure* (London, 1567).
35 On the popularity and influence of Painter's collections, see for example Neil Rhodes, 'Italianate Tales: William Painter and George Pettie', in *The Oxford Handbook of English Prose 1500–1640*, ed. Andrew Hadfield (Oxford: Oxford University Press, 2013), 92–105. For an indicator of the number of plays derived from Painter's collection, see John Robert Clements and Joseph Gibaldi, *Anatomy of the Novella: The European Tale Collection from Boccaccio and Chaucer to Cervantes* (New York: New York University Press, 1977), Appendix B. On Shakespeare's uses of Painter's collection as source material for plays like *All's Well That Ends Well* and *Romeo and Juliet*, see Stuart Gillespie, *Shakespeare's Books: A Dictionary of Shakespeare Sources* (Bloomsbury, 2016), ebook, 324–6.
36 See Jerry Brotton, *This Orient Isle: Elizabethan England and the Islamic World* (London: Penguin Books, 2016); Imtiaz H. Habib, *Black Lives in the English Archives, 1500–1677: Imprints of the Invisible* (Farnham: Ashgate, 2008); Jack D'Amico, *The Moor in English Renaissance Drama* (Tampa: University of South Florida Press, 1991); and Matar, *Britain and Barbary*.
37 Brotton, *This Orient Isle*, 272.
38 As Matar has shown, the appearances of Moors on the English stage often corresponded with ambassadorial visits. See *Britain and Barbary*, 13–16 and 23.
39 Habib, *Black Lives*.
40 Matar, *Britain and Barbary*, 30.
41 I borrow the phrase 'reading Muslim-ness onto' from Garner and Selod. See 'The Racialization of Muslims', 12.
42 Christopher Marlowe, *Tamburlaine The Great [. . .] Divided into two Tragicall Discourses* (London, 1590).

43 Garner and Selod, 'The Racialization of Muslims', 14.
44 Ibid.
45 Ibid.
46 Thomas Kyd, *The Spanish Tragedie* (London, 1592), fol. K1r.
47 Matthew Dimmock, *New Turkes: Dramatizing Islam and the Ottomans in Early Modern England* (Abingdon: Ashgate, 2005), 107–11.
48 Garner and Selod, 'The Racialization of Muslims', 12.
49 Zareena Grewal, *Islam Is a Foreign Country: American Muslims and the Global Crisis of Authority* (New York: New York University Press, 2013), 8.
50 Ibid., 298.
51 Ibid.
52 Maheen Haider, 'The Racialization of the Muslim Body and Space in Hollywoord', *Sociology of Race and Ethnicity* 6 (2020): 388.
53 Ibid.
54 Ibid., 392.
55 Ibid.
56 Ibid., 393.

PART III

Imagining freedom with Shakespeare

7

Shakespeare in and on exile

Politicized reading and performative writing in the Robben Island Shakespeare

Kai Wiegandt

Together with Nelson Mandela and other opponents of apartheid, Sonny Venkatrathnam was incarcerated in the 1970s on Robben Island, a prison island 12 kilometres from Cape Town. Prisoners were only allowed one book, which had to be of a religious nature. Having covered his Alexander edition of Shakespeare's works with motifs from the Hindu festival of light, Diwali, Venkatrathnam managed to smuggle it past a guard, whom he tricked into believing that the book was his 'Bible'.[1] Over the following three years, the volume circulated among the inmates of the small solitary cell wing where several leaders of the resistance movement were held. Venkatrathnam asked his comrades to mark a passage of their choice, so that, when he was released in 1978, a total of thirty-three fellow prisoners had highlighted sections of Shakespeare's texts and signed their names, often together with the date.

In his seminal study *Hamlet's Dreams: The Robben Island Shakespeare* (2013), David Schalkwyk discusses the parallels between the sense of imprisonment that pervades *Hamlet*, on the one hand, and the situation of prisoners on Robben Island and of the Black population during apartheid, on the other. For Schalkwyk, the bad dreams that haunt Hamlet express the prisoner's dependence on other people who alone can assure him of his identity, a dependence that proves highly problematic under conditions of permanent imprisonment.[2] Whereas Schalkwyk emphasizes the proximity of the Robben Island Shakespeare to prison literature, I want to trace a thematic pattern that is not identified in *Hamlet's Dreams*, although it runs through even more passages than the theme of imprisonment. The passages I discuss deal with the subject of exile and a feeling of banishment fed by the experience of not feeling at home in one's own country although still living in it. In Joyce's *Ulysses*, Stephen Dedalus points out that Shakespeare's plays deal with the theme of exile in manifold ways: 'The note of banishment, banishment from the heart, banishment from home, sounds uninterruptedly from *Two Gentlemen of Verona* onward till Prospero breaks his staff, buries it certain fathoms in the earth and drowns his book.'[3] The marked passages in the Robben Island Shakespeare reveal which political meanings Shakespeare's dramatizations of these themes acquired in the specific contexts of apartheid and the situation on Robben Island.

Following some brief remarks on my method, the first three parts of my chapter examine the meanings of the marked passages concerned with exile and banishment in the South African context. In the first section, I interpret a marked passage from *The Tempest* and the signatures on the front page of the Robben Island Shakespeare and at the end of Peter Alexander's introduction as symbolic attempts to end exile. The highlighted section allows an alternative view of colonial history, a view that emphasizes the exilic status of the colonizers themselves and thus questions the legitimacy of colonization. In the second section, I deal with marked passages from *As You Like It* and *King Lear*, where Shakespeare variously dramatizes the fact that the experience of exile is also possible on the land and in the country one perceives as one's own. I show how these dramatizations can be productively related not only to the situation of prisoners on Robben Island in particular but also to that of Black South Africans under the apartheid regime in general.

The third section focuses on passages from *Henry V* and *Hamlet* and the ways in which they suggest a connection between exile and nationalism, with a particular focus on the different nationalisms of the National Party and the African National Congress. Finally, the fourth section deals with the question of what it actually means to attach one's signature to a passage from Shakespeare's texts and how such an act relates to postcolonial rewritings of Shakespeare. From there, I will return to *The Tempest*. The play mirrors the prisoners' exile in their own country, and Caliban's desire to sign Prospero's 'book of power' anticipates the literal act of signing the Robben Island Shakespeare as a canonical text of the English-speaking colonial rulers. As I will demonstrate, what the Robben Island Shakespeare and postcolonial rewritings of *The Tempest* have in common is that they open up alternative views on colonial history.[4]

Method

The signatures of the thirty-four prisoners are distributed among very different plays: *A Midsummer Night's Dream*, *The Merchant of Venice*, *As You Like It*, *Twelfth Night*, *Richard II*, *Henry V*, *Julius Caesar*, *Macbeth*, *Hamlet*, *King Lear*, *Antony and Cleopatra* and *The Tempest*. Several sonnets were also selected. Some prisoners, Schalkwyk argues, may have remembered lines learned by heart at school, while others may have seen in a particular passage a welcome opportunity for lyrical escape from their surroundings or may have found it especially relevant to their current situation. For others, Shakespeare may have provided moral support.[5] In the final analysis, Schalkwyk writes, the motives for the selection cannot be identified with certainty, since three variables are at play, each of which is difficult enough to assess on its own: Shakespeare's text in all its ambiguity; the signature and its individual history; and the critic, who cannot claim an objective point of view.[6]

Schalkwyk concludes from this that one can at best read the marked passages for patterns in which a collective unconscious expresses itself. I will try to trace the thematic pattern of exile without recourse to the category of the unconscious or even to the *individual* motives of the prisoners. My basic assumption is that the chosen passages acquired their meanings in a specific historical and political context. While the prisoners' choices may have depended on their individual motives, these motives were themselves not independent of the context of Robben Island and apartheid. The question of if and to what extent this context consciously or unconsciously influenced the prisoners' choice must remain open. In this reading, the relevance of the selected passages does not primarily derive from the notion that they express general human virtues or dilemmas: they were relevant precisely because they were illuminating and critical of the specific situation on Robben Island and in South Africa. As will become clear, the prisoners sometimes had to read a particular passage out of the context of the play in which it is embedded to establish meaningful references to the South African context. Often the passages form part of plays which, when viewed as a whole, do not appear particularly apposite to the prisoners' circumstances. One can also observe a detachment of the quoted lines from the characters speaking them. Indeed, some of the highlighted passages are voiced by characters with whom identification on the part of the signatories seems rather unlikely. An example of this is Julius Caesar, who appears set to become a tyrant when he speaks the words marked by Mandela:

> Cowards die many times before their deaths:
> The valiant never taste of death but once.
> Of all the wonders that I yet have heard,
> It seems to me most strange that men should fear,
> Seeing that death, a necessary end,
> Will come when it will come.
> (*Julius Caesar*, 2.2.32–7)[7]

Symbolic undoing of exile: *The Tempest* and two signatures

Billy Nair, a member of the armed wing of the African National Congress (ANC), chose a passage from *The Tempest*:

CALIBAN   This island's mine, by Sycorax my mother,
          Which thou tak'st from me. When thou cam'st first,

> Thou strok'st me and made much of me, wouldst give me
> Water with berries in't, and teach me how
> To name the bigger light, and how the less,
> That burn by day and night; and then I lov'd thee,
> And show'd thee all the qualities o' th' isle,
> The fresh springs, brine-pits, barren place and fertile.
> Curs'd be I that did so! All the charms
> Of Sycorax, toads, beetles, bats, light on you!
> For I am all the subjects that you have,
> Which first was mine own king; and here you sty me
> In this hard rock, whiles you do keep from me
> The rest o' th' island.
>
> PROSPERO   Thou most lying slave,
> Whom stripes may move, not kindness! I have us'd thee,
> Filth as thou art, with humane care, and lodg'd thee
> In mine own cell, till thou didst seek to violate
> The honour of my child.
>   (1.2.332–49)

Caliban's speech can be related to the situation of any colonial subject. In the 1960s, numerous African and Caribbean authors began to adopt the play in the form of rewritings in which they emphasized Caliban's right to the land and to cultural self-determination. Caliban reclaims expropriated land by invoking inherited rights and can thus be read as a symbolic figure of decolonization. Far from complaining that his colonial father, Prospero, has abandoned him, Caliban would actually prefer to be left completely alone.[8]

In the context of South Africa, the passage evokes associations with expropriation and exile. Even before the National Party seized power in 1948 and introduced apartheid, the dispossession of the Black majority and their forced resettlement in barren 'homelands' was supported by large parts of the white minority. The Natives Land Act of 1913 divided the population of South Africa into categories according to racial characteristics and set quotas for land ownership. Only 13 per cent of the total area was granted to the

Black population. Responding to demands from white landowners, the law turned much of the Black rural population into farm workers or miners who were only allowed to visit their families in homelands such as the Transkei on holidays.[9] On the one hand, the Act could be seen as both an expression of and a means to enforce a blood-and-soil ideology that rested on Christian and nationalist foundations. According to this ideology, the Calvinist 'Boers' were destined by providence to settle in South Africa: Afrikaner nationalists conceived of themselves as a chosen people and saw the Great Trek as an exodus from British rule in the Cape region to the promised land of the Boer Republics.[10] On the other hand, English-speaking white South Africans also supported the Natives Land Act. The segregation of the Black population was official government policy from the founding of the Union of South Africa in 1910; in fact, its roots reach far back into the nineteenth century under British colonial rule, and, according to some historians, even further. As Saul Dubow points out, many scholars believe that the continuities between the era of racial segregation before 1948 and apartheid are so clear that apartheid cannot be seen as an innovation but as a consolidation of the racial order of the time.[11] Under apartheid, large sections of the English-speaking white population were complicit with or even lent active support to the regime. In 1961, one year after the Sharpeville massacre, both Afrikaans- and English-speaking white South Africans voted for the National Party in sufficient numbers to hand it an absolute majority for the first time. Dubow comments:

> One of the factors in this victory was the support for the government of English-speakers, responding to the call for 'national unity'. The republican campaign did indeed reveal that English-speaking South Africans were far less wedded to Britain and the multi-racial Commonwealth than they had been a generation or more before. It also demonstrated the government's willingness to expand insular Afrikaner nationalism into a greater defiant white nationalism.[12]

The policy of dispossession and expulsion was thus supported by most of the white population throughout the twentieth century, regardless of whether this support had its roots in the claim of Afrikaner nationalism to divine providence or in the idea of the superiority of the white race promulgated by Englishmen like Cecil

Rhodes and Rudyard Kipling. With his selection from *The Tempest*, Nair confronts both ideologies with Caliban's origin-based claim to his homeland, a claim that does not depend on God and dubious moral arguments.[13]

This observation does not exhaust the passage's critical potential: in his response to Caliban's speech, Prospero portrays the island dweller as a non-human being in order to justify his banishment after the attempted rape of Miranda. At the same time the play undermines Prospero's own humanity. The exiled person's full humanity was denied as early as Aristotle's *Politics*: 'He that is unable to live in society, or who has no need because he is sufficient for himself, must be either a beast or a god; he is no part of the state.'[14] Thus understood, the exiled Duke of Milan bears the stigma of inhumanity as much as Caliban, whose mother was expelled from her own country. Thanks to his books, which give him magical powers, Prospero seems to be in a god-like, not an animal-like position.[15] Yet the fact that Sycorax was banished from Algiers for practicing magic (1.2.264–8) undermines this claim; instead, the text suggests that his sorcery makes Prospero as inhuman as the witch.[16] Nor does it appear to be an expression of humanity when Prospero teaches Caliban the words for sun and moon. Rather, the colonial idea of language as a gift that transforms the animalistic natives into humans is unmasked as a pretext. What is really at stake is the training of servants capable of understanding the orders of their masters. This form of education was familiar to the prisoners on Robben Island: when Nair signed the passage on 14 December 1977, only a year and a half had passed since the student uprising in Soweto, a protest – against the introduction of Afrikaans as the second compulsory language of instruction besides English – whose bloody suppression by the South African security organs had claimed hundreds of lives.[17] Afrikaans developed in the eighteenth century in the region around Cape Town out of the Dutch Boers' daily interactions with their slaves and servants; it was a language in which colonial masters gave their orders. The fact that Prospero taught Caliban in English (the language that the Soweto protesters preferred when compared to Afrikaans) does not militate against the interpretation of Prospero as stand-in for the Afrikaans-speaking colonizer. Rather, in his capacity as the Duke of Milan, Prospero can stand for *any* colonial ruler who instructs his subordinates in his language, whether it be Italian, English or

Afrikaans. Against the backdrop of the political events of the day, Caliban's speech, in which he reclaims stolen land and alludes to Prospero's lessons in the same breath, can be read as a revealing commentary on the education policies introduced by the National Party. It emphasizes the exilic status of the oppressors, but the passage also contains criticism of teaching in English, the medium of instruction in the supposed 'civilizing mission' of British colonial education. In any case, Caliban destabilizes a clear distinction between colonial master/god on the one hand and servant/animal on the other.

Caliban's narrative of rebellion against captivity on his own island had to fall on particularly fertile ground among the inmates of Robben Island. Imprisonment there cut them off from the Black South Africans on the mainland who had been driven off their land entirely, or who were now working on it as wage labourers. Nair's highlighting of Caliban's lament about the loss of his island *on* this very island ('here you sty me / In this hard rock, whiles you do keep from me / The rest o' th' island') illustrates that exile on Robben Island can ultimately be understood to speak metonymically of the suffering of the Black majority as a whole. The prisoners' exile makes an affective disposition geographically visible: a disposition that affects not only those deported to Robben Island but also those who still live in the place they came from, although they cannot feel at home there anymore.

The apparently contradictory but in fact metonymic relationship of Robben Island to the South African mainland has its own history. From the early days of colonization, the island was part of South Africa, but functioned as a detached space for the outcasts of South African society: in the seventeenth and eighteenth centuries these were indigenous groups who resisted British and Dutch colonial rule, in the eighteenth and nineteenth centuries people whose sexuality was perceived as deviant, people who were deemed mentally disturbed, and lepers. From 1961 until the end of apartheid, the island served as a detention facility for political prisoners.[18] Simultaneously belonging to South Africa and not belonging to it, Robben Island can be said to be what Jacques Derrida calls a 'supplement': a denied part of the community, containing that from which the community has been officially cleansed; a peripheral zone that is also central to the construction of white South Africa. The mechanisms of the apartheid regime as a whole were reflected in condensed form in the conditions on Robben Island, where a large number of Black inmates were at the mercy of a small group of white guards.[19]

One last remark in this context: it is impossible to overlook the possessive gesture contained in Nair's highlighting and signing with which he claims not only the passage from *The Tempest* for himself but also Shakespeare in a broader sense. This claim of ownership is also clearly evident in the signatures of Sonny Venkatrathnam and Kadir Hassim: the owner of the Robben Island Shakespeare put his name next to those of author and editor on the front page, while Hassim signed Alexander's introduction to the plays. Indeed, every signature in the previously untouched complete edition, whether it highlights a single passage of text or is found in the middle of the title page, can be understood as an act of appropriation of Shakespeare – who, for a long time, had served white South Africans, especially English-speaking ones, as a prime example of white superiority and who was instrumental in underpinning the racial ideology propagated by the National Party during apartheid.[20] When it comes to divesting Prospero of his magic powers, Caliban warns Stephano: 'Remember / First to possess his books' (*The Tempest*, 3.2.92–3). On Robben Island, Venkatrathnam and his fellow inmates owned a book that was valued by white South Africans complicit with apartheid. Writing in the book and signing it, they made it their own.

Exile in and on one's own land: *As You Like It* and *King Lear*

The prisoner Sandi Sijake chose Orlando's speech at the beginning of *As You Like It*:

> As I remember, Adam, it was upon this fashion bequeathed me by will but poor a thousand crowns, and, as thou say'st, charged my brother, on his blessing, to breed me well; and there begins my sadness. My brother Jaques he keeps at school, and report speaks goldenly of his profit. For my part, he keeps me rustically at home, or, to speak more properly, stays me here at home unkept; for call you that keeping for a gentleman of my birth that differs not from the stalling of an ox? . . . He lets me feed

with his hinds, bars me the place of a brother, and as much as in him lies, mines my gentility with my education.

(1.1.1–23)

As in Caliban's speech, the object of complaint is the deprivation of the inheritance to which the speaker is entitled – here by his own brother – and as with Caliban, this deprivation goes hand in hand with the denial of learning. Instead of taking care of his brother's education, as his late father had instructed him to do, Oliver has Orlando eke out a living as a foreign servant who has to slave like an ox on the land which should by rights be his. Robbed of his status, his chivalric origins, his property and all education, Orlando sees his home turned into a foreign place. His eventual escape into exile in the forest of Arden thus only represents the choice of another exile, one which involves a change of location but is still easier to bear than banishment in one's own birthplace. When he chose Orlando's speech, Sijake, like Billy Nair, picked a passage that decries imprisonment on Robben Island as an illegitimate banishment from one's own land in one's own land. What is more, the speech links the claim to a share in the land with the claim to participation in its culture.

The theme of exile in one's own land also features prominently in *King Lear*, which is one of the most frequently highlighted works in the Robben Island Shakespeare. The prisoner Frank Anthony marked the entire opening scene. Justice Mpanza and Mohamed Essop both chose Edgar's closing statement:

The weight of this sad time we must obey;
Speak what we feel, not what we ought to say.
The oldest hath borne most; we that are young
Shall never see so much yet live so long.

(5.3.322–5)

The choice of beginning and end suggests that the entire play seemed relevant. In the opening scene, events cast their shadows ahead as the banishment of Cordelia and Kent is sealed and the conspiratorial agreement between Goneril and Regan lays the ground for Lear's exile in his own land. Edgar's concluding words, in turn, invite the audience to evaluate what has happened and reflect on the consequences. Over thirty years ago, when only a handful of former prisoners knew of the existence of the Robben Island

Shakespeare, Martin Orkin pointed out the parallels between *King Lear* and the exiling of the Black majority through the Natives Land Act.[21] Cordelia, Kent and later Lear himself are all exiles: Cordelia in France, Kent outside the kingdom and Lear in a way that must have reminded South Africans forcibly resettled in 'homelands' of their situation and the prisoners on Robben Island of theirs.

At this point, it is worth taking a closer look at the literary models that were available to Shakespeare for his depiction of exile in *King Lear* and *As You Like It*. In both plays, the outcasts of society found their own society. Their exile in the open countryside indicates that Shakespeare drew on the pastoral and bucolic theatre traditions of the early modern period. Yet not even in *As You Like It* does Shakespeare stage exile as idyllically as the conventions of the pastoral genre would demand: the forced stay in the forest of Arden remains marked by fear, since the forest is not only characterized from the beginning as a lawless space but is also immediately infiltrated by the courtly world.[22] The deprivations of exile are tangible; economic hardship plagues the old shepherd Corin, who has precious little to say about the joys of life in the forest of Arden.

In keeping with the ambivalence of life outside civilization articulated here, and in keeping with *King Lear*'s prominent position in the Robben Island Shakespeare, the prisoner Mobbs Gqirana chose a passage from *As You Like It* that can be read as a half-serious, half-serene version of Lear's exile in the wilderness:

> Now, my co-mates and brothers in exile,
> Hath not old custom made this life more sweet
> Than that of painted pomp? Are not these woods
> More free from peril than the envious court?
> . . .
> Sweet are the uses of adversity;
> Which, like the toad, ugly and venomous,
> Wears yet a precious jewel in his head;
> And this our life, exempt from public haunt,
> Finds tongues in trees, books in the running brooks,
> Sermons in stones, and good in everything.
>
> (2.1.1–17)

In the context of Robben Island, the Duke's appeal evokes the prisoners' suffering during the winter months. Here Shakespeare makes use of the classical genre of *consolatio*, a genre especially popular with the Stoics. As Jane Kingsley-Smith has pointed out, the influence of Seneca's *De Providentia* is particularly evident in the Duke's speech, which also shows traces of Epicurean ideas and of Ovid's *Tristia*, the most influential classical reflection on exile. In *As You Like It*, it becomes clear just how much a comic view of exile depends on earthly comfort. This applies not only to the tradition of consolation literature after Epicure but also to the pastoral *topos* of the happy return from exile.[23]

In the final analysis, the passage from *As You Like It* ('Sweet are the uses of adversity') expresses wishful thinking, which is also a key feature of *King Lear*. There, however, it is of a much more sombre variety. Lear's exile in the wilderness takes place in a setting that is a lot more menacing than the forest of Arden, and it is final. If Lear is ultimately denied pastoral amenities and the possibility of return, this denial exposes an exile that must do without the comforting fiction of heaven; an existential exile which, according to Kingsley-Smith, all humans must face. In Lear's permanent exile, the distinction between home and exile collapses. One could argue that it is precisely this quality that spoke to the prisoners on Robben Island. The fact that Lear's exile in his own land is more incisive than Cordelia's in France illustrates (as does Orlando's lament) that being cut off from one's roots, country and past does not necessarily entail physical separation. The prisoners on Robben Island may be isolated from the mainland – and yet this island belongs to South Africa as its metonymic supplement. The situation of the prisoners thus makes visible a more fundamental exile that applies to all Black South Africans: the exile *from* their own land *in* their own land.

Exile and nationalism: *Henry V* and *Hamlet*

Ahmed Kathrada, a close friend of Mandela, selected a passage from *Henry V*:

> Once more unto the breach, dear friends, once more,
> Or close the wall up with our English dead.
>   [. . .] On, on, you noblest English,
> Whose blood is fet from fathers of war-proof –

Fathers that like so many Alexanders
Have in these parts from morn till even fought,
And sheath'd their swords for lack of argument.
Dishonour not your mothers; now attest
That those whom you call'd fathers did beget you.
Be copy now to men of grosser blood,
And teach them how to war. And you, good yeomen,
Whose limbs were made in England, show us here
The mettle of your pasture; let us swear
That you are worth your breeding – which I doubt not;
For there is none of you so mean and base
That hath not noble lustre in your eyes.
I see you stand like greyhounds in the slips,
Straining upon the start. The game's afoot:
Follow your spirit; and upon this charge
Cry 'God for Harry, England, and Saint George!'

(3.1.1–34)

At first glance, it appears strange that this passionate invocation of English dead and English blood, of the English patron saint St George, even of English greyhounds, was highlighted by a political prisoner of Muslim faith who resisted white 'Christian' oppressors in South Africa. The passage certainly oozes a militant English nationalism defined by place ('in England'), blood, English history (embodied by the 'yeomen' who, as a social class, were a peculiarity of England in the late Middle Ages and the early modern period) and inextricably linked to Christianity. While this specifically English brand of nationalism may well have remained foreign to the resistance fighters, the nationalist sentiment expressed in the passage nevertheless struck a powerful chord with the prisoners.

The fact that the prisoners strongly felt South Africa to be their nation is also underlined by the passage selected by Saths Cooper. It is Hamlet's lament about his uncle's drunkenness and gluttony that casts a bad light on Denmark:

This heavy-headed revel east and west
Makes us traduced and taxed of other nations.

(*Hamlet*, 1.4.17–18)

Many of the prisoners on Robben Island were members of the African National Congress, a nationalist party whose claim to South Africa was based on the notion of a country that had been jointly inhabited for generations by a people with common values. Moreover, as Edward Said has shown, exile and nationalism are interdependent:

> Nationalism is an assertion of belonging in and to a place, a people, a heritage. It affirms the home created by a community of language, culture, and customs; and, by so doing, it fends off exile, fights to prevent its ravages. Indeed, the interplay between nationalism and exile is like Hegel's dialectic of servant and master, opposites informing and constituting each other. All nationalisms in their early stages develop from a condition of estrangement.[24]

No longer feeling at home in one's own country, no longer recognizing it: these are the slogans of burgeoning nationalism. Yet nationalism does not only position itself in exile. Exiles, those described by Said as 'cut off from their roots, their land, their past', in turn almost inevitably tend towards nationalism:

> Exiles feel . . . an urgent need to reconstitute their broken lives, usually by choosing to see themselves as part of a triumphant ideology or a restored people. The crucial thing is that a state of exile free from this triumphant ideology – designed to reassemble an exile's broken history into a new whole – is virtually unbearable.[25]

On Robben Island, too, exile and nationalism were mutually contingent. Nationalism had taken hold of the freedom fighters long before they became prisoners: the unifying idea of a shared nation was a prerequisite of the struggle, its goal the restored integrity of that nation. As Dubow has shown, the nationalism of the ANC shared the National Party's claim to South Africa as a state and as a territory.[26] However, while Afrikaner nationalism took a highly exclusionary and discriminatory stance in regard to ethnicity, language and culture, the nationalist resistance movement led by the ANC united a multi-ethnic following (of Black African, Indian, white and 'coloured', i.e. so-called mixed descent) by embracing shared values and a shared vision of the future of South Africa as a nation. Exile on the prison island made this identification with land

and values a vital matter. It welded together a group of men who, in such difficult circumstances, could have easily turned against each other. Kathrada's choice is therefore more than a call to arms in a common struggle. It reflects a nationalism that goes hand in hand with the experience of exile.

The Robben Island Shakespeare and postcolonial rewritings

The pattern of exile and banishment I have traced so far runs through seven passages and includes the signatures on the book's title page and at the end of the editor's introduction. The Diwali cards glued to its cover by Venkatrathnam can also be understood as part of the same pattern. The Hindu festival of lights celebrates the return of the god Rama after fourteen years of exile, so that the cards not only disguise Shakespeare as a 'Hindu Bible' but also express a possibly religiously inspired hope for a return from imprisonment on the Island.[27] While the thematic thread I have identified does not run through all of the thirty-two highlighted and signed passages, and while one should not deduce from this pattern a straightforward intent on the part of those who highlighted and signed, it has nonetheless become clear that Shakespeare's grappling with exile spoke poignantly to the conditions in South Africa under the apartheid regime, especially on Robben Island.[28]

What does it mean, then, to sign a passage from a Shakespeare play? What did it mean when a political prisoner on Robben Island did so? First of all, every signature – regardless of *what* has been signed – implies the presence of the signatory at a time in the past. If we consider the signatures of Venkatrathnam and his fellow prisoners in the Robben Island Shakespeare, however, the evocation of their singular presence proves problematic. As Derrida has shown, every signature must have a repeatable and imitable form in order to be read as a signature at all. The signature belongs to the impersonal system of language, which allows it to be detached from the original act of signing, and therefore signals the absence of the signatory as well as his presence.[29]

Detention on Robben Island meant that while prisoners lived close to their compatriots on the mainland – when the wind was favourable, they could hear the sounds of the city – they remained separated from them by an unbridgeable chasm. The signatures in the Robben Island Shakespeare reflected back to the prisoners this painful absence-in-presence, which is the thematic core of the passages examined. Moreover, any signature that is not erased is destined to outlive the signatory. The signature always anticipates the death of the signatory and, after his or her passing, expresses his or her intentions, which in turn can serve as instructions for those living on.[30] With the release of Venkatrathnam, the Robben Island Shakespeare and its signatures returned to the South African mainland, while the remaining prisoners could not be sure whether they, too, would return or die on the island. In Edward Said's words, exile is 'like death but without death's ultimate mercy'.[31] The haunting experience of exile as a kind of death *and* as a state in which actual death could be imminent at any time must have been vividly present in the minds of the prisoners when they attached their signatures to Shakespeare's texts on Robben Island.

The signing of a text represents a performative act of writing, the function of which depends on the context.[32] Thomas Macho distinguishes between two performative functions of signatures: they serve to *authorize* a text, as in an official decree; and they serve to *claim authorship*, as in a letter.[33] Compared to an official decree or a letter, however, the marked text passages in the Robben Island Shakespeare constitute a highly unusual case, unusual to the point where there are no established conventions to help us determine the meaning of these signatures. Schalkwyk therefore compares the Robben Island Shakespeare to what were known as 'commonplace books' in Shakespeare's time: popular books in which certain passages were highlighted for their special meaning, beauty or moral significance.[34] In the act of signing, according to Schalkwyk, prisoners identified themselves with the sections of text they had highlighted, although this identification proves to be unstable: signatures stand for presence and absence alike, and as Schalkwyk has argued, the highlighted words 'belong' simultaneously to Shakespeare, to a particular dramatic character and to the prisoner who selected the passage.[35]

In this sense, the signatures claim a kind of co-authorship, however unstable it may be: to identify with a passage means to make it your own. However, other performative functions of signatures seem equally important. As already mentioned, signatures in a book can *claim material ownership* of the object. Such a claim can also include the ideas expressed in the book in the sense of co-ownership, a claim that is clearly distinct from authorship. In addition, signatures can *signal consent*. This, too, is a performative function that differs from the claim to authorship and from authorizing actions: the signatory expresses consent to the content of a text passage without being willing or able to authorize it. Again, a comparison with the 'common-place book' could be drawn: signing a passage in such a book implies consent at least as much as a claim to co-authorship; and this consent in turn enables the signatory to identify with the passage.

Considering that the first readers of the signatures were other prisoners who proceeded to add their own, one could also compare the Robben Island Shakespeare to an eclectic code of honour in which the signatures not only express consent but formally *oblige* the signatory to live up to his or her choice. In this sense, Mandela's signature alongside Julius Caesar's speech is Mandela's vow not to fear death, but it also serves as a reminder of a moral obligation to the other readers in prison. The same applies to Gqirana's signature next to Duke Senior's remarks on the 'sweet uses of adversity'.

Finally, it could be argued that signatures also fulfil the performative function of *authorization*. Such an assertion may come as a surprise; the signature of a king or official can authorize a document, whereas Mandela and his fellow prisoners had lost all status and rights. It should not be forgotten, however, that for the majority of the South African population and for a large number of supporters worldwide, the prisoners had already become moral and political authority figures. By signing passages of Shakespeare's plays, the prisoners not only made Shakespeare's words their own; they also lent these words, and thus Shakespeare, the moral and political cachet the prisoners had acquired through personal sacrifice. This, it seems to me, is the signatures' performative function that made the Robben Island Shakespeare so attractive to the British Museum when it presented the volume in an exhibition entitled 'Shakespeare: Staging the World' during the London Olympics of 2012: the signatures served as proof that, in the hands of freedom fighters, Shakespeare's plays were capable of transcending their aesthetic appeal and being turned into powerful sources of inspiration for political activism.

As my examples of the performative functions of claiming authorship and property as well as expressing consent and authorization demonstrate, the position of a signature – on the title page or next to a text passage – and the content of the passage highlighted by a signature can only serve as rough clues as to which function or functions a signature does or does not fulfil. However, the history of education in South Africa does allow for more robust conclusions on related issues. It suggests that the prisoners highlighted and signed sections of text that they interpreted primarily in political terms, and that they often chose 'their' passage without taking into account in which situation the highlighted speech was made or by which dramatic character it was uttered. Many of the prisoners had attended mission schools, where syllabi and teaching methods were constantly being renegotiated between students and teachers, Christians and non-Christians, Black and white South Africans. In the politicized school circles to which the prisoners belonged, Shakespeare was discussed from a decidedly political angle, with passages frequently taken out of context. As Isabel Hofmeyr has shown, this approach continued to inform the handling of Shakespeare's texts by the prisoners on Robben Island: first, the plays provided an opportunity to discuss current events, thereby broadening the horizon of the debates that played a key role in the training of future freedom fighters; second, they were thought to contain lessons about political leadership, responsibility and authority; and third, they served as a source of mottos, maxims, quotations and rhetorical tricks, the effective application of which was studied and repeatedly practiced.[36] The strong emphasis on leadership, responsibility, authority and proverbial aphorisms makes it plausible that the selection of passages in the Robben Island Shakespeare tended to be politically motivated and that consent, obligation and authorization were indeed important performative functions of the signatures in the service of political mobilization.

The politically motivated decontextualization of textual passages is a trait the Robben Island Shakespeare has in common with many postcolonial rewritings of Shakespeare's plays. This is particularly true of *The Tempest* and its reworking by writers such as Aimé Césaire (*Une Tempête*, 1969) and George Lamming (*Water with Berries*, 1971). These rewritings are based on re-readings that focus heavily on certain passages, while others recede into the background. In light of this tradition, the Robben Island Shakespeare can be described as a (post)colonial *re-reading* of Shakespeare's works that did not result in a *rewriting*. And yet the act of highlighting and signing already includes an operation that is characteristic of the aforementioned rewritings: in portraying how the European colonizers force the rightful inhabitants into exile in their own country and on their own land, thus imposing their status as exiles on their colonial subjects, the passages in question permit an alternative view of colonial history that questions the legitimacy of colonization.

Notes

1 It must be added that there are different accounts of how the book arrived on the island, when it was at risk of being removed or banned, and what the guard's or guards' role was. These differing narratives are all ostensibly based on Sonny Venkatrathnam's recollection but suggest slightly different forms of possession or ownership of the Robben Island Shakespeare, its story and its significance.

2 David Schalkwyk, *Hamlet's Dreams: The Robben Island Shakespeare* (London: Bloomsbury, 2013), 74–119. Another important study is Ashwin Desai's *Reading Revolution: Shakespeare on Robben Island* (Pretoria: UNISA, 2012). Drawing on interviews he conducted with some of the former prisoners, Desai focuses on the prisoners' life stories rather than the marked Shakespeare passages. Matthew Hahn's *The Robben Island Shakespeare* (London: Methuen, 2017) is a dramatic adaptation that has helped to popularize the story of the Robben Island Shakespeare.

3 James Joyce, *Ulysses* (London: Penguin, 1992), 272.

4 In the course of my argument, I draw on my previously published 'Shakespeare im und über Exil: die "Robben Island Bible"', *Shakespeare Jahrbuch* 155 (2019): 165–87.

5 Schalkwyk, *Hamlet's Dreams*, 13–17 and 23–4.

6 In interviews, some former inmates could not recall why they had chosen a certain passage at that time. Schalkwyk interprets this as an indication that memory is not a reliable source. If you countersign a passage, you tie your identity to it; but your own identity changes, so that identification can cease (20–1).

7 Quotations from Shakespeare's plays are taken from Richard Proudfoot, Ann Thompson, David Scott Kastan and H. R. Woodhuysen, eds, *The Arden Shakespeare Complete Works, Third Series* (London and New York: The Arden Shakespeare, 2021).

8 See Rob Nixon, 'Caribbean and African Appropriations of *The Tempest*', *Critical Inquiry* 13, no. 2 (1987): 566.

9 See Martin Orkin, 'Cruelty, *King Lear*, and the South African Land Act 1913', *Shakespeare Survey* 40 (1987): 135; and Schalkwyk, *Hamlet's Dreams*, 58.

10 See Martin Prozesky and John de Gruchy, *Living Faiths in South Africa* (London: C. Hurst & Co., 1995), 27–55. Boer literally means 'farmer', but the word has a range of connotations and when used today it tends to carry a pejorative taint. It became a term of pride and defiance among Afrikaners following the South African (or so-called Anglo-Boer) War; later, its association with Afrikaner nationalism made it synonymous with the security police and supporters of the apartheid regime.

11 Saul Dubow, *Apartheid, 1948–1994* (Oxford: Oxford University Press, 2014), 11–12 and 31.

12 Ibid., 85.

13 Ruth Morse and David Schalkwyk argue that the words 'earth' and 'land', as used by Sol Plaatje and Nelson Mandela, come much closer to their meanings in Shakespeare than the blood-and-soil ideology. Their article refers to the Robben Island Shakespeare, but focuses primarily on the works of Plaatje and on Mandela's autobiography *Long Walk to Freedom*. See Ruth Morse and David Schalkwyk, 'This Earth, This Land, This Island . . .', *Archiv für das Studium der neueren Sprachen und Literaturen* 252, no. 2 (2015): 294–313.

14 Aristotle, *The Politics and the Constitution of Athens*, ed. Stephen Everson, trans. Benjamin Jowett (Cambridge: Cambridge University Press, 1996), 14.

15 Jane Kingsley-Smith, *Shakespeare's Drama of Exile* (Houndmills: Palgrave, 2003), 163.

16 Ibid., 166.

17 See Carrol Clarkson, *Drawing the Line: Toward an Aesthetics of Transnational Justice* (New York: Fordham University Press, 2014), 69.

18 See Harriet Deacon, *The Island: A History of Robben Island, 1488–1990* (Cape Town: David Philip, 1996), 1–6; and Schalkwyk, *Hamlet's Dreams*, 26.

19 Monika Fludernik, 'Caliban Revisited: Robben Island in the Autobiographical Record', in *In the Grip of the Law: Trials, Prisons and the Space Between*, ed. Fludernik and Greta Olson (Frankfurt a. M.: Peter Lang, 2004), 278.

20 See David Johnson, *Shakespeare and South Africa* (Oxford: Clarendon, 1996), 74–180.

21 Martin Orkin, *Shakespeare against Apartheid* (Craighall: Ad. Donker, 1987), 130–80.

22 See Kingsley-Smith, *Shakespeare's Drama of Exile*, 106–7 and 110–11.

23 Ibid., 112–17 and 136.

24 Edward Said, *Reflections on Exile and Other Literary and Cultural Essays* (London: Granta, 2000), 176.

25 Ibid., 177.

26 Dubow, *Apartheid*, 69 and 295.

27 See Tim Dowley and Christopher Partridge, *Introduction to World Religions*, 3rd edition (Minneapolis: Fortress, 2018), 565.

28 Significantly, as mentioned in note 6, some former inmates did not remember in interviews why they chose a certain passage at the time. Ahmed Kathrada even disavowed the Robben Island Shakespeare's significance, and the ANC distanced itself from the book and its mythos via Jackson Mthembu as spokesperson some years ago.

29 Jacques Derrida, 'Signature Event Context', in *Limited Inc* (Evanston: Northwestern University Press, 1988), 20.

30 Thomas-Michael Seibert, 'Politik der Unterschrift', in *Die Schreibszene als politische Szene*, ed. Claas Morgenroth, Martin Stingelin and Matthias Thiele (Munich: Fink, 2012), 280.

31 Said, *Reflections on Exile*, 160.

32 Seibert, 'Politik der Unterschrift', 281.

33 Thomas Macho, 'Handschrift – Schriftbild: Anmerkungen zu einer Geschichte der Unterschrift', in *Schrift: Kulturtechnik zwischen Auge, Hand und Maschine*, ed. Gernot Grube, Werner Kogge and Sybille Krämer (Munich: Fink, 2005), 413.

34 Schalkwyk, *Hamlet's Dreams*, 21.

35 Ibid., 22.

36 Isabel Hofmeyr, 'Reading Debating/Debating Reading: The Case of the Lovedale Literary Society, or Why Mandela Quotes Shakespeare', in *Africa's Hidden Histories: Everyday Literacy and Making the Self*, ed. Karin Barber (Bloomington: Indiana University Press, 2006), 269–70.

8

'Men at some times are masters of their fates'

The Gallowfield Players perform *Julius Caesar*

Rowan Mackenzie

The Gallowfield Players is a cooperative prison-theatre company (founded in 2018) that edits, adapts, rehearses and performs the works of Shakespeare. *Julius Caesar* was the Players' second production, performed in 2019, featuring a heavily edited text and a toga-clad cast. In recent years this play has enjoyed renewed popularity, addressing as it does the themes of power, ambition, politics and honour. Against a backdrop of Brexit, the Trump administration and growing concerns over political leadership across the globe, *Julius Caesar* has seemed to speak to audiences in a way that is at once timeless and contemporary. In the United Kingdom, for instance, Angus Jackson directed the play for the Royal Shakespeare Company in 2017 and 2018 saw Nicholas Hytner's promenade performance at the Bridge Theatre, with many other performances staged by professional, semi-professional and amateur companies. In 2017 Phyllida Lloyd directed it at the Donmar

Warehouse, where 'to "justify" an all-female *Julius Caesar* . . . [she] came in with the idea of setting the play in a female prison'; it became the first in a trilogy of Shakespeare plays performed in this vein.[1] Lloyd engaged Clean Break, a theatre company that works with women connected with the criminal justice system, in the adaptation process. The appeal of *Julius Caesar* extends, of course, beyond the Anglophone world. It was also the subject of the Taviani brothers' award-winning film *Cesare deve morire* (2012), set within Rome's Rebibbia prison.[2] Building on the years of work director Fabio Cavalli has done within the high-security wing of the prison, this film interwove a translation of Shakespeare's play with scripted episodes to demonstrate 'how precarious the atmosphere of good-natured camaraderie actually is in a prison setting'.[3]

Prison theatre and prison Shakespeare specifically are not new phenomena, but in recent years interest has burgeoned, both in terms of practice and academic inquiry.[4] The politics and ethics of incarceration are fraught with complexity, and there is not sufficient space to explore this fully here, but a brief explanation of my own perspective is pertinent to understanding the work of the Gallowfield Players. Ashley Lucas describes 'the global crisis of incarceration' which sees millions imprisoned around the world in cases where non-custodial sentences would have been more appropriate and provided more humane alternatives.[5] I am not an abolitionist; I believe that there are instances when the temporary removal of a person from society is required for the safety of others. However, I also believe that the experience should not be further dehumanizing than it already is by its very nature. Although incarceration is the deprivation of liberty, it should not be the deprivation of humanity – yet often those who are imprisoned feel that they lose their very identity within the penal system. As Michael, one of the Gallowfield Players, explains:

> Upon crossing the threshold of prison we instantly become less, we are stripped of our clothes, our dignity and even our humanity. Our lives prior to incarceration instantly rendered worthless. All our experience, our knowledge debased. However, within the setting of the Gallowfield Players these trends are reversed.[6]

The aspiration with my work in prisons is to reverse these dehumanizing trends through collaborative theatre companies and a belief that every person has the ability to 'become something more or different than what we are today'.⁷

This chapter considers the ways in which members of the Gallowfield Players have encountered Shakespeare during times of personal struggle as they have contended with their lives separated from family and loved ones – often dealing with the trauma their crimes have caused. Throughout, I use the term 'inmates' as a generic description of the people I work with inside the prison system; inmate is the term the actors prefer, and it fulfils the gender neutrality required in a company that includes a transgender woman. The focus here is on the practicalities and impact of creating a trauma-informed theatre company within the male English prison estate. The principles which underpin trauma-informed practice are 'safety, trustworthiness and transparency, peer support, collaboration and mutuality, empowerment and choice and cultural, historical and gender issues'.⁸ It is important to understand that these are not meant as a 'checklist'; they need to be embedded in the design of any trauma-informed initiative and they have to be consistently and continually demonstrated. In the UK, Her Majesty's Prison and Probation Services (HMPPS) are initiating trauma-informed practices across the estate, using the principles listed earlier as 'the scaffolding by which a service can implement their trauma-informed vision'.⁹ There are, naturally, challenges to implementing these principles within an estate which was designed for the containment of offenders and not the treatment of traumatized individuals, but the high prevalence of serious trauma within the prison estate – estimated to be between 4 per cent and 32 per cent in male and 16 per cent and 58 per cent in female prisoners – highlights the importance of embedding them into practice.¹⁰ The Probation Service recognizes that 'desistance is rooted in the life course and development of an individual and focuses on the ways that they can learn to stop offending and change their lives'; this applies throughout the criminal justice system, not merely in probation.¹¹

My role as artistic director of the Gallowfield Players has always taken precedence over my role as a researcher during the actual sessions in the prison, and at the outset I made the conscious decision to be guided by James Thompson's wisdom on balancing practice and research. He states in *Digging Up Stories*, 'I do not test theories in my practice, but practice to meet the contingencies of each moment – and then reflect hard on the challenges emerging from these moments.'[12] While this was written in the context of theatre in war zones it resonates with me and applies equally to prison theatre, another area in which Thompson has worked extensively. My research as practice in multiple English prisons has enabled me to utilize ethnographic methods of data-gathering: observations, detailed note-taking after each session, rehearsal diaries, semi-structured interviews with participants and feedback sheets from inmates, staff and families. This chapter draws on such sources to assess how the Gallowfield Players has enabled participants to harness what is frequently described as the 'transformative power of arts and culture in criminal justice settings' in a trauma-informed way.[13] The United Nations asserts, 'there is clearly a universal dimension to social justice, with humanity as the common factor'; the aim of the Gallowfield Players is to encourage this sense of shared humanity among those incarcerated by supporting people to find their own voices.[14] Participation, equity, diversity and access to the process of creating theatre through Shakespeare are cornerstones of the work we do together.

Of course, Shakespeare is not a panacea. Indeed, using Shakespeare is a double-edged sword. Writing about *Cesare deve morire*, Maurizio Calbi observes that the film presents Shakespeare as 'both poison *and* cure' and that this depiction is 'far removed from the incontrovertibly salvific "Shakespeare" as catalyst of spiritual growth, reformation and redemption that emerges from previous "prison Shakespeare" films'.[15] Shakespeare's characters, language and plots offer much richness and, as Azar Nafisi observes, great writing 'heightens your senses and sensitivities to the complexities of life and of individuals, and prevents you from the self-righteousness that sees morality in fixed formulas about good and evil'.[16] There is, however, a danger that choosing Shakespeare for this work may be seen as an affirmation of his cultural capital, established in a patriarchal, white-dominated culture which has facilitated the development of deeply entrenched social injustices over centuries. My own intention in using Shakespeare with marginalized communities is to draw on this cultural capital as a way of creating heterotopias from the juxtaposition of Shakespeare's plays with a group of people ostracized by society.[17] Shakespeare is used as a communication methodology to enable the inmates to speak and to be heard by society, staff, relatives and peers. The work we do involves adapting the plays to reflect elements of the inmates' lived experience within the prison and to make the production appeal to a diverse audience who may not be regular theatre-goers.

The establishment in question is a category B prison with an operational capacity of 707 inmates serving life or indeterminate sentences, predominantly for murder. The 2017 Inspectorate report acknowledged that it 'holds some very challenging prisoners, often with complex mental health problems and long-term needs'.[18] The impact of staff shortages on meaningful activity and offender management was also noted, along with safety risks for inmates and staff; 90 per cent of inmates were assessed as 'presenting a high or very high risk of harm to others'.[19] It was in this environment that the Gallowfield Players was formed in 2018. Over a number of months, we established a cohesive core as we worked on *Macbeth*. I have written a separate account that documents much about this formative period, which culminated in the governor announcing that the initiative was to become a permanent fixture following the inaugural performance.[20] The participants immediately elected to form a theatre company and chose a name reflecting a combination of their location (the prison stands on Gallow Field Road) and the Shakespearean connection (Players to echo the terminology describing actors in Renaissance England). The continuance of the work, not as a short-term project but as a long-term feature in the prison, gave the trauma-informed principles to which I have referred the time needed to flourish. Whereas I had agreed with the governor on the choice of the inaugural play, subsequent decisions have always been made collectively with the actors, as empowerment and choice are fundamental to the company ethos.

Multiple discussions were held, both in our Friday rehearsals and during association time on the wings, about what should be our next work. The consensus was *Julius Caesar* because of the interplay of power, pride and honour which the company wanted to explore (although we are a collective unit of sixteen actors, I try to avoid influencing decisions within the company, so I do not participate in any votes).[21] I was out of the country for a month shortly afterwards and rehearsals were suspended as there was no supervision available. Despite this interruption in the weekly sessions, I returned to discover that two actors had already begun the editing process, gathering input and opinions from the wider group, and had a shortened script of approximately eighty minutes. Some comical prison references were added, such as Brutus declaring his lack of sleep the night Cassius broaches the subject of conspiracy to be because 'the mattresses in this house are wafer thin' rather than the result of a restless mind.[22] Prisons are usually places of mistrust and cynicism, but during our work the company formed deep bonds with each other and with me; this enabled a freedom of expression of emotion, vulnerability and honesty rarely encountered in the penal system. The physical safe space and the continuity of rehearsals acted as a catalyst to encourage the actors to explore both their abilities and their sense of humour, and to include this within the performance.

Recent research from the Prison Reform Trust states a number of prisoner-identified initiatives that are endorsed as enabling positive change, many of which closely align with the principles for trauma-informed approaches listed by SAMHSA (Substance Abuse and Mental Health Services Administration). Two of these have specific resonance for the Gallowfield Players:

> The arts and creativity have a key place in prison to support engagement, tackle isolation and build optimism.

> Prisoner-led initiatives are vital to increase agency, a sense of ownership and responsibility for the health of the prison community. Prisons should create space and opportunities for prisoners to demonstrate that they can be trusted, including by involving prisoners in decision making and scrutiny functions.[23]

The inmates' engagement was evident in the ownership of the script-editing in my absence. Rehearsal diary comments such as 'we are like a family' are testimony to the way the company actively combats isolation.[24] This feeling of familial connectivity, peer support and belonging has been crucial for many participants, giving them the opportunity to develop healthy and sustaining relationships which in turn have fostered emotional resilience. The comments made by the actors during rehearsals for *Julius Caesar* and in their diaries showed that the group fostered 'pride in contributing to group discussions and increasing intellectual and emotional vulnerability', which have been identified as criteria for success in prison arts programmes.[25] The group became incredibly supportive of each other, providing emotional support during rehearsals and on the wings. For example, when one member of the company, Richard, had a dispute with his family, others in the group took time to sit and talk through it with him, facilitating a reconciliation.

The Gallowfield Players differs from the majority of prison arts projects in that it is treated entirely as a collaborative initiative; the decisions are made with the cooperation of every member of the group. Loss of autonomy is synonymous with imprisonment, but it must be emphasized that this is both a source of frustration during a sentence and an impediment to people living independent lives upon release – particularly for those who are serving, or have served, long sentences. This loss of autonomy and 'the fundamental trauma of being deprived of liberty' were identified as the most difficult aspects of imprisonment for those serving long sentences in Ben Crewe et al.'s comprehensive study.[26] There is a considerable body of work on the complex ways in which order is maintained in prisons, whereby 'prisoners are increasingly encouraged to self-govern and assume responsibility for the terms of their own incarceration, in a way that represents neither direct coercion or autonomous consent.'[27] The intention of the company was to allow the actors to operate with some degree of autonomy within the framework of the prison system, enabling them to take ownership of the work performed together. Through this ethos of mutuality and empowerment they were encouraged to make their own decisions and to act in a way which benefitted the entire collective. Michael describes the group as a 'co-operative endeavor':

> all involved have a sense of ownership of it, at times a possessiveness over a beautiful organism that grows in unexpected and wondrous ways. This means there is a sense of responsibility bestowed on everyone involved to act in a certain manner; to promote the best 'us' we can be in order to reap the rewards this initiative has to offer.[28]

Such shared ownership is something rare in the criminal justice system, both the ability to have ownership – 'the right of possession' – and the notion of sharing something.[29] With the production of *Julius Caesar* the actors possessed every element of the work: designing and making costumes and props, contributing to the blocking of scenes and taking turns directing, writing and performing the musical accompaniment which precedes the appearance of the ghost of Caesar. Prisoners have many of their rights and possessions removed when they enter the penal system so the ability for them to develop and influence this group, which had no pre-determined outcomes beyond a desire to put on some form of performance, had a significant effect on their self-worth. Wayne comments: 'I'm proud to say my identity has changed from being a Gallowfield Player', showing how for him the ability to move beyond the label of prisoner to the identity of actor has been a powerful one.[30] Michael's articulation of the way the members of the company felt they should behave related to their internalization of the values of the group (created by them, not imposed on them by an external agency). His description of it as a 'beautiful organism' suggests the creation of something which was both theirs to own and also an independent phenomenon in its own right, a collective larger than the sum of their individual contributions. This concept of creating a shared experience was also important; traditionally among those incarcerated there is often a reticence about sharing. During my first prison workshop I was told that prisoners in educational settings will usually only engage with the teacher and avoid peer collaborations.[31] While, in my experience, this is a rather monochromatic perspective of what is in fact a more nuanced reality, there is an element of truth in that much of prison life discourages the formation of close interpersonal bonds and people therefore shy away from sharing too much. Keith's honesty about his nervousness regarding joining the group demonstrates this issue succinctly. His diary entry documents an apprehension about understanding Shakespeare as a non-native English speaker but also, moreover, a concern about his 'inability to fit in and fear of possible rejection'.[32] Pierre Bourdieu's concept of 'habitus' as a sense of belonging is relevant to Keith's insecurities about language and about his ability to be accepted by a group of Shakespearean actors.[33] The vulnerability of inmates appears to be the primary reason that many avoid engaging with their peers and fear becoming involved in new activities; they are scared of exposing themselves as vulnerable to other inmates or to officers, or alternatively of developing attachments to a project which is then discontinued. Michael writes of the 'insidious oppression of prison life', making it difficult for inmates to trust anyone.[34] He describes the contrast the company has offered through the 'intangible sense of community, of coming together in a wondrous melting pot to *create*'.

The creative autonomy of the members of the company is noted by Rob, who in his rehearsal diary describes a moment when Martin inadvertently missed his cue in Act 5 Scene 5 and ran across stage muttering, 'Argh, I'm meant to be in this scene!' – which subsequently became an integral part of the staging. Rob writes: 'This is a good example of what I find special about this group – our ability to contribute and influence the play and in so doing truly [make] this our own.'[35] Rob joined the group during rehearsals for *Julius Caesar*, as did a number of other inmates. Rob was asked by Michael if he wanted to participate 'and surprised himself by saying yes!' as he undertook his first foray into acting since 'the obligatory roles in primary school'.[36] Each member of the group was given the opportunity to help shape and influence the production and in rehearsals every voice was given equal credence, each suggestion listened to and discussed, allowing what Michael describes as being 'given a voice, no longer shadows in the daylight but people once more'.[37] That this should happen during the rehearsals for a play in which the dynamics of voices and the power of rhetoric are prominent seems particularly poignant. In rehearsals, each actor was individualized as well as being part of a supportive community.

The new joiners quickly integrated themselves into the group. Keith comments: 'Within the first few minutes of arriving I was quite shocked by the atmosphere that was oozing from the group' as he realized that the rehearsal space really was one of support.[38] Many of the actors had longstanding mental health issues and spoke freely in the sessions about the resilience which they developed from being part of the company and the continued support it provided. It is difficult to estimate accurately the scale of mental health challenges within the general population due to problems with diagnosis, but the last UK-wide study estimated there to be over 8.2 million cases of anxiety disorders, 1 million cases of substance addiction and over 4 million cases of personality disorders in 2013.[39] The number of those incarcerated who experience mental health difficulties is disproportionately higher:

> The most comprehensive study of prison mental health in England and Wales found that approximately 90% of prisoners experienced one of the five categories of psychiatric disorder studied – four times the corresponding rate in the wider

community. Some 70% of prisoners had two or more of these problems.[40]

The psychiatric disorders included in the study quoted here were psychosis, neurotic disorders, personality disorders, hazardous drinking and drug dependency, and it is estimated that reception screening on imprisonment identifies less than a third of those with mental health needs.[41] Understandably the threat of self-harm, suicide or attempted suicide in the criminal justice system is significant. Her Majesty's Inspectorate of Prisons Annual Report 2018–19 highlights a 15 per cent increase in self-inflicted deaths in custody in the male estate and a 25 per cent increase in self-harm from the previous year, with over 45,000 instances logged in 2018.[42] In the Gallowfield Players' third production, *The Merchant* (an adaptation of *The Merchant of Venice*), the company would choose to address this issue openly by adapting Shylock to be a released lifer, charting the challenges of his reintegration into society and the impact on his familial relationships, and adding an epilogue focused on the increasing incidents of self-harm and suicide within prisons.[43]

Academic research confirms 'imprisonment itself is a stressful experience, entailing separation from family and friends, living at close quarters with other prisoners, and a lack of constructive activity'.[44] Added to that is the challenge of living with the internalization of 'the people I've hurt, the choices I've made, the guilt, disgust, self-loathing to name but a few emotions' – as an actor in Emergency Shakespeare, another of my prison theatre companies, has eloquently described it.[45] The struggle to cope with isolation from loved ones, the pressures of prison life and the emotional fallout of being a perpetrator of serious crime take their toll, and many of the inmates have commented on the 'refuge' provided by the Gallowfield Players.[46] Wayne, the youngest member of the company, reflects that 'in a place where there's judgement and violence at every turn, there's also a place of peace, fun and tranquility, a place better known as The Gallowfield Players'.[47] During the rehearsal process for *Julius Caesar*, Wayne began to address the emotional issues which had contributed to his index offence and agreed that he should enter the Therapeutic Community (TC) where he would undertake intensive therapy to help address his violent behaviour. Over the course of many rehearsals he discussed with other members of the company the possibility of enrolling in the TC, stating that he felt this was 'a safe space' in which to talk.[48] Will, who had successfully completed the programme, offered encouragement and expounded the benefits while Malcolm, who had removed himself from the TC after nine months, offered the opposing but also supportive stance that it was helpful for some but he had personally found more benefit from the Gallowfield Players: 'I learned much about what went wrong in my index crime. I would say the therapeutic value of Macbeth is far greater than my nine months in the Therapeutic Community.'[49] Here it may be noted that Malcolm later elected to leave the Gallowfield Players due to 'issues that have roots in my life with [his previous partner, against whom his index offence was committed], it all comes from the way she used Shakespeare to belittle me.'[50] His resignation letter contained detailed reflections on the arguments sparked by her perceived superior exposure to ('high') culture in comparison to his and how this had contributed to the situation in which his crime was committed. He felt that she had wielded this superiority over him; playing the title role in *Macbeth* enabled him to attempt to redress the seeming imbalance he had experienced. During his time as a member of the company, Malcolm re-established contact with his children and began to apply for repatriation to his native country in a bid to build links with them during the remainder of his sentence. Wayne, for his part, made the decision to undertake therapy with TC – but obtained permission not to have to take a leave of absence partway through a production in order to start therapy, and it was agreed that his place as a Gallowfield Player would be held for him to return to eighteen months later. He felt empowered to make this decision because within the group the inmates are all treated 'as equals and . . . as if failure didn't exist', giving him the self-confidence to embark on a journey that would require him to deal with some very serious challenges.[51]

The rehearsals themselves were not without difficulties and disagreements, but encouraging the inmates to deal with these amicably and respectfully helped to equip them for their eventual release. The group was a place in which differences could be discussed and resolved without the need to resort to violence, as is often the case within prisons. Yvonne Jewkes explores the rationale for 'engagement in gratuitous violence which is characteristic of much underclass masculinity' across the carceral estate in her monograph, *Captive Audience*.[52] With the exception of one physical assault of an actor inmate by another inmate during the very early days of the *Macbeth* rehearsals, which I have documented elsewhere, the members of the group have always conducted themselves with respect for each other and for me.[53] Whenever an issue has been raised it has been given serious consideration and a resolution found which is acceptable to all involved. For example, some concerns were raised by the group that they had not enjoyed a session where we talked through each line to consider the meaning and inject more feeling into the words. Rob recalls, 'I recognized the importance of this but did find the session quite tedious', as attention lapsed for many members of the group.[54] We were able to agree a resolution and move forward. Authenticity on my part as facilitator has been an important aspect of building trust within the company and has helped to create rehearsal spaces where everyone can feel comfortable raising issues, opining on them and being a proactive part of the resolution strategy. What in many prison programmes could have resulted in disengagement, in the Gallowfield Players has been an opportunity to demonstrate conflict resolution skills.

The benefits of the Gallowfield Players were summarized by a senior member of staff as providing 'a sense of meaning, purpose, collective vision, hope and life beyond Gartree, a vision of a different and better self'.[55] The positive impact of the company was noticed by staff throughout the prison and epitomized when in May 2019 I was unable to attend a rehearsal due to speaking at the 'Shakespeare and Social Justice' conference in Cape Town. The prison was notified of this absence in advance and I had requested that someone be allocated to sit in the library with the actors to enable the rehearsal to go ahead. However, there were insufficient resources to allow that to happen and instead the rehearsal was relocated to the Education Department, where the actors were allowed to rehearse with minimal supervision. They worked alone for much of the session, with an officer checking in periodically but not physically present throughout. The actors were delighted to have this level of trust given to them by the prison and repaid that by focusing diligently and achieving significant progress. Many of their rehearsal diaries record the level of contribution from the whole company and how much they achieved in the first rehearsal held without my input. Differences of opinion relating to the inclusion of Monty Python's Black Knight scene as a humorous interpretation of Lucilius's claim to be Brutus in Act 5 Scene 4 were addressed and resolved positively by the company through democratic discussion (in the performances the audience were delighted with this humorous interlude).[56] This rehearsal in many ways embodied the extent to which the trauma-informed methodology enabled the group members to develop their interpersonal skills, collaboration and empowerment. Their focus on developing and enhancing the production took priority over their personal positioning within the social context of prison, which Crewe describes as acutely exposing 'the terms of friendship, conflict, loyalty and alienation'.[57]

The focus of this chapter has been on the rehearsal process for the Gallowfield Players' production of *Julius Caesar*, and particularly the emotional resilience developed by and among members of the company during this period. A full analysis of the performances themselves is not appropriate, but they deserve at least a brief consideration. There were two performances, one in the morning in the chapel for attendance by fellow inmates and staff, and then a second one in the Visits Hall to which a number of players invited their families. A prison-wide lockdown for security reasons in mid-June curtailed planned rehearsals and we did not even manage a full dress-rehearsal, but despite all of the challenges of prison theatre (widely experienced and acknowledged by prison practitioners across the globe) the performances took place and gave all of us an opportunity to be rightfully proud.[58] The Gallowfield Players demonstrated that we were a cohesive group: missed lines were covered and cues were given and gratefully received as we 'took an audience to Rome', resulting in standing ovations after both performances.[59] The feedback was exemplary and the buzz among the actors and audience after each performance was truly joyous. For a short space of time these inmates were not being judged by the label of 'offender' but were commanding rapt attention as actors. The damaging impact of labelling people is widely acknowledged and is something the group and I have discussed multiple times; I do not see the members of the company as 'murderers' but as 'people who have committed murder' – a subtle yet fundamental difference.[60] Their entire life cannot and should not be distilled into one act, and the Gallowfield Players allows them to explore and share other facets of themselves.

At the end of the family performance I was presented with a beautiful drawing of the company, adorned with personal messages from each actor, which hangs in pride of place in my living room. The thank-you speech reduced the majority of the audience to tears as Michael spoke of 'the community which has brought joy into a somber place and shows us there is more to the world than prison'.[61] Wayne wrote in his diary after the performances that 'it has been the best day that I've ever had in prison', describing the pleasure he took in seeing his family show pride in him for the first time since his incarceration as a juvenile.[62] After the families had left we carried the props and costumes back to the main prison. The actors were unwilling to leave, preferring to stand in the corridor talking rather than break the magic they had created by returning to their cells. Ben's reflection on the day seems a poignant one with which to end this consideration of what the Gallowfield Players meant to the actors during our rehearsals for *Julius Caesar*. 'I can honestly say,' Ben wrote, 'that during our performance to our loved ones I forgot that I was in prison, forgot I was a prisoner, so much so that when it was over and I stepped back into the main prison it was like my first day in prison again.' There is an ambivalence to this experience of returning to his first day of incarceration: it produced 'an echo of how deep I've entered into this place', leaving Ben with 'an empty feeling', although this in turn was a reminder of 'why The Gallowfield Players are so important – a rare breath of fresh air in an otherwise suffocating situation'.[63]

'Men at some time are masters of their fates', Cassius tells Brutus (*Julius Caesar*, 1.2.139).[64] In appropriating this line for the title of my chapter, I have sought to affirm that, while the actors of the Gallowfield Players may lack agency in the context of the wider prison system, in their ownership of the theatre company they have been – at some times at least – masters of their own fates.

Notes

1. Harriet Walters, *Brutus and other Heroines: Playing Shakespeare's Roles for Women* (London: Nick Hern Books, 2016), 159.
2. Paolo and Vittorio Taviani (directors), *Cesare deve morire* (Rome: Rai Cinema La Talee Stemal Entertainment, 2012).
3. Mariangela Tempera, 'Shakespeare Behind Italian Bars: The Rebibbia Project, *The Tempest*, and *Caesar Must Die*', in *Shakespeare, Italy,*

and *Transnational Exchange: Early Modern to Present*, ed. Enza De Francisci and Chris Stamatakis (London: Routledge, 2017), 273.

4 See Murray Cox, ed., *Shakespeare Comes to Broadmoor* (London: Jessica Kingsley Publishers, 1992); James Thompson, ed., *Prison Theatre* (London: Jessica Kingsley Publishers, 1998); Jean Troustine, *Shakespeare Behind Bars* (Michigan: University of Michigan Press, 2004); Michael Balfour, ed., *Theatre in Prison* (Bristol: Intellect, 2004); Amy Scott-Douglass, *Shakespeare Inside* (London: Continuum, 2007); Jonathan Shailor, ed., *Performing New Lives* (London: Jessica Kingsley Publishers, 2011); Laura Bates, *Shakespeare Saved My Life* (Naperville: Sourcebooks, 2013); Niels Herold, *Prison Shakespeare and the Purpose of Performance* (Basingstoke: Palgrave Macmillan, 2014); and Rob Pensalfini, *Prison Shakespeare* (Basingstoke: Palgrave Macmillan, 2016).

5 Ashley E. Lucas, *Prison Theatre and the Global Crisis of Incarceration* (London: Methuen, 2021).

6 Michael, 'Experiencing Freedom within the High Security Estate', The Gallowfield Players, 22 March 2019 [unpublished]. Names of incarcerated individuals have been changed; in order to ensure anonymity while maintaining humanity, pseudonyms are used throughout.

7 Lucas, *Prison Theatre*, 16.

8 Substance Abuse and Mental Health Services Administration, U.S., *SAMHSA's Concept of Trauma and Guidance for a Trauma-Informed Approach* (Rockville, MD, 2014). Available online: https://www.cdc.gov/cpr/infographics/6_principles_trauma_info.htm.

9 Vicky Jervis, 'The Role of Trauma-Informed Care in Building Resilience and Recovery', *Prison Service Journal* 242 (Special Edition: Recovery in Prison, March 2019): 20.

10 G. Baranyi, M. Cassidy, S. Fazel, S. Priebe and A. P. Mundt, 'Prevalence of Posttraumatic Stress Disorder in Prisoners', *Epidemiologic Reviews* 40, no. 1 (2018): 134–45.

11 Shadd Maruna and Ruth Mann, *Reconciling 'Desistance' and 'What Works'* (HM Inspectorate of Probation Academic Insights 2019/1), cited in Kieran F. McCartan, *Trauma-informed practice* (HM Inspectorate of Probation Academic Insights 2020/05, 07 July 2020). Available online: https://www.justiceinspectorates.gov.uk/hmiprobation/wp-content/uploads/sites/5/2020/07/Academic-Insights-McCartan.pdf.

12 James Thompson, *Digging Up Stories* (Manchester: Manchester University Press, 2005), 8.

13 National Criminal Justice Arts Alliance commissioned report, *Enhancing Arts and Culture in the Criminal Justice System: A Partnership Approach* (June 2019). Available online: https://www.art sincriminaljustice.org.uk/wp-content/uploads/2019/06/Enhancing-arts -and-culture-in-the-criminal-justice-system.pdf.
14 United Nations, *Social Justice in an Open World* (2006), 13. Available online: https://www.un.org/esa/socdev/documents/ifsd/SocialJustice .pdf.
15 Maurizio Calbi, '"In States Unborn and Accents Yet Unknown": Spectral Shakespeare in Paolo and Vittorio Taviani's *Cesare Deve Morire* (Caesar Must Die)', *Shakespeare Bulletin* 32, no. 2 (2014): 236.
16 Azar Nafisi, *Reading Lolita in Tehran: A Memoir in Books* (New York: Random House, 2003), 112.
17 See Michel Foucault, 'Of Other Spaces: Utopias and Heterotopias', trans. Jay Miskowiec, *Architecture/Mouvement/Continuite* (October 1984): 4. Online: https://web.mit.edu/allanmc/www/foucault1.pdf.
18 HM Chief Inspector of Prisons, 'Report of Unannounced Inspection of HMP Gartree' (13–23 November 2017): 4. Available online: https:// www.justiceinspectorates.gov.uk/hmiprisons/wp-content/uploads/sites /4/2018/03/HMP-Gartree-Web-2017.pdf.
19 Ibid., 5.
20 Rowan Mackenzie, '"Action is Eloquence": Creating Space for Shakespeare in HMP Gartree', *Drama Research* 11 (Spring 2020). Available online: http://www.nationaldrama.org.uk/journal/current -issue/.
21 The Gallowfield Players, discussion during rehearsal (HMP Gartree, 26 October 2018).
22 The Gallowfield Players, *Julius Caesar* (February 2019), 2.1.27. See William Shakespeare, *Julius Caesar*, ed. David Daniell (London: The Arden Shakespeare, 1998).
23 Lucy Wainwright, Paula Harriott and Soruche Saajedi, *What Do You Need to Make the Best Use of Your Time in Prison?* (Prisoner Policy Network, Prison Reform Trust, July 2019). Available online: http:// www.prisonreformtrust.org.uk/Portals/0/Documents/PPN/What_do _you_need_to_make_best_use_of_your_time_in_prisonlo.pdf.
24 Wayne, 'Rehearsal Diary for *Julius Caesar*', The Gallowfield Players, 26 April 2019 [unpublished].
25 Geraldine Brown and Paul Grant, 'Hear Our Voices: We're More Than the Hyper-Masculine Label', in *New Perspectives on Prison*

Masculinity, ed. Matthew Maycock and Kate Hunt (Cham: Palgrave Macmillan, 2018), 145–68, 150.

26 Ben Crewe, Susie Hulley and Serene Wright, *Life Imprisonment from Young Adulthood: Adaptation, Identity and Time* (Cham: Palgrave Macmillan, 2020), 155.

27 Ben Crewe, 'The Sociology of Imprisonment', in *Handbook on Prisons: Second Edition,* ed. Yvonne Jewkes, Jamie Bennett and Ben Crewe (London and New York: Routledge, 2016), 95. Crewe's chapter contains a summary of the work done in this area.

28 Michael, 'Experiencing Freedom within the High Security Estate'.

29 Della Thompson, ed., *Oxford Concise English Dictionary* (Oxford: Oxford University Press, 1997), 977.

30 Wayne, 'Rehearsal Diary for *Julius Caesar*', The Gallowfield Players, 19 June 2019 [unpublished].

31 Paul Johnston (Cluster Head of Learning, Skills and Employment HMP Leicester and HMP Gartree), interview with the author, 18 October 2017.

32 Keith, 'Rehearsal Diary for *Julius Caesar*', The Gallowfield Players, 12 June 2019 [unpublished].

33 Pierre Bourdieu, *Outline of a Theory of Practice,* trans. Richard Nice (Cambridge: Cambridge University Press, 1977).

34 Michael, 'A Sense of Freedom', The Gallowfield Players, May 2019 [unpublished], 3.

35 Rob, 'Rehearsal Diary for *Julius Caesar*', The Gallowfield Players, 5 April 2019 [unpublished].

36 Rob, 'Rehearsal Diary for *Julius Caesar*', 11 January 2019 [unpublished].

37 Michael, 'Rehearsal Diary for *Julius Caesar*', The Gallowfield Players, 14 April 2019 [unpublished].

38 Keith, 'Rehearsal Diary for *Julius Caesar*', The Gallowfield Players, 12 June 2019 [unpublished].

39 Mental Health Foundation, *Fundamental Facts about Mental Health 2016* (London: Mental Health Foundation, 2016) citing N. Fineberg et al., 'The Size, Burden and Cost of Disorders of the Brain in the UK', *Journal of Psychopharmacology* 27, no. 9 (2013): 761–70.

40 Alice Mills and Kathleen Kendall, 'Mental Health in Prisons', in *Handbook on Prisons: Second Edition,* ed. Yvonne Jewkes, Jamie Bennett and Ben Crewe (London and New York: Routledge, 2016), 188, citing N. Singleton, H. Meltzer and R. Gatward, *Psychiatric Morbidity Among Prisoners* (Office of National Statistics, 1998).

41 See C. Brooker, J. Repper, C. Beverley, M. Ferriter and N. Brewer, *Mental Health Services and Prisons,* (Sheffield: University of Sheffield School of Health and Related Research, 2002).
42 Peter Clarke, *HM Chief Inspector of Prisons for England and Wales, Annual Report 2018–2019* (Crown Copyright, July 2019), 25. Available online: https://www.justiceinspectorates.gov.uk/hmiprisons/wp-content/uploads/sites/4/2019/07/6.5563_HMI-Prisons-AR_2018-19_WEB_FINAL_040719.pdf.
43 The Gallowfield Players, *The Merchant: An Adaptation of William Shakespeare's The Merchant of Venice,* performed at HMP Gartree 27–29 January 2020 [script unpublished].
44 Mills and Kendall, 'Mental Health in Prisons', 187.
45 Brody, 'Rehearsal Diary for *The Merry Wives of Windsor*', Emergency Shakespeare, 18 May 2020 [unpublished].
46 Ben, 'No Drama', The Gallowfield Players, July 2019 [unpublished]; Rob, 'Rehearsal Diary for *Julius Caesar*', The Gallowfield Players, 19 April 2019 [unpublished]; Wayne, 'Rehearsal Diary for *Julius Caesar*', The Gallowfield Players, 15 February 2019 [unpublished].
47 Wayne, 'The Gallowfield Players: A Reflection', The Gallowfield Players, May 2019 [unpublished].
48 Wayne, The Gallowfield Players, verbal comment made during rehearsal, 24 May 2019.
49 Malcom, The Gallowfield Players, verbal debrief following performance of *Macbeth*, HMP Gartree, 19 October 2018.
50 Malcolm, The Gallowfield Players, letter of resignation from the company written to the author, 7 September 2019 [unpublished].
51 Wayne, 'The Gallowfield Players: A Reflection', The Gallowfield Players, May 2019 [unpublished].
52 Yvonne Jewkes, *Captive Audience: Media, Masculinity and Power in Prisons* (Cullompton: Willan Publishing, 2002), 54.
53 See Mackenzie, 'Action Is Eloquence'.
54 Rob, 'Rehearsal Diary for *Julius Caesar*', The Gallowfield Players, 25 January 2019 [unpublished].
55 Regional Learning and Skills Manager, HMPPS Long Term and High Secure Estate, feedback form completed following performance of *Julius Caesar*, HMP Gartree, 19 June 2019.
56 The text of *Julius Caesar* 5.4.7–32 was interspersed with text and physical actions from Monty Python's Black Knight Scene (see https://www.montypython.net/scripts/HG-blkscene.php).

57 Crewe, 'The Sociology of Imprisonment', 77.

58 In Shailor's *Performing New Lives*, John McCabe-Juhnke (127–42), Curt L. Tofteland (213–30) and Elizabeth Charlebois (256–69) each include acknowledgements of the challenges of prison theatre, including permissions for props and costumes, inmates being moved, segregation and administrative challenges.

59 'Gallowfield Players took an audience to Rome', *The Grapevine: HMP Gartree Magazine*, July 2019 [unpublished].

60 See Alexandra Cox, 'The Language of Incarceration', *Incarceration* 1, no. 1 (2020). Available online: http://repository.essex.ac.uk/27518/; P. S. Bedell, M. So et al., 'Corrections for Academic Medicine: The Importance of Using Person-First Language for Individuals Who Have Experienced Incarceration', *Academic Medicine* 94, no. 2 (2019): 172–5; and J. G. Bernburg, 'Labeling Theory', in *Handbook on Crime & Deviance*, ed. M. D. Krohn, A. J. Lizotte and G. P. Hall (Cham: Springer, 2009), 187–207.

61 Michael, The Gallowfield Players, post-performance thank you speech, 19 June 2019.

62 Wayne, 'Rehearsal Diary for *Julius Caesar*', The Gallowfield Players, 19 June 2019 [unpublished].

63 Ben, 'No Drama', The Gallowfield Players, July 2019 [unpublished].

64 Richard Proudfoot, Ann Thompson, David Scott Kastan and H. R. Woodhuysen, eds, *The Arden Shakespeare Complete Works, Third Series* (London and New York: The Arden Shakespeare, 2021).

PART IV

Scrutinizing gender and sexual violence

9

The 'sign and semblance of her honour'

Petrarchan slander and gender-based violence in three Shakespearean plays

Kirsten Dey

Violence against women is a global concern of epidemic proportions. The World Health Organization's 2013 report on the global and regional estimates of violence against women in over eighty countries revealed that approximately '35% of women worldwide have experienced either physical and/or sexual intimate partner violence or non-partner violence'.[1] Statistics such as these were only exacerbated by the outbreak of Covid-19 in 2020. Early studies in China's Hubei province, for example, discovered a dramatic surge in domestic violence reports, which tripled in February 2020.[2] It is true that the past thirty years, in particular, have seen an increase in local and international energies devoted to recognizing, researching and addressing the realities faced by a third of the world's women; however, it is also true that gender-based violence is still a pervasive, systemic phenomenon which evidently requires the international community to improve upon and expand its response to the causes and consequences of this social injustice.

Violence against women is certainly not new to world history and has consequently been given voice throughout time by the various artists who have borne witness to its embodiment in their specific epochs. In the 1590s and 1600s, William Shakespeare exploited Petrarchan rhetoric, as the dominant love language of his day, to dramatize the destructive potential of romantic relationships in which the female beloved is idealized, silenced and slandered. That is not to say that all of Shakespeare's works advocated for the equal and humane treatment of women, *The Taming of the Shrew* being one example of a work that has troubled feminist scholars and theatre-makers. Nonetheless, there are plays that expose the structural violence intrinsic to the Petrarchan 'theatre of desire'[3] directed by the male gaze, and which require us to imagine and thereby take action against a system in which the 'passive position [is] feminised and thus disempowered, reduced, weakened . . . in a model of domination where the subject is male'.[4]

Petrarchism flourished in England in the 1590s, primarily in the form of the Elizabethan love sonnet. The sonnet sequence which has won the most renown, and is still the most widely read, is *Shakespeare's Sonnets* (1609). However, the influence of Petrarchism is not limited to *Shakespeare's Sonnets* but is widespread across his works – in his narrative poems such as *Venus and Adonis* and throughout his plays – but especially his comedies, in which besotted Petrarchan lovers are satirically portrayed as falsely idealistic and melodramatic. Leonard Barkan links Petrarch directly to Shakespeare's drama in a suggestive way. Invoking the concept of 'transdiscursive' authors or texts of wide and pervasive influence, a term coined by Foucault with reference to Marx and Freud, Barkin describes Petrarch's *Canzoniere* as one of a 'body of important works of such universal presence within early modern civilisation . . . that they are present everywhere in the formation of [Shakespeare's] plays via some deep acculturation'.[5] Few critics, however, have explored what David Schalkwyk refers to as the '"necessary embodiment" of the poetic voice' in the 'dramatised sonneteer'.[6]

This chapter endeavours to contribute to this critical tradition by focusing on Shakespeare's engagement with an *enacted* Petrarchism in order to demonstrate that Shakespeare's early imagining of Petrarchan relationships often foregrounded and critiqued their destructive potential to result in intimate partner violence. Indeed, not all of Shakespeare's plays, and certainly not his sonnets, engaged with Petrarchism in this manner; in his sonnets, for example, Shakespeare experimented with the tropes of Petrarchism, exploring the possibilities of a greater realism in its depiction. By contrast, many of his comedies simply made a mockery of the fops and dandies who made elaborate, Petrarchan declarations of love which were not imbued with the heart's sincerity. There are a few of his plays across genres, however, in which the treatment of Petrarchism is more serious and chilling: these texts explicitly illustrate and consider the dangers of Petrarchan rhetoric when the idealization it provokes and justifies is not limited to the poetic landscape but brought to life on the stage in ways which are representative of the world beyond it.

This analysis will consider Shakespeare's portrayal of a destructive Petrarchism, which operates at varying and increasing levels of intensity, beginning with his comedy *Much Ado about Nothing*, followed by his romance *Cymbeline*, and his tragedy *Othello*, so as to investigate the ways in which the plays centre violence against women. In each case, Shakespeare imagines a Petrarchan lover who converts his mistress into a heavenly envoy of chastity and unwavering virtue, and this spiritual idealization releases pathological forces which unleash an irrational and violent anguish in the lover when suspicion is cast on her purity. Usually this doubt is triggered by some form of slander on the mistress, and for this reason, it can be argued that Shakespeare appropriated and developed his own variation of 'the calumny romance'[7] or the 'slandered heroine' plot,[8] a popular motif within romance narratives, in order to explore this aspect of Petrarchism. Valerie Wayne defines the calumny romance as a 'story of a woman accused of being unchaste until some agent, earthly or providential, proves her innocence and reveals the charges against her to be false, usually slanderous'.[9] I begin with a brief discussion of Hero and Claudio's relationship in *Much Ado about Nothing*, a comedy in which 'the slander prompts social confusion but no deaths'.[10] This is followed by a fuller analysis of Innogen and Posthumus's relationship in the tragicomedy *Cymbeline,* in which the slandered wife is recovered in the context of other losses. Finally, Othello and Desdemona's relationship in *Othello* is examined as an aptly tragic example of Shakespeare's imagined climax of this aspect of Petrarchism. In each case, Shakespeare emphasizes the vulnerable position women occupy as representatives of purity and virtue by considering the consequences of descending from idealized to abhorred when they deviate from their prescribed roles. In all of this, the intention is to demonstrate Shakespeare's early engagement, by means of Petrarchan rhetoric, with the phenomena of gendered idealization and gender-based violence, which were as integral to his age as they are to our own. Through his creation of disenchanted Petrarchan lovers who either plan or perpetrate violence against their intimate partners, Shakespeare makes a case for justice for women, thereby calling upon his audience – then and now – to take urgent action.

The dangerous rage of the disillusioned Petrarchan lover is initially presented and explored within the context of the calumny romance in *Much Ado about Nothing*, in which Don John tricks Claudio into thinking that Hero has been unfaithful. From the outset of the play, Claudio is infatuated with and uses Petrarchan terms to describe Hero – drawing attention to her virtue when he calls her a 'modest young lady' (1.3.157) as well as to her beauty when he uses a metaphor to describe her as a 'jewel' (171) and identifies her as the 'sweetest lady that ever [he] looked on' (177).[11] Yet his perception of her is altered in Act 3 when Don John 'pours his sexual slander of Hero into the credulous ears of Don Pedro, Claudio and Leonato',[12] calling her 'disloyal' (3.3.94) and then asserting:

> The word is too good to paint out her wickedness. I could say she were worse. Think you of a worse title, and I will fit her to it. Wonder not till further warrant. Go but with me tonight, you shall see her chamber window entered, even the night before her wedding day.
>
> (3.3.98–103)

Claudio responds: 'If I see anything tonight why I should not marry her, tomorrow, in the congregation where I should wed, there will I shame her' (113–15). Even at the initial stages, when faced with the possibility of Hero's tainted reputation, Claudio reveals a destructive desire to make Hero suffer socially – if not physically – for her supposed sins. Such a public shaming would damage her reputation of virtue and worth, producing far-reaching consequences in her life by denying her the prospect of marriage with any other man. She would probably be relegated to a life in a nunnery or in her father's household. Hence, while Claudio might not threaten a violent death, he does promise social annihilation at the very least. This is precisely what happens at the start of Act 4 in the church at Hero and Claudio's wedding after Don John's successful staging of Hero's infidelity the night before. Claudio asserts:

> There, Leonato, take her back again.
> Give not this rotten orange to your friend.
> She's but the sign and semblance of her honour.
> Behold how like a maid she blushes here!
> O, what authority and show of truth
> Can cunning sin cover itself withal!
> Comes not that blood as modest evidence
> To witness simple virtue? Would not you swear,
> All you that see her, that she were a maid,
> By these exterior shows? But she is none.
> She knows the heat of a luxurious bed.
> Her blush is guiltiness, not modesty.
>
> (4.1.31–42)

Indeed, Hero's fate is an 'exemplary case of femininity fashioned between praise and slander: most praised as an ideal woman, hers is the deepest fall'.[13] In these lines, Shakespeare illustrates Hero's precarious position as the embodiment of chastity whose value has suddenly deteriorated to that of a 'rotten orange'. Claudio is particularly preoccupied with the 'gap between inner being and outward seeming' in Hero, who is described as the hollow shell of a modest woman – a woman whose beauty is 'but the sign and semblance of her honour'. The sexualizing of a woman he once idealized in Petrarchan terms as 'Dian in her orb, / As chaste as is the bud ere it be blown' (4.1.57–8) horrifies him and he rejects her as a bride before the congregation, calling her more 'intemperate in [her] blood / Than Venus or those pampered animals / That rage in savage sensuality' (59–61). Claudio's inverted perception of Hero is reflected in the mythological metaphors he uses to describe her. Initially, she is compared to Diana – the goddess of the hunt, moon and nature, who guarded her chastity – and is thus associated with that which is physically and metaphorically transcendent. This, however, is replaced by his likening of her to Venus – the goddess of love, sex, beauty and fertility – and to lower beings, animals, so that she is transformed into a representative of the carnal and the physical.

Furthermore, when Hero attempts to defend herself by denying the accusations against her, at Claudio's behest that she answer honestly, '[w]hat man . . . talked with her / Out at [her] window betwixt twelve and one' (84–5) the night before, Claudio does not believe her. Instead, he states:

> But fare thee well, most foul, most fair, farewell
> Thou pure impiety and impious purity.
> For thee I'll lock up all the gates of love,
> And on my eyelids shall conjecture hang
> To turn all beauty into thoughts of harm,
> And never shall it more be gracious.
>
> (103–8)

Hero consequently collapses at the wedding and is believed to be dead by the community, including Claudio, who exits the church with no sign of remorse. While the comic structure of the play prevents a tragic conclusion, as Hero survives and is married to Claudio at the end of the play, Claudio and Hero's relationship calls upon the audience to recognize and address the dangers of a rhetoric, and indeed a reality, which not only enables and justifies a rigid idealization of women, making them vulnerable to the consequences of deviating from that ideal, but also invalidates their voices – even when they are present.

Later in Shakespeare's career, the romance genre enabled him to explore the slandered heroine and demonized Petrarchan lover dynamic to a greater extent, as is evident in his romance *Cymbeline*. Both J. M. Nosworthy and Valerie Wayne acknowledge Shakespeare's debt to the romance tradition and the wager plot, a form of the calumny romance, in their prefaces to *Cymbeline*. Wayne notes that the 'sources of the wager plot in *Cymbeline* have long been recognized as Tale 9 of Day 2 in Boccaccio's *Decameron*, which appeared first in Italian in 1349-1351 and was widely disseminated',[14] and defines the wager plot as a form of the calumny romance in which a man 'initiates a bet [and] doubts that any woman can be faithful and then offers false proof of his success in seducing a targeted woman',[15] thus slandering the heroine. This is precisely what occurs in *Cymbeline*, but Shakespeare develops and presents his own version of this standard plot by portraying Posthumus and Innogen as Petrarchan lover and beloved, so that the dangers of Petrarchan spiritual idealization are emphasized and explored when they threaten to result in gender-based violence.

At the start of the play, Innogen's husband Posthumus has been banished for marrying Innogen without her father King Cymbeline's permission. Innogen's value, her virtue, is announced immediately by the two gentlemen in the opening scene:

> To his mistress,
> (For whom he now is banish'd) her own price
> Proclaims how she esteem'd him; and his virtue
> By her election may be truly read
> What kind of man he is.
>
> (1.1.50–4)

Innogen appears to be associated with and characterized in terms of the ideal constancy of the Petrarchan mistress before Posthumus can present himself as her counterpart Petrarchan lover in his idealization of her. However, when he goes to Rome and meets Iachimo and a group of foreigners who are boasting about their country's women, he is explicit in his veneration of Innogen. According to a Frenchman, Posthumus has already vouched 'his [lady] to be more fair, virtuous, wise, chaste, constant, qualified and less attemptable than any of the rarest . . . ladies in France' (1.5.55–8). In addition, Posthumus calls himself Innogen's 'adorer' (66). Colin Burrow glosses 'adorèd' in this context as: 'worshipped as a deity (with a suggestion of idolatry)', which draws attention to Posthumus's spiritually idealizing perception of Innogen.[16] Hence, Posthumus uses typically Petrarchan topoi to describe both himself and his beloved – associating Innogen with the physical and moral perfection of the Petrarchan mistress and himself with the reverence of the Petrarchan lover. The fact that Posthumus associates Innogen with what amounts to a spiritual ideal is evident when he calls Innogen the 'gift of the gods' (1.5.82). In other words, he cannot perceive Innogen in human terms, but only in terms that exalt her. However, Posthumus's public idealization of his wife initiates the wager plot. Iachimo states: 'I will lay you ten thousand ducats to your ring, that, commend me to your court where your lady is, with no more advantage than the opportunity of a second conference, and I will bring from thence that honour of hers, which you imagine so reserv'd' (1.5.124–8).

The narrative then unfolds in accordance with the conventions of the wager plot. When Iachimo goes to England, attempts to seduce Innogen and is unsuccessful, he decides to gather information in order to trick Posthumus into thinking that he managed to corrupt Innogen's chastity. To do so, Iachimo hides in a trunk in Innogen's bedroom and emerges while she is asleep to study her room as well as her half-naked body, creating an 'inventory' (2.2.30) and taking Posthumus's bracelet off her arm. He notes:

> On her left breast
> A mole cinque-spotted: like the crimson drops
> I'th'bottom of a cowslip. Here's a voucher,
> Stronger than ever law could make; this secret
> Will force him think I have pick'd the lock, and ta'en
> The treasure of her honour.
>
> (2.2.37–42)

When Iachimo returns to Rome, he informs Posthumus that 'the ring is won' (2.4.45), and continues to present Posthumus with his inventory of Innogen's bedroom, to which Posthumus replies that 'the description / Of what is in her chamber nothing saves / The wager [Iachimo] has laid' (93–5). In response, Iachimo reveals the bracelet he took from Innogen's arm; Posthumus is profoundly dismayed, asserting that the 'vows of women / Of no more bondage be to where they are made / Than they are to their virtues, which is nothing' (110–12). However, Philario is not as ready to accept Iachimo's evidence, and tells Posthumus that one of Innogen's handmaids could have stolen her bracelet, so that Posthumus begins to waver between faith in Innogen's fidelity and despair at her supposed 'incontinency' (127). Nonetheless, Philario remains certain that Iachimo has not provided enough evidence and attempts to assure Posthumus of Innogen's chastity. Crucially, Posthumus's extreme Petrarchism appears to make him more vulnerable to the possibility of the tainting of Innogen's honour, pointing to the dangers inherent in the spiritual idealization of the

Petrarchan mistress to the extent that her lover loses his sense of rationality and sound judgement. Furthermore, after Iachimo is prompted by Philario's uncertainty into revealing his knowledge of the mole under Innogen's left breast, a 'seismic shift . . . convulses [Posthumus], as his faith in [Innogen is finally] undermined'.[17] His despair mutates into destructive impulses, exposing the psychic disturbance and split personality that extreme Petrarchan idealization can provoke, and revealing the demonic alter-ego of the Petrarchan lover, when he says: 'O, that I had her here, to tear her limb-meal! / I will go there and do't, i'th'court, before / Her father' (2.4.146–8). Posthumus thus develops a disturbing desire not only to kill her but to do so with an extremity of violence that matches the extremity of his idealization. While there is no explanation presented as to why his despair should transform into the desire to murder Innogen, his impulse suggests that Innogen's value to him, as an object he possesses, has been eradicated; his rage is that of a cuckold whose pride has been wounded, whose power has been undermined by his mistress, subsequently catalysing the instinct to eliminate the source of his disillusionment. In addition, Posthumus's dismay at the corruption of his ideal, the 'nonpareil of [the] time' (160), appears to bleed into his perception of all women when he calls all men 'bastards' (154) and asserts, Hamlet-like, that '[a]ll faults . . . that hell knows' belong to women, including 'flattering', 'deceiving', 'lust', 'rank thoughts', 'revenge', 'ambitions', 'covetings', 'change of prides', 'disdain', 'nice longings', 'slander' and 'mutability' (175–9). Hence, even Posthumus's lexicon registers the Janus face of the Petrarchan lover and the mutation of his devotion into disgust, through the change in the nature of his epideictic rhetoric, in which he substitutes a language of praise with that of blame. In this way, the play emphasizes the precarious, unjust position occupied by women, like Innogen, who fall victim to their partners' violence when they appear to escape the strict boundaries determined by their gender.

In Act 3, the audience discovers, however, that Posthumus does not literalize his desire to 'tear [Innogen] limb-meal', but that his outrage leads him to request that his servant, Pisanio, murder Innogen on his behalf. In his shock, Pisanio wonders:

O master, what a strange infection
Is fall'n into thy ear! What false Italian

(As poisonous tongu'd as handed) hath prevail'd
On thy too ready hearing? Disloyal? No.

(3.2.3–6)

Here, Pisanio is able to recognize that Innogen has been slandered, and accuses Posthumus of having 'too ready hearing' – of being too quick to accept falsified evidence against Innogen. Pisanio and Philario's comparatively more willing faith in Innogen is significant in that it draws attention to Posthumus's particular vulnerability to the possibility of Innogen's infidelity, a vulnerability rooted in his rigid idealization of her. Yet, despite his despair, Posthumus does not intend to murder her himself. It is possible that he cannot bring himself to murder her, but it is equally likely that he simply cannot enter England since he has been banished. More intriguingly, however, his absence, which effectively denies Innogen the chance of defending herself, points to the recurring trope of the silencing of the Petrarchan mistress in favour of the 'omnipotent male' lover.[18] Posthumus's actions suggest that he does not require Innogen's voice to decide her fate but believes it his right as her husband to order her death. This emphasizes the destructive implications of a system, as represented by Petrarchism, that privileges the male over the female voice, and grants him the permission, as her keeper, to discipline and punish her for her sins – a system which has had far-reaching implications in the world's long history of gender-based violence. On a more pragmatic level, Posthumus's absence, which leaves him unable to act out his murderous thoughts, saves Innogen and the drama from a tragic outcome, for Pisanio decides not to obey his master's orders. In Act 5 of *Cymbeline*, the focus is on restoration, recovery and redemption, as befits a romance. Posthumus is informed of Innogen's innocence and is reunited with her after believing her to be dead, so that, narrowly avoiding the destruction of his beloved and himself, he experiences not only a recovery of Innogen but a renewal of himself, as is evident when he says: 'Hang there like fruit, my soul, / Till the tree die' (5.5.262–3).

While Shakespeare did not explore the tragic outcome of a destructive Petrarchism in *Cymbeline* (1610), just six years earlier he had depicted in *Othello* (1604) what would happen if a disillusioned lover fulfilled his threat of murdering the beloved. The tragic genre is precisely what enabled Shakespeare to imagine the climax of an extreme Petrarchism that spiritually idealizes the beloved to the extent that the possibility of her sexual corruption acts as a catalyst for an irrational despair that does not consider her voice or defence, but erupts into the physical realm as violence against his intimate partner.

From the outset of the play, Othello appears to be preoccupied with associating both himself and Desdemona with the spiritual as opposed to the sexual. After Desdemona asks the Senate to accompany him to Cyprus, Othello asks that her request be heard, but not without explicitly denying his sexuality and arguing that desire will not determine his behaviour. He calls upon 'heaven' to '[v]ouch with [him]':

> Let her have your voice.
> Vouch with me, heaven, I therefore beg it not
> To please the palate of my appetite,
> Nor to comply with heat, the young affects
> In me defunct, and proper satisfaction,
> But to be free and bounteous to her mind.
>
> (*Othello*, 1.3.261–6)

The fact that Othello calls upon heaven makes evident from the outset his desire to associate himself and Desdemona, as well as their relationship, with that which is spiritual, higher and virtuous. He dissociates himself from his 'appetite' and 'heat', indicating that he is 'too old for the pleasures of young love', and that he wants to be available to Desdemona's *mind* as opposed to her *body*.[19]

Desdemona is similarly characterized by others as the quintessence of female virtue, as is made evident by her father's reaction to her elopement; Brabantio is '[u]nable to reconcile his daughter's revolt with his notion of her as a female paragon, incapable of either self-will or appetite':[20]

> A maiden never bold,
> Of spirit so still and quiet that her motion
> Blushed at herself; and she, in spite of nature,
> Of years, of country, credit, everything,
> To fall in love with what she feared to look on?
> It is a judgement maimed and most imperfect

> That will confess perfection so could err
> Against all rules of nature ...
>
> (1.3.95–102)

According to Brabantio, Desdemona does not *represent* perfection, but *is* perfection. This perception is reinforced by Cassio when he tells Montano that Othello

> hath achieved a maid
> That paragons description and wild fame;
> One that excels the quirks of blazoning pens
> And in th'essential vesture of creation
> Does tire the inginer.
>
> (2.1.61–5)

Cassio 'celebrates her as one who surpasses all other textual constructions of exemplary women',[21] portraying Desdemona as the ideal Petrarchan beloved. In fact, when Desdemona's ship reaches Cyprus before Othello's does, Cassio attributes her safe journey to her 'divin[ity]' (2.1.73) and, in welcoming her to Cyprus, kneels and salutes her:

> O, behold,
> The riches of Cyprus is come on shore:
> You men of Cyprus, let her have your knees!
> Hail to thee, lady, and the grace of heaven,
> Before, behind thee, and on every hand
> Enwheel thee round!
>
> (2.1.83–8)

E. A. J. Honigmann argues that this 'comes close to being a "Hail Mary", and [that] her identification with heaven continues to the end of the play'.[22] When Othello reaches Cyprus, his Petrarchan perception of Desdemona is made evident by his statement upon seeing her: 'O my fair warrior!' (2.1.179) As Honigmann indicates, in the Petrarchan tradition, 'the woman is sometimes addressed as a warrior (in love)', citing Spenser's *Amoretti* 57.1, when 'the speaker addresses his beloved: "Sweet warriour! when shall I have peace with you?"'[23] This idea is further emphasized by Cassio when he refers to Desdemona as 'a most exquisite lady', 'right modest' and 'perfection' (2.3.18–25), drawing attention to her physical and moral *perfection*, which are the primary qualities attributed to the ultimate Petrarchan lady.

The fact that Othello idealizes Desdemona spiritually is especially evident when he says: 'Perdition catch my soul / But I do love thee! and when I love thee not / Chaos is come again' (3.3.90–2). In this context, 'Perdition' and 'Chaos' can be understood as damnation or the nothingness of destruction, which would associate Desdemona with that which is heavenly, higher and spiritual. In Othello's mind, 'it is only Desdemona who stands between him and the "Chaos" or "Perdition" that he associates with his former state. Thus, it is not simply Cassio's habit of courtly hyperbole that licenses the lieutenant to dress her in the poetry of Marian adoration.'[24] In fact, according to Honigmann, Othello's words not only suggest that he views Desdemona as a spiritual envoy but in fact imply 'a willingness to give "all for love", a worship of God's creature rather than God'.[25] Significantly, the idealization of a woman before God is a dilemma that affected Petrarch, especially in the later sonnets of his *Canzoniere*. Stephen Minta indicates that

> [a] love as miserable as Petrarch's for Laura must be a fundamentally wrong kind of love, and in the final poem of the *Canzoniere*, under the threat of approaching death, Petrarch renounces his love and turns to the Virgin Mary in the hope that she will intercede for him and save him from the consequences of his sin.[26]

However, unlike Petrarch, Othello does not realize that his spiritual idealization of Desdemona is potentially harmful, but rather embraces his dependence on their love as the only barrier between him and 'Perdition'. What makes this statement particularly poignant is the fact that it occurs just before Othello begins to doubt Desdemona due to Iago's slanderous insinuations that Desdemona has been unfaithful, catalysing the 'Chaos' that is to come again in the form of Othello's unquestioning despair and violence against Desdemona.

In Act 3, Iago suggests that Cassio ought not to be trusted with Desdemona, and then exclaims:

O beware, my lord, of jealousy!
It is the green-eyed monster, which doth mock

> The meat it feeds on. The cuckold lives in bliss
> Who, certain of his fate, loves not his wronger,
> But O, what damned minutes tells he o'er
> Who dotes, yet doubts, suspects yet strongly loves!
>
> (3.3.168–73)

Although Othello responds with 'misery', he notes that he will 'see before [he] doubt[s]' (74). Hence, Othello does not appear to be overcome with jealousy or despair at first, and rather consoles himself with the idea that he will obtain proof before he acts, much as Posthumus does in *Cymbeline*; Othello desperately clings to the hope that 'Desdemona's honest' (229) and states that even if Iago proves that she is guilty of infidelity, Othello will 'whistle her off and let her down the wind / To prey at fortune' (266–7). Nevertheless, he cannot prevent himself from exclaiming: 'O curse of marriage / That we can call these delicate creatures ours / And not their appetites!' (272–4). Evidently, Othello's perception of Desdemona has already been tainted by Iago, as he appears, for the first time, to associate Desdemona with that which is sexual as opposed to spiritual. He continues with this newly sexualized rhetoric in relation to Desdemona when he says that he would rather 'be a toad / And live upon the vapour of a dungeon / Than keep a corner in the thing [he] love[s] / For others' uses' (274–7). Desdemona has rapidly become but a 'thing' to Othello – as opposed to his 'warrior' and paragon of virtue – revealing the irreversible reduction in her value as the object of his love.

Othello's despair appears to escalate at an alarming rate, which is exacerbated by Iago when he fuels Othello's imagination by telling Othello that he has overhead Cassio dream of Desdemona and their supposed affair. Othello begins to uncover the demonic alter-ego of the Petrarchan lover when he responds: 'I'll tear her all to pieces!' (3.3.434) This is the first sign of Othello's violent intent, and, in fact, closely resembles Posthumus's violent reaction to the possibility of Innogen's infidelity in *Cymbeline* ('O, that I had her here, to tear her limb-meal!') Both lovers use the word 'tear' – a verb associated with brutal action – to signify the extremity of their destructive anguish at the thought of their wives' tainted virtue. Othello's rage is both intensified and solidified when Iago informs Othello that he has seen Cassio 'wip[ing] his beard' with the handkerchief that was

Othello's 'first gift' to Desdemona (3.3.439–42). In response to this statement, Othello states:

> My bloody thoughts with violent pace
> Shall ne'er look back, ne'er ebb to humble love
> Till that a capable and wide revenge
> Swallow them up. Now by yond marble heaven
> In the due reverence of a sacred vow
> I here engage my words.
>
> (3.3.460–5)

Othello continues to present himself as a demonic incarnation of the Petrarchan lover by indicating that his intentions have grown violent even though the only proof he has exists in Iago's deceptive words. Othello then vows by 'heaven' to achieve 'revenge' in acquiring 'some swift means of death / For the fair devil' (480–1). Crucially, Othello's assumption that she has been demonized is what catalyses his own demonic transition. Furthermore, Othello indicates that his violent intentions are 'sacred' or right because they are aimed at eliminating the tainted and unspiritual, which is how he perceives his actions until he realizes that Desdemona is innocent after he murders her at the end of the play. He views it as his responsibility or right to eliminate her sin as her husband, amalgamating his role as a soldier and Petrarchan lover who, as a defender of spiritual love, ought to eliminate its enemy – Desdemona. In this way, Shakespeare reworks the love-as-war and woman-as-warrior allegory of Petrarchism, affirming the dangers inherent to its rhetoric, which has the potential to justify violence against women.

Consequently, events appear to conspire against Desdemona and only serve to make Othello more suspicious: she champions Cassio's cause and cannot find her lost handkerchief even though she assures Othello that she has not lost it. Othello then sees the handkerchief he gave Desdemona in Bianca's hand after Iago planted it in Cassio's chamber. This is sufficient for Othello to reiterate that 'she shall not live' (4.1.179), even if he cannot help acknowledging that she is 'delicate with her needle, an admirable musician' (185) and can 'sing the savageness out of a bear' (186), which are among the unlimited accomplishments of the typical Petrarchan beloved. In this way, he reminds himself of her supposed deviation from the ideal, perhaps to rationalize his intention to murder her. He subsequently instructs Iago to obtain 'some poison' (201). However, Iago suggests that he should rather 'strangle [Desdemona] in her bed – even the bed she hath contaminated', to which Othello responds: 'Good, good, the justice of it pleases' (204–6). Michael Neill observes:

> The place of love will be transmuted into the place of punishment; and the ironic 'justice' of the suggestion 'pleases' the Moor because it converts his murder into a species of abstract ritual – not so much the killing of a woman as the ceremonial cleansing of a polluted place.[27]

Iago thus enables Othello to justify his murder of Desdemona to himself once more, so that he can view himself as a warrior or priest of a higher, more spiritual love, who is responsible for its sanctity. To Othello, Desdemona ought to suffer the consequences of her sin, and his role as her husband is to take responsibility for her punishment. To the audience witnessing Othello's attempts at justifying his violent impulses, the sheer *injustice* of his terrifying power over her fate is self-evident, and indeed representative of the realities of many women throughout the world and its history, whose intimate partners have similarly rationalized their violent intent.

When Othello finally speaks to Desdemona and commands her to '[s]wear [she is] honest',[28] she responds: 'Heaven doth truly know it'.[29] Although Desdemona is unaware of the deed to which Othello is referring, she can still vow that she is a faithful and chaste wife. Like Hero, Desdemona is given a voice and an opportunity to be heard – although, to Othello, Desdemona's words are meaningless. He has been convinced by Iago and has convinced himself into believing that Desdemona is unfaithful, revealing that women can be disempowered and treated as an absence even if their voices are indeed present. Othello has resolved to murder Desdemona, and not even her avowal that she is faithful can deter him from his intention. After instructing Desdemona to go to bed, and saying that he will meet her in their chamber, Othello reminds himself of the ritualistic aspect of the murder he is about to commit when he states that their bed, 'lust-stained, shall with lust's blood be spotted' (5.1.36), drawing attention to his belief that only the shedding of blood can cleanse and purify that which is contaminated. In this way, Othello not only affirms the binary pathologies of the Petrarchan lover – that a woman can only be virginal and pure, or promiscuous and degraded – but also exposes their violent potential.

As the play draws to its conclusion, its tragic structure allows for the terrifying fulfilment of Othello's threats. When he enters their bedroom in the final scene of the play while Desdemona is asleep, Othello, 'committed as he thinks he is to noble action',[30] is still justifying his actions to himself: 'It is the cause, it is the cause, my soul!' (5.2.1) Furthermore, he states:

> Yet I'll not shed her blood
> Nor scar that whiter skin of hers than snow
> And smooth as monumental alabaster:
> Yet she must die, else she'll betray more men.
>
> (5.2.3–6)

In these lines, it is not simply that Othello is 'tragically invoking Desdemona's beauty',[31] but that he is doing so specifically through the use of Petrarchan imagery, comparing the beloved's skin to 'snow' and 'monumental alabaster'. Othello is focusing on the conventional Petrarchan attributes perhaps to remind himself of Desdemona's deviation from the spiritual ideal and 'maintain his guise as . . . priest rather than murderer' who is 'sacrificing Desdemona to save her from herself' and from the other men he believes she would seduce and betray.[32] The idea that this murder is 'sanctified by heavenly sorrow' and that he is a heavenly agent is even further emphasized when he asserts: 'This sorrow's heavenly, / It strikes where it doth love' (5.2.21–2).[33] When Desdemona awakes upon Othello's entrance, she is given a voice once more in saying that she does not know 'guiltiness' (39). She also denies giving the handkerchief to Cassio 'by [her] life and soul' (49), but Othello does not trust her and ultimately smothers her, telling her that it is simply 'too late', even for 'prayer' (82). Othello thus invokes that which is spiritual at the point of murder, making explicit the paradox inherent in his impulse to destroy, which is at the root of a despairing spiritual idealization of the Petrarchan mistress.

In *Much Ado about Nothing*, *Cymbeline* and *Othello*, Shakespeare exploits the Petrarchan tradition to reveal the dangers of gendered romantic idealization that is so rigid that the female beloved can be only wholly pure or wholly impure, and easily descend from idealized to despised. It is in this way that voice is given to the silenced women who suffer the violent consequences of such dichotomous classification and face the terrifying injustice of their position in patriarchal systems. Indeed, contemporary readers of these texts may learn much from Shakespeare's dramatization of a system, which prioritizes the power and opinions of men over those of women, and a discourse – or 'transdiscourse' – which restricts the roles available to women to that of pious virgin or rank temptress. By breathing life into the causes and consequences of gender-based violence, Shakespeare initiated a call to action whose echoes need not be restricted to the sixteenth and seventeenth centuries, but which, through careful study and consideration, can provide us with a means to understanding and addressing the long history of violence against women throughout the world.

Notes

1 Claudia Garcia-Moreno, et al., *Global and Regional Estimates of Violence Against Women: Prevalence and Health Effects of Intimate Partner Violence and Non-Partner Sexual Violence* (Geneva: WHO Press, 2013), 1.

2 Neetu John, Sara E. Casey, Giselle Carino, and Terry McGovern, 'Lessons Never Learned: Crisis and Gender-Based Violence', *Developing World Bioeth* 20 (2020): 66.

3 Gary F. Waller, 'Struggling into Discourse: The Emergence of Renaissance Women's Writing', in *Silent but for the Word: Tudor Women as Patrons, Translators, and Writers of Religious Works*, ed. Margaret P. Hannay (Kent: Kent State University Press, 1985), 242.

4 Natasha Distiller, *Desire and Gender in the Sonnet Tradition* (Basingstoke: Palgrave Macmillan, 2008), 30.

5 Leonard Barkan, 'What Did Shakespeare Read?', in *The Cambridge Companion to Shakespeare*, ed. Margreta de Grazia and Stanley Wells (Cambridge: Cambridge University Press, 2001), 43.

6 Sara Morrison and Deborah Uman, 'Setting the Stage', in *Staging the Blazon in Early Modern English Theater*, ed. Sara Morrison and Deborah Uman (Abingdon: Routledge, 2013), 4.

7 Helen Cooper, *The English Romance in Time: Transforming Motifs from Geoffrey of Monmouth to the Death of Shakespeare* (Oxford: Oxford University Press, 2004), 219.

8 Ina Habermann, *Staging Slander and Gender in Early Modern England: Women and Gender in the Early Modern World* (Aldershot: Ashgate, 2003), 135.
9 Valerie Wayne, 'Introduction', in Shakespeare, William, *Cymbeline*, ed. Valerie Wayne, Arden Third Series (London: The Arden Shakespeare, 2017), 7.
10 Ibid., 16.
11 Citations from works by Shakespeare are taken from Richard Proudfoot, Ann Thompson, David Scott Kastan and H. R Woodhuysen, eds, *The Arden Shakespeare Complete Works, Third Series* (London and New York: The Arden Shakespeare, 2021).
12 Ina Habermann, *Staging Slander and Gender in Early Modern England: Women and Gender in the Early Modern World* (Aldershot: Ashgate, 2003), 10.
13 Ibid., 11.
14 Wayne, 'Introduction', 5.
15 Ibid., 7.
16 Colin Burrow, 'Notes', in William Shakespeare, *The Complete Sonnets and Poems*, ed. Colin Burrow (Oxford: Oxford University Press, 2002), 248.
17 Wayne, 'Introduction', 86.
18 Heather Dubrow, *Echoes of Desire: English Petrarchism and Its Counter Discourses* (Ithaca: Cornell University Press, 1995), 24.
19 Maurice Charnay, *Shakespeare on Love and Lust* (New York: Columbia University Press, 2000), 100.
20 Michael Neill, 'Introduction', in William Shakespeare, *Othello*, ed. Michael Neill (Oxford: Oxford University Press, 2006), 170.
21 Valerie Wayne, *The Matter of Difference: Materialist Feminist Criticism of Shakespeare* (Ithaca: Cornell University Press, 1991), 160.
22 E. A. J. Honigmann, 'Introduction', in William Shakespeare, *Othello*, ed. E. A. J. Honigmann, Arden Third Series (London: Nelson, 1997), 107.
23 Ibid., 174.
24 Neill, 'Introduction', 172.
25 Honigmann, 'Introduction', 52.
26 Stephen Minta, *Petrarch and Petrarchism: The English and French Traditions* (Manchester: Manchester University Press, 1980), 4.
27 Neill, 'Introduction', 157.

28 Shakespeare, *Othello*, (IV, ii, 38).
29 Shakespeare, *Othello*, (IV, ii, 39).
30 Honigmann, 'Introduction', 84.
31 Charnay, *Shakespeare on Love and Lust*, 21.
32 Charnay, *Shakespeare on Love and Lust*, 21 and Honigmann, 'Introduction', 84.
33 Neill, 'Introduction', 173.

10

Open-gendered casting in Shakespeare performance

Abraham Stoll

From its inception Shakespeare performance tested gender, casting boy actors in such roles as Juliet, Rosalind and Cleopatra. And its history has seen a number of further challenges to prevailing gender assumptions, from the advent of female actors on the Restoration stage to the recent all-male, original practices productions by the Globe. But we may now have entered a new moment, in which female actors are cast in male roles with increasing regularity – in which they are cast and walk the stage with the sense that such a move is increasingly not a pointed challenge but a standard thing.[1]

Women playing Hamlet is hardly new. From Sarah Siddons and Sarah Bernhardt on, it has been estimated that there have been more than 200 female Hamlets in professional productions.[2] But in recent years Maxine Peake played Hamlet at the Royal Exchange in Manchester (2014), Laura Walsh Berg played the role at the Idaho Shakespeare Festival (2017), Michelle Terry performed it at the Globe in London (2018) and Ruth Negga at the Gate Theatre in Dublin (2018), reprised at St. Ann's Warehouse (2020). In Australia Bell Shakespeare has announced a *Hamlet* for the 2021 season, with Harriet Gordon-Anderson in the lead.

Bell Shakespeare also cast Kate Mulvany as Richard III, at the Sydney Opera House (2017). On Broadway, Glenda Jackson played

King Lear (2019). There have been two recent productions of *Othello* with all-female casts: by the Harlem Shakespeare Festival, with Debra Ann Byrd as Othello (2015), and *Othello: A Woman's Story*, by the Cape Town company Mish Mash Media Productions, with Annitha Judith Kontyo as Othello (2018). The Public Mobile Unit did an all-female-identifying, all-Black, *Measure for Measure*, with Grace Porter as the Duke (2019). There have been several female Prosperos, including Helen Mirren in Julie Taymor's 2010 film, and Harriet Walter in Phyllida Lloyd's *Tempest* at the Donmar Warehouse in 2017. In 2018 Martha Henry played the role in Stratford, Ontario, while Kate Burton did so at the Old Globe in San Diego. Lloyd's *Tempest* was the third in a trilogy of all-female productions, preceded by *Henry IV* and *Julius Caesar*. Beginning with Walter's Brutus in 2012, and all the actors in that superb production, Lloyd's trilogy deserves a great deal of credit for making open-gendered casting almost impossible to avoid in contemporary Shakespeare theatre. Equally important, Terry, as the new artistic director of the Globe, has made a policy of gender equity in casting.[3] In a trip to England in 2019, open-gendered casting was a feature of every Shakespeare and early modern production I saw. Anna-Maria Nabirye played Macduff at the Globe's Wanamaker Theatre. In Stratford at the Royal Shakespeare Company, Timon was played by Kathryn Hunter (who famously played Lear in 1997). Charlotte Josephine played Mercutio for the RSC in London. Jocelyn Jee Esien and Pauline McLynn played Doctor Faustus and Mephistophiles respectively for the Globe. This is to skip the many other mid-level roles and ensemble parts that were cast across gender, too many to name.

The sheer number of women playing leading male roles, and in so many leading theatres, indicates how open-gendered casting has become a standard part of the landscape of Shakespeare performance. Accordingly, it has also become basic to the work we do at the Old Globe and the University of San Diego Shiley Graduate Theatre Program. We are a classical acting programme, a conservatory known for its focus on Shakespeare and one that is striving to update classical theatre for the twenty-first century. We admit seven actors each year and offer a practical training programme focused on performance, aimed at preparing them to get work in American theatres. We have made a commitment to open-gendered casting and are in the process of exploring what it means.

Our motivations are largely practical. Among the benefits to an acting conservatory is the simple fact that open-gendered casting creates more opportunities for female actors – more roles to audition for, to understudy and to play over the course of their degree. It also gives greater scope to our repertoire. We have tended over the years towards producing the comedies and romances, simply because they have more female characters – open-gendered casting makes possible the histories and the tragedies as well. And perhaps most practically, if today's Shakespeare theatre is increasingly turning to open-gendered casting, then the Old Globe-USD MFA must do so too in order to prepare our actors for employment in the real world.

While 'cross-gendered' casting has been the common critical term, this chapter uses 'open-gendered' in order to be non-binary.[4] The cases discussed here mainly involve female actors playing male roles, consonant with the practical needs of the theatre today. However, these cases may also teach us something about male actors playing female roles, as well as the permutations introduced by non-binary actors and non-binary characters. And even within the process of a female actor taking on a male character, gender often resists binaries. The acting work, at its imaginative core, requires an investment in the openness and fluidity of gender.

This chapter takes a practical approach, by considering open-gendered casting in two interrelated areas, dramaturgy and acting. It is meant to be exploratory, a first stab at thinking about the practice, based on our programme's first two intentional attempts, *Julius Caesar* in 2018 and *Twelfth Night* in 2019, both produced by the Old Globe Theatre in San Diego. It will, however, blend practice with theory by returning to the construct most central to recent theorizations of gender: Judith Butler's argument that gender is performative. Butler's concept of performativity, to the degree that performativity overlaps with performance, may serve as a theoretical foundation for open-gendered casting. In Butler's subtle reworkings of the original concept, moreover, we can find vocabulary and dynamics that help to explore the practical tasks of dramaturgy and acting within open-gendered casting.

Such a valorisation of queer theory may already seem in tension with this chapter's initial claim that open-gendered casting is becoming standard in Shakespeare theatre. To suggest that it is becoming normalized, however, is not to say that the politics of gender equity are thereby solved, or that open-gendered casting does not continue to pursue radical ends. Open-gendered casting cannot help but be political – as Gemma Miller has argued, it 'constitutes a bold feminist activism that audiences, academics and critics alike have found difficult to ignore'.[5] Moreover, in this moment of increasing normalization, we can perceive in open-gendered casting a widening front in feminist and queer activism, one that may have the potential to temper some of the rigidities that Robyn Wiegman and Elizabeth Wilson describe as 'the politics of oppositionality'.[6] Normalization, in this moment, describes not a blunting of activism or a settling for mediocrity but a fluid and productive state of events. It introduces new challenges, and the detailed work done to meet these challenges has the potential for spectacular artistic results, the kind of results that are already making this generation of Shakespeare theatre extraordinarily transformative.

Dramaturgical choices

The initial choice to cast with openness to gender calls forth a number of dramaturgical choices, which can yield a brief taxonomy. Simplifying and recognizing that these categories blend and break down in practice, we can name three approaches. The first is what could be called the Unacknowledged Approach, in which no changes are made to the text, and nothing in the production explains or frames the casting choice. The second could be called the Edited Approach, in which a character's gender is changed, necessitating edits in the script. These can include changes in pronouns and addresses such as 'My Lord', and they can include more substantial interventions in the plot, for example to create a backstory. And third would be the Framed Approach, in which a frame or metatheatrical intervention acknowledges the fact of the open-gendered casting.

The Unacknowledged Approach has been used widely for minor characters, as available actors fill out ensemble parts. It was notably used in the recent Globe *Hamlet*, where Michelle Terry played Hamlet, as a man, with no changes to pronouns or other gendered references in the script. Several other roles were cast openly and without any textual changes, including Shubham Saraf, who played an affecting Ophelia, and Catrin Aaron as Horatio and Bettrys Jones as Laertes. In the Old Globe-USD production of

Twelfth Night, Claire Simba played Orsino, Jocelyn Vammer played Fabian and Summer Broyhill played Feste in this unacknowledged way, although the first two each had a brief frame, which will be discussed later. Without stage business to mark the casting, with only the programme doing so, it is possible for a change of gender to go unnoticed, for the performance to 'pass'. Jennifer Drouin describes a kind of passing that is 'neither parody nor an intentional exposure of normativity', in distinction from drag.[7] Such passing, however, refers only to Shakespearean characters shifting genders within the mimesis, not to the work of the actors. The cross-dressing of actors is 'a theatrical convention of which we are always aware'.[8] The Unacknowledged Approach steers away from the spectacle of drag, with its parody and intentionality. But arguably it rarely achieves a total sense of passing. With the intimacy of live theatre, and given our attunement to the gestures that go into the performance of gender in the world, arguably the audience will quite often read an actor's identified gender, and so discern the shifting of gender from actor to character.

Always at stake in the Unacknowledged Approach is the location in which gender is scanned. Within the mimesis of *Twelfth Night*, Claire Simba's Orsino was male and was presumably scanned that way much of the time. But when the audience happened to see through the character to the actor, reading Simba as a woman, that gender was scanned outside of the mimesis. Even if the audience mostly saw male Orsino, each night there were surely a number of times that they also saw female Simba. In such moments the actor diverges from the character, as gender precipitates a falling out of the immediacy of the play's story, a fall from mimesis to stage business. Or, instead of the sudden fall, it may be that the audience attained what Alisa Solomon calls a 'double vision' of this divergence, so that the audience was able to commit to the mimetic male Orsino and all the while retain an awareness of the female Simba.[9] In either case, this breaking of the mimesis by an awareness of stage business, a moment of metatheatricality often aligned with Brechtian alienation, leads to a critically productive instability, one that has been central to feminist discussions of open-gendered casting.[10]

In the Edited Approach, the characters themselves undergo gender changes. In the RSC *Timon of Athens*, Kathryn Hunter was Lady Timon, and accordingly the script was edited for pronouns and other incidentals. In some ways this is the more unobtrusive choice, as the edits do the work of fixing the gender in place for the audience, avoiding any divergences between the gender of the actor and the gender of the character. Avoiding moments of falling out of the mimesis allows the director and actors to move towards naturalness, away from alienation. In this spirit, the editing of the script left Hunter free to play Timon as a misanthropic old woman – and it was a brilliant performance. Mirren's filmed Prospera was similarly shaped by an edited script, helped by the addition of a blank verse backstory as the studious sister of the Duke of Milan. In both cases the actors made no gender transition; the shift took place entirely in the script, stabilizing the world of the mimesis.

The Old Globe-USD production of *Julius Caesar* also took the Edited Approach, by transforming both Brutus and Cassius into female characters, played by Hallie Peterson and Yadira Correa respectively (Figure 10.1). These gender shifts in this play, however, created instabilities that made the casting both complicated and ambitious. A key complexity was history. Transforming Brutus and Cassius into female Romans meant taking a large imaginative leap into a new version of Rome. In historical Rome, women were denied the vote, could not serve in the Senate and military and were required

FIGURE 10.1 *Hallie Peterson (left) as Brutus and Yadira Correa (right) as Cassius in* Julius Caesar, *directed by Allegra Libonati (The Old Globe Theatre, San Diego). Photograph by Daren Scott.*

to have either a husband or a male guardian. In our historical fiction, Roman women had world-shaping power – female soldiers, thinkers, assassins and revolutionaries walked our stage and did so with the assumption of normativity. Based on talk-backs and other comments, it seemed that a desire for historical authenticity bubbled up in the audience – an authentic Rome, of course, that Shakespeare hardly achieved. Moreover, during rehearsal we were struck by the fact that the production challenged the gender politics not only of ancient Rome and Elizabethan England but also of America today. Still mindful of Trump's defeat of Clinton, for example, we often felt the degree to which our Rome was striving against American gender discourses. This striving sharpened the audience's focus on the female Brutus and female Cassius, increasing awareness of the open-gendered casting. Throughout the production, the possibility loomed that such foregrounding of the casting would pull the audience, as well as the actors, out of the mimesis into a state of metatheatricality or alienation.

Editing of the script could not entirely stabilize such bouts of alienation – nor did we always want it to. We rather chose to be unsystematic with gendered language, taking it on a case-by-case basis. Pronouns were changed: 'he', 'him' and 'his' with respect to Brutus and Cassius became 'she', 'her' and 'hers' respectively, with no disruption to the metre. 'My lord', which for example Lucius and Portia both use when addressing Brutus, sounded wrong as 'My Lady', both in tone and metre. We played with this in rehearsal, and in Act 4 Scene 3 landed on Lucius using 'madam', as he uses for Portia in Act 2 Scene 4. Portia, however, retained 'my lord' in Act 2 Scene 1, which pinged with a bit of gender queerness. We also could not see clear to rewriting Antony's iconic 'Brutus is an honorable man' (3.2.83 ff).[11] 'Brutus is an honorable woman' would be a metrical problem, and too distractingly iconoclastic of one of those Shakespearean phrases that everyone already knows. So we kept the original. We then ended up with the line 'And sure she is an honorable man' (3.2.100), admitting inconsistency, which played as an explicit acknowledgement to the audience that they were watching open-gendered casting.

'Brutus is an honorable woman' is unlikely to have presented itself as an option in Phyllida Lloyd's *Julius Caesar*, because that production developed a Framed Approach, the third category in this taxonomy. Harriet Walter was not just playing Brutus, she was playing Hannah, a prisoner with a revolutionary backstory, who had been cast in a prison production.¹² The frame of a woman's prison, which Donmar carried on through the entire trilogy, meant that the gender shift was enacted within the mimesis, by the device of the framing. As in the Unacknowledged Approach, no pronouns were changed in the script. As in the Edited Approach, the gender of the actor and the gender of the framing character did not diverge. The imaginative web of the performance was reinforced by the self-awareness created by the frame. Metatheatre, the play within the play, served to explain, to provide occasion for, the gender shifts. It rendered them part of the performance rather than a falling off. And Lloyd's production made frequent recourse to that awareness, including moments such as a lockdown siren and the guards beating one of the performers, bringing the audience back to the fact of the prison.

Our *Twelfth Night* also developed a frame: the play began in a rehearsal space with street clothes and evolved into a fully costumed production. The casting of Simba as Orsino (Figure 10.2) received a brief treatment in the frame, a moment when Simba the 'actor' seizes the role of Orsino, to the surprise of the 'director'. But this

FIGURE 10.2 *Bibi Mama (left) as Viola and Claire Simba (right) as Orsino in* Twelfth Night, *directed by Jesse Perez (The Old Globe Theatre, San Diego). Photograph by Daren Scott.*

was so understated as to have little lasting effect on the audience. Jocelyn Vammer's casting as Fabian, however, was given a bit more metatheatrical spin. Vammer, in a brief return of the frame, shows up late for rehearsal. Still in her street clothes, she interrupts Toby, Maria and Andrew in Act 2 Scene 3 and has to find a seat in the audience, before joining the action in Act 2 Scene 5. This tinge of theatrical awareness stuck with Vammer's performance, creating a knowing mood to her Fabian. It was a male Fabian, always a 'he'. And just as he always seemed to know a bit more than everyone else, even more than Olivia and Feste in Act 5, Fabian also, metatheatrically, seemed to know, along with the audience, that a gender shift was in the offing.

Compared to *Julius Caesar*, the comic mode, with its easy metatheatrical awareness, opens the door quite a bit wider for gender shifts, precisely by making the theatrical business of the casting more easily seen. Awareness of gender fluidity does not interrupt or destabilize, so much as add to the comic mode. Indeed, *Twelfth Night* absorbs gender fluidity into its very plot – Viola becomes Caesario and the audience knows all about it, laughing and thinking along with her. However, in our production we became aware that throwing open the door of gender awareness and metatheatricality could have diminishing returns. Bibi Mama, who played Viola, commented afterwards that casting a woman as Orsino, alongside her Caesario/Viola, sometimes felt like 'putting a hat on a hat'. Were we extending the comedy of Caesario/Viola's escapades also to Orsino/Simba? Was the pathos felt in such lines as 'Disguise, I see thou art a wickedness' (2.2.27) also applicable to Orsino's character, or to Simba's casting? As Simba developed her version of Orsino in rehearsal, when she called attention to her own open-gendered casting she risked overlapping with Viola, in ways that were often interesting, but also often distracting.

Our director, Jesse Perez (also Director of the MFA programme), sensed the problem and worked with Simba to shift Orsino towards a more plain masculinity – that is, towards a gender representation that did not call attention to itself and was not edited or framed. Any divergence between the actor's and the character's gender went unacknowledged. The realization of such an Orsino turned on combating metatheatricality. And so, as with Cassius and Brutus, we found ourselves looking for ways to make open-gendered casting blend in. Avoiding awareness of gender, finding a gender shift that does not call attention to itself – this meant avoiding drag. Drag is a rich, highly theatrical mode of gender presentation, one that comes readily and is capable of doing much important political work. The director of *Julius Caesar*, Allegra Libonati, had directed the long-running disco and drag show, *The Donkey Show*, in which four women play all the roles of *A Midsummer Night's Dream*, with much dancing and glitter. But drag, with its self-conscious hyperbole and parody, was essentially the opposite of what she was seeking in this production.[13] Similarly, as Perez led rehearsals, a constant refrain was, 'Get used to it!' This was usually an imaginary conversation Perez had with our future audience, issuing a political challenge to accept gender fluidity, and an aesthetic challenge to see what was in front of them, and then become accustomed it. To stop noticing the casting would be to give permission for the storytelling to envelop the stage. Perez also wanted the same for his actors: for Simba to get used to being male, so that the gender could become increasingly natural, and for the actors on stage with her to get used to her as such, to the point that collectively they could achieve the level of comfort that is essential to their craft.

This is not to make a case against drag, which is a powerful kind of performance and should remain a fundamental choice in open-gendered casting. Rather, it is to describe an important way that open-gendered casting can settle in as a norm. As it becomes familiar and widespread, open-gendered casting must also be capable of being not-drag. Working to make gender shifts feel ordinary and natural, rather than exaggerated and parodic, is a way for Shakespeare performance to 'get used to it'. To find the vocabulary for such a normative mode, we might borrow from Judith Butler, whose encounters with drag have yielded the useful alternative, the theoretical concept of 'citation'.

From drag to citation

'Gender reality is performative, which means, quite simply, that it is real only to the extent that it is performed.'[14] I would speculate that a fundamental cause of today's turn to open-gendered casting in Shakespeare performance is our widespread cultural engagement with the performativity of gender. Since *Gender Trouble* was published in 1990, Judith Butler's argument has been one of the most influential in literary theory. It has been central to much subsequent feminist criticism, to cultural studies, queer theory and many other disciplines in the academy. And few academic ideas have entered so fully into general cultural and political discourse, whether we trace it in the mainstreaming of drag (from the New York ballrooms to *Paris Is Burning* to *RuPaul's Drag Show*), or we trace it through the increasingly trenchant politics of trans rights and gender nonconformity. Not only might Butler's work explain the normalization of open-gendered casting, but it accounts for its ongoing political and cultural impact, as James Bulman argues: 'Transvestitism in the theater, therefore, serves to mirror the cultural constructedness of gender identity and thereby to reveal to spectators the instability of what they may have taken for granted.'[15]

In Bulman's description, cross-dressing, or open-gendered casting more generally, becomes noticeably artificial and so holds a mirror up to real-world gender identity that is itself constructed, or performative. As in Alisa Solomon's 'double vision', or the use of Brechtian alienation, many feminist critics valorise the way open-gendered casting becomes self-conscious about its own stage business.[16] Such metatheatricality would seem to pull open-gendered casting towards the habits of drag. With its hyperbole and parody, drag makes the constructedness of gender very clear – and so has served as one of the most persuasive cases in Butler's argument. When, in the final pages of *Gender Trouble*, Butler turns to performativity, she describes it in terms more theoretical than theatrical, focusing on the way bodily gestures are made out of 'signs and other discursive means'.[17] But she enters into the discussion with an epigraph that views Greta Garbo as a drag performer, and in the subsequent pages her main example is drag. Nothing explains the performativity of gender quite so well: 'In imitating gender, drag implicitly reveals the imitative structure of gender itself – as well as its contingency.'[18]

Butler, however, became dissatisfied with drag as an emblem of gender performativity. In *Bodies That Matter*, she is concerned to correct a reception that had focused too much on drag. Her reading of *Paris Is Burning* backs off the stronger claims she made in *Gender Trouble* for subversiveness, by arguing that drag can often reinforce, rather than just subvert, hegemonic gender norms.[19] Drag proves ambivalent in part because it is too easily deployed, even by heterosexual normativity, as an intentional choice. As an emblem of performativity, drag misleads us into thinking that gender is intentionally performed, adopted by a subject who can too easily simply put on the clothes. Instead, 'performativity must be understood not as a singular or deliberate "act", but rather, as the reiterative and citational practice by which discourse produces the effects that it names'.[20] Performativity takes place not through drag but through what Butler calls citation – through the slow, accumulating, forced repetitions of existing norms. Citation is an iterative process of referring to pre-existing power and symbol, to what has already taken shape in existing discourses. Furthermore, citation materializes sex out of discourse, creating the sense that a sexed body forms an essential ground for gender. And it similarly creates the sense of an essential subjectivity.[21]

In reframing performativity as citation rather than drag, Butler moves it away from theatre: 'Moreover, this act is not primarily theatrical. . . . Within speech act theory, a performative is that discursive practice that enacts or produces that which it names.'[22] Although Butler's original formulation of gender performativity appeared in *Theatre Journal*, she eventually eschews the theatrical context. In doing so, she points instead to what many critics feel is the more important source for her concept of performativity: J. L. Austen's speech act theory.[23] Making room for Butler's ideas in their full development, therefore, can mean making room on the stage for what feels less like traditional drama and more like theory. As Elin Diamond argues, 'Though "performativity" is not an "act" but a "reiteration" or "citation", why should we restrict its iterative sites to theory and to the theorist's acts of seeing? Theater, too, is theory.'[24] Admittedly, the uneasy relationship between Butler's performativity and theatrical performance can feel like a version of the longstanding tension between performance studies and theatre practice. But it may be worth taking seriously the possibility of incorporating Butler's theory of citation in the practice of open-gendered casting. If its increasingly widespread utilization calls for acting possibilities beyond drag, and for productions that can choose other modes than epic theatre, if we are to expand the palette of open-gendered casting, we may do so by finding room in the actor's work for Butler's theory of citation.

So can citationality be acted? Or must the performativity of gender inevitably appear as drag or self-conscious stage business? Does citation, with its theoretical complexity, alienate us from the theatre? We might say yes to the last question, if we are thinking about the way the body disappears in Butler's account of performativity and citation. Biological sex and the materiality of the body itself are not essential or naturally there, but are constructed out of discursive norms: 'the regulatory norms of "sex" work in a performative fashion to constitute the materiality of bodies and, more specifically, to materialize the body's sex.'[25] This has led to a trans critique of Butler that wants to insist on 'the materiality of the sexed body'.[26] Similarly, actors, using their breath and bodies as their instruments, may be disinclined to let go of materiality to this extent; theatre as a whole, devoted to bringing embodiment to a script, also may have less patience with the wide scope of Butlerian discursivity. W. B. Worthen captures this tendency in the theatre to cling to what, from the perspective of literary theory, feels like a traditional understanding of the body and what is natural. Actor training, he argues, valorises 'the native state of the pre-ideological body'.[27] It 'assumes an integrated and organic "subject" which can be discovered through the body, beneath the blockages and obstructions of culture'.[28]

For Worthen, the centring of the actor's work on a natural body, one that is believed to be outside of ideology and prior to the ideological construction of the subject, is naïve. It means that the actor finds only a narrow freedom: 'The body is freed into its nature only to have the more deeply ideological version of identity inscribed within it.'[29] Worthen's strong insight is to align the creation of a traditionally conceived character with the ideological construction of the subject, a 'hailing' such as Althusser describes.[30] But while Worthen aims at revealing the false consciousness of such notions of character, it seems to me that the role of ideology may actually have a practical use. It may give us a way to describe how citation enters into the actor's art. For Butler understands the citational process not only as creating gender but also as creating the subject itself. Indeed, it is precisely the entrance of subjectivity and ideology together that forms the medium in which discourse, through citation and reiteration, produces gender: 'Subjected to gender, but subjectivated by gender, the "I" neither precedes nor follows the process of this gendering, but emerges only within and as the matrix of gender relations themselves.'[31] If the creation of what the audience would see as a natural, realistic character on the stage goes through ideology, as Worthen suggests, then the creation of what appears to be a naturally gendered character also does. The existing discourses that regulate and create gendered subjects can be cited on stage, as part of the creation of character. This becomes a pathway for the actor playing within open-gendered casting.

Acting citation

In both *Twelfth Night* and *Julius Caesar*, we found ourselves working on gender crossings that steered clear of the self-conscious mode of drag. For the plays to unfold to their fullest potential, not as mere commentaries on gender politics but as productions that engaged with the full gamut of emotions and ideas that are to be found in such great plays, we needed everyone to feel as though the casting was not itself the whole point. We needed everyone, actors as well as audience, to feel that the casting was a normal part of the theatre – we needed, as Perez would say, to 'get used to it'. While important steps can be taken in that direction through dramaturgical choices such as edited scripts or metatheatrical frames, the most important work belongs to the actors. For it is through their meticulous efforts in training and rehearsal that gender can be layered into the emerging character. In a mimesis of Butlerian citation, the actor can work iteratively to discover the gestures that materialize and naturalize gender. The actor can become present in a character of another gender, and the audience can thereby become well enmeshed in the character and story, by the patient layering in of citation, through voice and gesture, across the days and weeks of the rehearsal process.

In *Twelfth Night*, Claire Simba's interpretation of Orsino evolved in just this way. She began by conceiving of Orsino as an assigned-at-birth female who passes as male – everyone in Illyria was deceived, though the audience would probably not be. At first this drag-inflected Orsino made for a fresh version of the character's aestheticism and histrionic wooing of Olivia. But as rehearsal progressed, it increasingly entailed story problems – for example does Viola figure out (and like) Orsino's cross-dressing, or is she going to be surprised on their wedding night? Working to solve this and other problems, Simba found that Orsino's motives and actions were too often shaped by the fact of cross-dressing; drag had become an insistent fact in too many scenes. As a result, Simba reinvented her Orsino as male, just as he is in the text. Moving the gender shift out of the mimesis seemed to clarify her work considerably. It allowed her to take up many elements of character and story in a more direct relationship to the language of the play. And it seemed to free her physically, by toning down the self-conscious quality of her gestures.

In developing the gestural vocabulary for her Orsino, Simba had first turned to several familiar markers of masculinity. She swaggered, spread and displayed a peacock's sexuality. But once Orsino the character left behind expressions of drag, Simba began to find a quieter set of gestures. Among these new gestures, I would like to focus on just one that I noticed, which seemed particularly effective. This was something Simba developed with her chin: when she addressed another character, her chin rose up and tilted down (as actors learn in Alexander), she squared her shoulders, and she allowed her breath to carry her words straight forward, without indirection, to their target. Her voice projected with strength, and her language travelled a straight trajectory to the other characters. This gesture of the chin was very understated, but it created in Orsino an expectation of command, and created in the ensemble, among Valentine, Viola and the others, a prevailing sense of Orsino's authority. The gesture was not full of the sense of display, was not an invitation to be looked at – it did not have the performativity of drag. But for its quietness, it was all the more loaded with an assertiveness, an imperative mood, that carried her towards the gestures of masculinity that prevail in our culture.

Importantly, I do not think Simba was intentionally gesturing with her chin; she was not coached into it, and did not consciously decide to use it, as she had done with the swagger. By the same token, the audience, I am supposing, did not read the chin in the same way as it would have read the swagger. The swagger performed a familiar and masculine gesture, and was for both actor and audience a conscious idiom. The swagger, like drag, inevitably served as a reminder that a female actor was acting a male character. The chin, on the other hand, cited a gesture that is not part of the familiarly deployed indications of masculinity. It undoubtedly did communicate masculinity as our society sees it, but without referring to obvious gestural idioms. In this way it brought Simba nearer to the process of citation. As Butler makes clear, citation of regulatory gender discourses cannot be volitional.[32] Gender can only be layered into character, and so experienced more naturally on stage, when it is allowed to build, without volition, through the accretions of a reiterative process.

Luckily such a process is fundamental to the actor's art, which in rehearsal often depends on improvisation, where things are discovered, not planned, and on patient repetition. The citation of gesture has to be found by the actor through that instinctive sense of naturalness that ultimately guides so many acting choices. In this process of citation, the actor feels her way towards what works, through trial and error, and then discovery. Within an improvisational field of actions, the actor begins to explore a set of vocal and gestural idioms. When these idioms echo, or cite, existing discourses of gender, they will begin to feel as if they are ringing true. Importantly this experience of truth will not be felt with the specificity that will allow the actor to point at the citation itself. Rather, it will begin to feel as if a truth has been discovered, that the character has been inhabited. As Simba discovered a way to inhabit Orsino, she simultaneously found Butlerian citation, and in this process created the sense of an embodied masculinity.

Integral to the discovery of citational gestures is the ensemble. If the actor does not choose a gesture, but rather discovers it in rehearsal, the gesture will begin to feel right to the actor when it begins to feel right to everyone else. The other actors on stage will respond to the gesture, take in the gender-constructing citationality of it (probably also not consciously), and reflect the gendered meaning back. Simba's chin gesture began to feel like a natural kind of masculinity because her scene partners began to feel it as such. In this way the ensemble creates on stage a shared pool of expectations and reactions that themselves originate in the larger discursivity of the culture beyond the stage. In other words, the ensemble implicitly brings into the rehearsal process the discursivity that in the larger society regulates subjectivity and imposes gender. On the level of gesture and attitude, the actor cites from society's discursive idioms. When a citation is effective, it is felt by the other actors as natural, and they convey back their engagement with the embodied gender. So a virtuous cycle can be formed, in which effective citation is established communally through a less-than-volitional process of trial and error and discovery.

The importance of the ensemble in the construction of gender became clear in our *Julius Caesar*. As noted earlier, Brutus and

Cassius were played by female actors, Hallie Peterson and Yadira Correa, as female characters. The ahistoricism of this dramaturgical choice meant that the actors had fewer points of contact with existing discourses of gender, female Roman Senators and generals being an unknown category. Rather than mirroring existing discourses and modelling gestures on familiar behaviours, in a sense Peterson and Correa had to invent new kinds of gender. They had to discover gestures and actions that would feel natural, without recourse to the familiar indications of drag, and with fewer of the well-worn discursive grooves to cite. This was an acting challenge, requiring significant imaginative work and an openness to moving fluidly within gender norms.

Correia, like Simba, began her work on Cassius with drag-like gestures, but felt dissatisfied. 'I know how to play a man', she said early in rehearsals, 'but I don't know how to be a woman Cassius'. Correia is a very physical actor, leading with a commanding voice and an openly emotional demeanour. Libonati, the director, recognized the physicality of her approach, and suggested studying female Olympic athletes, and the film *Wonder Woman*. As Correia explored such athleticism, she began to discover gestures that moved beyond mere physicality, that seemed to capture the character of the spare and hungry Cassius. The sharp and confrontational style of Cassius is quite externalized, which seemed to provide ample opportunities for Correia to find a persuasive character who was both Shakespeare's Cassius and a woman. Brutus, however, is far more inward, and the character's stoic, circumspect qualities offered Peterson fewer physical choices to work with. As she explored Brutus in rehearsal, Peterson appropriately began with a composed and buttoned-down approach. But her reserve, together with Brutus's reserve, left few places in which to discover the kinds of gestures that echo with gender discourses to become citation. It felt as though she was stuck outside of the character – until Peterson began working on Act 2 Scene 1, the scene with Portia.

Nona Truong played Portia, and she and Peterson built a remarkably nuanced exchange, which found an emotional centre in the fact of two female characters. This scene can be tough for modern sensibilities, as Portia's claims for strength and constancy can feel desperate, and Brutus can come across as coldly out of touch with Portia's humanity, as well as his own. But from the moment they began rehearsing, it became clear that open-gendered casting added some unexpected layers. The fact that in the Rome of this production a woman can become a political agent, and can take part in revolutionary secrets, meant that Portia was not being shut out by Brutus for reasons of gender hierarchy. Portia could become a soldier or a Senator, and she could become a conspirator too. Portia is shut out of Brutus's confidence not due to systemic inequity, then, but because of something in her own character, as well as Brutus's. What emerged was a fascinating study of a couple trying together to figure out how to exist in a revolutionary world. One had a strong (although tragically doomed) political orientation, and the other had a kind of private fragility that made her unsuited to politics. Brutus may not have understood her own political shortcomings, but she clearly saw Portia's, and lovingly protected her. The scene became intimate and authentic precisely to the degree that it was queered by the casting. Brutus's gender was therefore deeply integrated into her relationship to Portia, and integrated into the storytelling of the scene. The intimacy that sprung up between Portia and Brutus was the opportunity for Peterson to discover the authentic gestures of a female Brutus. As these felt true, they were reflected back by Truong. Together, as an ensemble, they found how to layer gender citation into the unique character of Brutus, a series of discoveries that seemed to provide a foundation for Peterson's entire performance.

* * *

The process of inhabiting characters in these open-gender productions required patient individual imagination, as well as committed ensemble work. Based on improvisation and discovery, the process had to be as fluid as gender itself. Indeed, the genders discovered by Peterson, Truong, Correa and the actors in *Twelfth Night*, Simba, Mama, Vammer and Broyhill – the genders these actors discovered and developed through citation were eclectic, and at times non-binary (making 'open-gendered' a more fitting term than 'cross-gendered' casting). Productions themselves are also fluid, so it can be anticipated that the next one will have different dramaturgical choices and different actors, which will evolve different processes to get to an authentic representation of gender. There is no point in mapping overly specific techniques, as citation must be discovered without such volition. But if we can give all that fluidity scope, the actors will find their ways.

After *Julius Caesar*, Peterson told me that she is putting Richard II into her audition repertoire, and that she found herself working on broadsword and rapier with more care, since she now feels there is a greater chance that she will need combat skills in her career. Open-gendered casting has been inspiring not just for those actors playing other genders but for every actor in our programme. The entire ensemble acts alongside those cast with gender shifts and participates in the construction of those characters' genders. The entire ensemble benefits from being part of a theatre that recognizes gender fluidity that is striving towards gender equity and working to improve upon generations of inequity in Shakespeare performance.

As the commitment to train actors within open-gendered casting itself requires experimentation and discovery, we must keep an eye out for where the pitfalls lie. After *Twelfth Night*, Simba shared that her initial desire to play Orsino as a woman was a response to her cumulative experience in theatre, in which Black women were more often cast in male roles than white women. She expressed concern that open-gendered casting does not pigeonhole Black female actors, based on a societal perception that their bodies may be more masculine than white female bodies. We also must be careful not to allow the normalization of open-gendered casting to proceed in an unexamined way. The emergence of open-gendered casting at so many mainstream theatres, the turn away from drag described here, this chapter's use of queer theory in the service of normalization – all of these could become politically retrograde. Many have warned against the institutionalizing of queerness, as Judith Butler does: 'normalizing the queer would be, after all, its sad finish'.[33] It will be important to be thoughtful about how open-gendered casting can become a norm without losing its queer and feminist potential, something the recent special issue of *differences*, 'Queer Theory Without Antinormativity', could inform.[34]

And finally, it will be important to see to it that this new moment is not lost. At the time of this writing, nearly all theatres are dark due to the coronavirus pandemic. What theatre itself will look like after the pandemic, no one knows. There is a risk that the increasing normalization of open-gendered casting, so apparent in recent years, could be lost in the cataclysm. Perhaps critical attention to the remarkable flowering of open-gendered casting can help sustain that momentum. And hopefully its artistic value, together with its practical benefits, will ensure that open-gendered casting will not prove a theatrical fashion, but will continue to be a defining quality of Shakespeare performance in the twenty-first century.

Notes

1 I would like to thank all the actors in The Old Globe and University of San Diego Shiley Graduate Theatre program, particularly Yadi Correa, Bibi Mama, Hallie Peterson and Claire Simba. Many thanks to Jan Gist, head of Voice and Speech, for her conversation on these topics. Thanks to the members of the 'After Queer Theory' seminar at the 2020 Shakespeare Association of America, and to the participants in the 2019 South Africa Shakespeare Congress on Shakespeare and Social Justice.

2 Tony Howard, *Women as Hamlet: Performance and Interpretation in Theatre, Film and Fiction*, 1st edition (Cambridge: Cambridge University Press, 2009), 11.

3 See Mark Brown, 'New Shakespeare's Globe Chief Promises Far More Diverse Casting', *The Guardian*, 18 August 2017, section Stage https://www.theguardian.com/stage/2017/aug/18/new-shakespeares-globe-chief-promises-far-more-diverse-casting-michelle-terry (accessed 30 October 2020). And Mark Brown, 'Shakespeare's Globe Casts Its Own Artistic Director as Hamlet', *The Guardian*, 11 April 2018, section Stage https://www.theguardian.com/stage/2018/apr/11/shakespeares-globe-casts-its-own-artistic-director-as-hamlet (accessed 30 October 2020).

4 Recent discussions of 'cross-gender' casting include James C. Bulman, ed., *Shakespeare Re-Dressed: Cross-Gender Casting in Contemporary Performance* (Madison, NJ: Fairly Dickinson University Press, 2008). Gemma Miller, 'Cross-Gender Casting as Feminist Interventions in the Staging of Early Modern Plays', *Journal of International Women's Studies* 16, no. 1 (2014): 4–17. Catherine Silverstone, '"It's Not About Gender": Cross-Gendered Casting in Deborah Warner's Richard II', *Women: A Cultural Review* 18, no. 2 (2007): 199–212. Analogously, 'cross-dressing' and 'transvestitism' have been explored by, among others: Samuel Crowl, '"Nobody's Perfect": Cross-Dressing and Gender-Bending in Svend Gade's Hamlet and Julie Taymor's *The Tempest*', in *The Oxford Handbook of Shakespeare and Performance*, ed. James C. Bulman (Oxford: Oxford University Press, 2017), 387–401. Marjorie B. Garber, *Vested Interests: Cross Dressing and Cultural Anxiety*, 1st Harper Perennial ed. (New York: Routledge, 1993). Jean E. Howard, 'Crossdressing, the Theatre, and Gender

Struggle in Early Modern England', *Shakespeare Quarterly* 39, no. 4 (1988): 418–40. Stephen Orgel, *Impersonations: The Performance of Gender in Shakespeare's England* (Cambridge; New York: Cambridge University Press, 1996).

5   Miller, 'Cross-Gender Casting as Feminist Interventions in the Staging of Early Modern Plays', 6.
6   Robyn Wiegman and Elizabeth Wilson, 'Queer Theory without Antinormativity', *Differences: A Journal of Feminist Cultural Studies* 26, no. 1 (2015): 13–14.
7   Jennifer Drouin, 'Cross-Dressing, Drag, and Passing: Slippages in Shakespearean Comedy', in *Shakespeare Re-Dressed: Cross-Gender Casting in Contemporary Performance*, ed. James C. Bulman (Madison, NJ: Fairly Dickinson University Press, 2008), 23–56.
8   Drouin, 'Cross-Dressing, Drag, and Passing', 23.
9   Alisa Solomon, *Re-Dressing the Canon: Essays on Theater and Gender* (London; New York: Routledge, 1997), 17.
10 Solomon argues that 'Plays that question their strategies of representation are ready sites for feminist resistance'. Solomon, *Re-Dressing the Canon*, 9. Elin Diamond says that 'A feminist practice that seeks to expose or mock the strictures of gender, to *reveal* gender-as-appearance . . . usually uses some version of the Brechtian A-effect'. Elin Diamond, *Unmaking Mimesis: Essays on Feminism and Theater* (London: New York: Routledge, 2006), 46.
11 Quotations from Shakespeare's plays are taken from Richard Proudfoot, Ann Thompson, David Scott Kastan and H. R Woodhuysen, eds, *The Arden Shakespeare Complete Works, Third Series* (London and New York: The Arden Shakespeare, 2021).
12 For Harriet Walter's account of the Donmar production, see Harriet Walter, *Brutus and Other Heroines: Playing Shakespeare's Roles for Women* (London: Nick Hern, 2016), 155–80. Also see Cary M. Mazer, 'Rosalind's Breast', in *Shakespeare Re-Dressed: Cross-Gender Casting in Contemporary Performance*, ed. James C. Bulman (Madison, NJ: Fairly Dickinson University Press, 2008), 96–115.
13 Judith Lorber: 'Drag's core elements are *performance* and *parody*. Drag exaggerates gendered dress and mannerisms with enough little incongruities to show the "otherness" of the drag artist. In the exaggeration lies the parody . . . . The joke in drag is to set up "femininity" or "masculinity" as pure performance, as exaggerated gender display – and then to cut them down as pretense after all.' Steven P. Schacht, Lisa Underwood and ProQuest (Firm), eds., *The Drag Queen Anthology: The Absolutely Fabulous but Flawlessly*

Customary World of Female Impersonators (New York: Routledge, 2004). Available online: http://ebookcentral.proquest.com/lib/sandiego/ detail.action?docID=1111319 (accessed 31 October 2020).

14 Judith Butler, 'Performative Acts and Gender Constitution an Essay in Phenomenology and Feminist Theory', *Theatre Journal* 40, no. 4 (1988): 527.

15 Bulman, *Shakespeare Re-Dressed*, 12.

16 Diamond describes 'a triangular structure of subject/actor – character – spectator. Looking at the character, the spectator is constantly intercepted by the subject/actor, and the latter, heeding no fourth wall, is theoretically free to look back'. Diamond, *Unmaking Mimesis*, 53–4. Miller describes the Donmar *Julius Caesar* as activist by virtue of its metatheatrical frame: 'The frame structure provided its own spectator/performer paradigm, whereby the female actors were not only the objects but also the subjects of the theatrical exchange.' Miller, 'Cross-Gender Casting as Feminist Interventions in the Staging of Early Modern Plays', 11.

17 Judith Butler, *Gender Trouble: Feminism and the Subversion of Identity* (New York: Routledge, 1990), 136.

18 Butler, *Gender Trouble*, 137.

19 'Although many readers understood *Gender Trouble* to be arguing for the proliferation of drag performances as a way to subverting dominant gender norms, I want to underscore that there is no necessary relation between drag and subversion.' Judith Butler, *Bodies That Matter: On the Discursive Limits of 'Sex'* (New York: Routledge, 1993), 125.

20 Butler, *Bodies That Matter*, 2.

21 'The process of that sedimentation or what we might call *materialization* will be a kind of citationality, the acquisition of being through the citing of power, a citing that established an originary complicity with power in the formation of the "I".' Butler, *Bodies That Matter*, 15.

22 Butler, *Bodies That Matter*, 12–13.

23 See Andrew Parker and Eve Kosofsky Sedgwick, *Performativity and Performance* (Hoboken: Wiley and Sons, 2013), 1–16 Available online: https://public.ebookcentral.proquest.com/choice/publicfullrecord.aspx?p=1542586 (accessed 4 September 2020).

24 Diamond, *Unmaking Mimesis*, 47.

25 Butler, *Bodies That Matter*, 2.

26 Jay Prosser, 'Judith Butler: Queer Feminism, Transgender, and the Transubstantiation of Sex', in *The Transgender Studies Reader*, ed. Susan Stryker and Stephen Whittle (New York: Routledge, 2006), 265. Also see Viviane K. Namaste, *Invisible Lives: The Erasure of Transsexual and Transgendered People* (Chicago: Chicago University Press, 2000).
27 William B. Worthen, *Shakespeare and the Authority of Performance* (Cambridge; New York: Cambridge University Press, 1997), 106.
28 Worthen, *Shakespeare and the Authority of Performance*, 110. Also see Mazer, 'Rosalind's Breast', 96–115.
29 Worthen, *Shakespeare and the Authority of Performance*, 110.
30 Louis Althusser, *Lenin and Philosophy, and Other Essays* (New York: Monthly Review Press, 1972), 173–4. On Althusser's concept of subjectivity operating in the theatre, see Étienne Balibar, 'Althusser's Dramaturgy and the Critique of Ideology', *Differences: A Journal of Feminist Cultural Studies* 26, no. 3 (2015): 1–22. Judith Butler, 'Theatrical Machine', *Differences: A Journal of Feminist Cultural Studies* 26, no. 3 (2015): 23–42.
31 Butler, *Bodies That Matter*, 7.
32 '(T)he account of agency conditioned by those very regimes of discourse/power cannot be conflated with voluntarism or individualism, much less with consumerism, and in no way presupposes a choosing subject.' Butler, *Bodies That Matter*, 15.
33 Judith Butler, 'Against Proper Objects. Introduction', *Differences: A Journal of Feminist Cultural Studies* 6, no. 2–3 (1994): 21.
34 Wiegman and Wilson, 'Queer Theory without Antinormativity'.

11

Teaching *Titus Andronicus* and Ovidian myth when sexual violence is on the public stage

Wendy Beth Hyman

How ought we teach *Titus Andronicus* when we recognize that sexual violence is not just the stuff of ancient myth and spectacular tragedy but also the lived experience of so many of our students? How do we teach works like this, or the plethora of Ovidian and Renaissance rape narratives, or really any Shakespearean comedies involving bed tricks, when the private agony of sexual coercion and violence is foregrounded on the world stage? How should we grapple with literary depictions of rape in ways that not only do justice to those texts but also empower rather than retraumatize? And for that matter, *why* should we do so? These were questions that became the centre of my pedagogical universe when, through grim happenstance, my class came to its discussion of Shakespeare's notorious play the very week of the United States Supreme Court Brett Kavanaugh hearings. As millions watched Christine Blasey Ford's heartbreaking testimony that the nominee for Supreme Court Justice had raped her, as academics simultaneously reeled from the revelation of the Avital Ronnell scandal, as new details about Junot Diaz's sexual transgressions emerged, as the serial rapes perpetrated by Harvey Weinstein and Bill Cosby unfolded on the front pages of every American newspaper, as sexual assault was normalized – actually bragged about – by the then-president of the United States, and as indeed seemingly half the nation staggered through relived trauma, my class turned to Week 5 of ENG 304 and Lavinia: raped, mutilated and silenced.[1]

First, I will be honest: this was not something I thought of as exactly a happy coincidence, at least not when I went into it. If you had told me when I drew up my syllabus that my teaching of Shakespeare's most traumatizing play (considering the frequency with which staged productions have caused audience members to faint, vomit or leave the theatre in distress) would coincide with national trials that had so many of my students reeling, I am not sure I would have proceeded.[2] But as the semester progressed and these asymptotic events barrelled towards each other, I recognized I had two choices: flinch and take it off the syllabus, or somehow lean in. The latter option sounded emotionally gruelling and risked further traumatizing vulnerable people. But the first felt like it would be an act of pedagogical bad faith, one which demoted Shakespeare's plays to a hermetically sealed past and, thereby, undermined the educational enterprise of teaching historical literature in the first place. Worse still, avoidance might signal a lack of confidence in my students' ability to grapple with difficult texts, tantamount to preemptively disempowering the very people I wanted to empower. Whatever my trepidations, it seemed to me that my only ethical course was to carry on with the play.[3]

This chapter shares some of the strategies I used to enable my students to process these awful events while also doing intellectual justice to Shakespeare's plays and the Ovidian myths that inspired them. The strategy included weaving together elements of *mythopoesis* and genre theory, that is, analyses that mitigate overidentification with suffering characters; historicizing Shakespeare's depictions of sexual violence while also addressing its ongoing structural presence in the academy and beyond; utilizing a flexible assignment structure that emphasized student agency and choice; and prioritizing trauma-informed pedagogical practices that incorporated, but de-emphasized, trigger warnings. What has emerged for me are both practical strategies and a theoretical framework for teaching *Titus Andronicus* and Ovidian rape myths with integrity to college students, many of whom are survivors and all of whom are still learning about consent. I suggest here that although studying potentially traumatizing material involves risk for both student and professor, and should therefore always be approached with care and humility, its potential rewards are also great. *Titus Andronicus*, many of my students found, contained within itself its own remedy: first, as a revenge tragedy that allegorizes a lust for justice; and second, perhaps even more powerfully, simply as the rare work of literature – from any era – willing to display the psychic horror of crimes so often erased. Some of my students recoiled from the play but continued to engage in profound ways, as I detail later in the following pages. But almost all have actually found it bracing to encounter a literary work whose sheer brutality enacted, as it were, a form of implicit validation. *Titus Andronicus*' lurid depictions of suffering spotlight a thing that is too often hidden, suppressed, or denied. As a student of mine put it, *Titus Andronicus* thereby uniquely gives trauma survivors – much as Lavinia's staff does in the play itself – 'something to point to'.[4] In a world of gaslighting presidents and Supreme Court 'Justices' accused of sexual assault, my students found the play's deployment of mythological excess a means of allegorizing emotional experience. In other words, many of my students responded positively to *Titus Andronicus* because they found that it told them the truth.

Bridging the gap between the historicist methods I was trained in and presentist concerns had been on my mind a lot, as I finished editing with Hillary Eklund a collection of original essays on Shakespeare and social justice.[5] We and our contributors wrote from the conviction that the Renaissance literature classroom provides great opportunities for our students to delve into rich historical texts while also seeing themselves as shapers of a just and equitable world. But how to do that with a play like *Titus Andronicus*, which makes a spectacle of female dismemberment and rape, subjugates a younger generation to the maw of bellicose nationalism, and bases its sole Black character on a medieval-style stage devil (albeit one who, unlike every other adult in the play, shows actual devotion to his child)? How can we acknowledge revenge tragedy's malevolence while also finding in its energetic release some beacon of transformative justice – if one whose specific mode of recourse we hardly wish to emulate?[6]

It is worth saying here that what social justice looks like for rape survivors does not adhere to any singular model, yet must as a baseline mean not dropping out of college, disassociating from the learning process, or feeling disempowered to enact change in their world. Beyond the trauma of rape, our students have grown up negotiating degrees of unconsent, the ubiquity of which accustoms young people to subjugation, or lacklustre acquiescence, as an unwritten norm. Given the appalling statistics, having survived sexual assault or coercive sexual contact may well be the single most commonly shared experience among our female and LBGTQ students. In the United States, the National Sexual Violence Resource Center reports that nearly one in five women are raped at some point in their lives. What might be less well known is that 'most female victims of completed rape (79.6%) experienced their first rape before the age of 25' and, in fact, 42.2 per cent of those victims were raped before the age of eighteen years. Although heterosexual and cis men are less likely to be victims of rape overall, 'more than one-quarter of male victims of completed rape (27.8%) experienced their first rape when they were 10 years of age or younger'.[7] Global rape statistics are equally grim. For instance, in South Africa, which in 2010 reported the highest rate of rape in the world (132.4 incidents per 100,000 people), 'approximately one in four men admitted to committing rape'.[8] Numbers like these, devastating as they are, do not account for what must be an even more ordinary experience for young people: initiating or reluctantly agreeing to unwanted sexual contact or receiving or giving consent under coercion. Reversing that norm, developing a just sense of outrage and a pathway towards agency, is the *sine qua non* for enabling other forms of engagement and action. The goal of my teaching is therefore not just to do no harm but to foster the confidence to *undo* harm. And that means, in part, teaching with an expectation that our classrooms include several students who have faced sexual assault or unwanted sexual contact, and quite possibly include some that have done the assaulting. I try to operate under the assumption that all of them are ready to learn more about consent.

The immediate context in which I was teaching the play in the Fall of 2018 was a class called Shakespeare and Metamorphosis, which considers a half-dozen Shakespeare plays alongside the Ovid and Apuleius myths that inspired them, and various later adaptations by authors like Rilke, Keats, Mary Zimmerman, Anne Carson, W. H. Auden, Frank Bidart, A. E. Stallings, Paisley Rekdal and Seo-Young Chu.[9] This material teaches exceptionally well in aggregate not only because it thematizes questions of transformation and change, a perennial theme for college students, but also because it demands a complex and variegated reading strategy. Bringing to these myths the expectation of novelistic realism is simply to be unable to read. Asking students to grapple with Ovidian or Apuleian sources therefore means making space for texts that are, in some ways, even more alien and alienating than *Titus Andronicus*. A challenge in that class, but also part of my solution, is thinking about the potentialities of reading mythologically: drawing on the allegorical and symbolic as a circuitous means for confronting the real.

As many readers of this chapter will know, Ovid's prototypical discourse for the complex processing of events, and for literary art as the most articulated of those responses, is rape. My students learn to grapple with these associations at the very beginning of the semester, when we encounter the tales of Apollo and Daphne, Jove and Io, Pan and Syrinx, and Pygmalion and Galatea, in fairly short succession. In all of these myths, women are raw material for poetic and artistic making, and their involvement with the gods is brought about through, at best, ambiguous consent. But as we read of Daphne as a source of the laurel wreath and figure for poetry, of Syrinx as source of the pan pipe, of Io the heifer as an emblem for self-identification through writing (remember her tracing in the sand the letters of her name – also the sound of the war cry – I, O?) and of Galatea as animated sculpture, we develop an archive that is more than the sum of its parts. Students begin to see that to over-identify any of the female 'realistic' 'characters' with proto-novelistic interiorities is to miss the meanings that supersede affective response. Instead, a structuralist approach that identifies patterns and persons surfaces how suffering is created by systems of power, and illuminates how suffering can be alchemized into action and transformation.

Myths always raise these questions and are indeed about these questions. Pygmalion is a story of perversion, about a man so unable to love real women that he cathects upon an inanimate idol. But it is also a story about the regenerative power of art so alive that it not only animates stone but also rebirths a metaphorical dead man. The myth of Persephone is about rape and the agonizing underworld of loss it drags one into. But it is also about the metaphorical death attendant on every *bildungsroman*, about the congruence between human life cycle and the seasons, and about all the ways that any catastrophe might – for a time – seize us and throw our lives into disarray, yet also become a means of our reinvention, what clinicians call 'post-traumatic growth'.[10] Reading these myths well thus means recognizing that they often hold conflicting epistemologies in tandem, which perhaps is a needlessly convoluted way of saying that they are good to think with, because they refuse to mean just one thing.

When we turn to Philomela in anticipation of *Titus Andronicus*, the students are ready to see how her story is not just about violation and trauma but also about creative expression as a supervening means of transformation. As a weaver, Philomela is a Penelope outwitting her obstreperous 'suitors'; she is Arachne speaking truth to power; she is Ovid himself creating a metamorphic *'textus'*. She is the nightingale whose magnificent song restores Philomela's lost voice. She is the furies seeking revenge. She is Psyche whose myth so deeply echoes; she is the soul turned into a bird. This is not to whitewash the brutality of the story – Ovid certainly doesn't – but it is to say that there is more here than victimhood, in part because suffering is transubstantiated into art and into action. In these terms, my students have found it especially helpful to take in Seo-Young Chu's 'A Refuge for Jae-in Doe: Fugues in the Key of English Major', a sometimes-excruciating account of sexual assault and its aftermath, articulated through Petrarchan lyrics, Donnean holy sonnets, Spenserian stanzas, Miltonic lullabies and more.[11] These literary forms not only enshrine centuries of misogyny and trauma, but importantly, they also become the gorgeous shards with which the author reconstitutes her world. Myth and *metapoesis* do not deny suffering. But they also elucidate that Philomela is not a *person* but the raw material of poetry. She is made out of art, she makes art and we make art from her story.

That perspective can and should be superseded in a reading of Shakespeare's dramatization of the myth in his figure of Lavinia. If Philomela can function in part as a mythological abstraction, the early modern stage puts concepts into bodies whose vulnerability we witness, an effect still discernible even when encountering a play on the page. In *Titus Andronicus*, Lavinia is subjected to even more brutality, even more dismemberment and a far less poetic apotheosis than her forebear(s).[12] But what many of my students came to see is that this dramatic strategy is not axiomatically misogynistic, and that, for all its inhumanity, the play's rendering of sexual assault is not gratuitous.[13] Instead, *Titus Andronicus* makes psychological trauma externally legible. Lisa Starks-Estes contends that Shakespeare's play 'exposes the horror of sexual violence' exactly because 'Lavinia's raped and mutilated body becomes the emblem of trauma itself'.[14] Its graphic depictions disallow looking away from the failures of justice in the world of the play. The play thus effectively catapults – like Titus's hopeless notes to the gods – the enormity of personal trauma into an almost existential void, forcing us to see the gulf between the Andronici's suffering and the negative space which that suffering drops into.[15] Like the racist violence of the play, it is a void shaped entirely by the inadequacy of public remedy, as scholars connecting *Titus Andronicus* to Black Lives Matter have also shown.[16] As one student put it, reading the play 'is therefore a radical feminist project, one which calls us to consider the ways in which we perpetuate violence communally and culturally'.[17] Such a consideration is illuminated by an intersectional analysis of the play's sometimes-victims, Tamora and Lavinia, who are fully interpolated within and energetically perpetuate racist and patriarchal power structures.[18] Aaron, too, unlike the diabolical devil figure of allegories old, does not stand outside and untouched by the world of the play, but is instead the target of its loathing and torture. All three figures, and for that matter Titus himself, are thus victims and victimizers, underscoring that the play is not so much about good and bad people, but about the reiterative nature of structural violence.

Reading *Titus Andronicus* after reading a good deal of Ovidian myths also enables students to theorize the distinctions between myth and tragic drama as meaning-making structures. As I mentioned earlier, by translating Ovidian narratives into staged actions, Shakespeare actualizes what Ovid mythologizes. As several of my students observed, tragedy thereby also eliminates Ovidian apotheosis. One student argued that we discern value in Lavinia's personhood exactly because she does not 'get transformation and beautiful song'. Instead, as Jenna wrote, 'her suffering is merely pain, not the beauty that can come from suffering, and thus the question becomes not what can you make out of your pain as an inspiration, but whether a person's pain is worthy of empathy and support merely because they're a person'.[19] The mute and murdered Lavinia forbids audiences an instrumentalized reading of her experience; her presence denies any attempt to justify, ameliorate or legitimize suffering by seeing it as fundamental to art. One can see that stripping bare as a meditation – actually affiliated with humanist philosophy and disability studies alike – on the irreducibility of human worth.

Making connections between Shakespeare's Rome and our own world is not hard. My students well understood the almost total discrepancy between the ubiquity of sexual assault and what is at best the indifference of the legal system, in which fewer than 1 per cent of rapes lead to a conviction, but nearly 90 per cent of sexual assault victims are left with varying degrees of anxiety or distress.[20] The Fall of 2018 highlighted an especially alarming correlation between Shakespeare's nightmarish play and our quotidian world, which a close reading of two scenes laid bare. The first was from *Titus Andronicus*, after the rape of Lavinia:

DEMETRIUS	So, now go tell, and if thy tongue can speak, Who 'twas that cut thy tongue and ravished thee.
CHIRON	Write down thy mind; bewray thy meaning so, An if thy stumps will let thee, play the scribe.
DEMETRIUS	See how with signs and tokens she can scrawl.
CHIRON	Go home, call for sweet water, wash thy hands.
DEMETRIUS	She hath no tongue to call, nor hands to wash, And so let's leave her to her silent walks.
CHIRON	And 'twere my cause, I should go hang myself.
DEMETRIUS	If thou hadst hands to help thee knit the cord.

(2.3.1–10)[21]

And the second was a transcript of an event that took place on 27 September 2018 in Room 226 of the Dirksen Senate Office Building, where Democrat Patrick Leahy asked Christine Blasey Ford to give testimony to the Senate Judiciary Committee about her strongest memory from the night that Supreme Court nominee Brett Kavanaugh allegedly assaulted her. 'Indelible in the hippocampus is the laughter', she explained.[22] 'The uproarious laughter between the two. They're having fun at my expense':

Patrick Leahy:	'You've never forgotten them laughing at you.'
Christine Blasey Ford:	'They were laughing with each other.'
Patrick Leahy:	'And you were the object of the laughter?'

Christine Blasey Ford: 'I was underneath one of them, while the two laughed.'[23]

Thinking about these two scenes playing out hundreds of years apart, my student Anna observed that 'looking beyond the appalling acts of violation and mutilation which Lavinia endures, we can see Shakespeare's narrative as a proto-sociological exploration of the way in which societal conditions perpetuate and exacerbate trauma even after the fact of the assault'.[24] This observation astutely reveals that what the fictional Lavinia and the very real Christine Blasey Ford both suffered was not rape alone but also the ongoing failure of all forms of legal redress, reparation or recognition. My students did not hold Shakespeare accountable for this failure. Instead, they saw that it was the failed and possibly unrecuperable legal system – the one that abandoned Lavinia and seated Brett Kavanaugh on the Supreme Court of the United States – that should itself be on trial.[25]

Faculty working through these troubling scenes with students can draw judiciously on Julie Taymor's extraordinary *Titus*, which chooses to emphasize rather than soft-pedal Chiron and Demetrius' cruel laughter, their bonding over Lavinia's suffering. It gives her, and the viewer, nowhere to hide. In other ways, too, her adaptation augments the sheer atrocity of the play through its gruesome depictions of violence that veer even towards the carnivalesque. Some of this is hard to watch. But it does the important work of 'making visible the disturbing', as Sandra Young has put it.[26] This making visible is, I am suggesting, part of the work of revenge tragedy. Deborah Willis, too, sees this as part of the purgative power of the play, its construction 'of hopeful action and a reconstituted community, in which the freaks, the losers, and the exiles, stubbornly persisting in the face of their losses and humiliation, find dignity in labor and "much to do": If healing is possible, perhaps it can be best accomplished through an embrace of the grotesque'.[27] Such an embrace brings us far from the world of literary realism but towards the almost comedic grandeur unleashed by allegorical excess. To further illustrate this principle, I often show students an incredible sequence from *Django Unchained*.[28] You might remember the one: it is where Jamie Foxx's character opens fire on scores of grotesque, cussing, white slaveholders, who, one after one, die in the most excessive way possible. Scores of bodies, gallons of blood, a cacophony of racial slurs, endless gore. But at a certain point in the long scene – at about the time that the film goes into slow motion, the Tupac/James Brown mash-up begins, the fourth gentleman's head is shot off like a pumpkin while the thirtieth receives a third bullet wound in the identical spot in his knee where he has been shot several previous times – they get it: this is over the top. This is an allegory. This has gone beyond gratuitous violence to symbolic form. It is a shooting gallery. It is a Senecan reprise. In its aesthetic rupture is a takedown of the entirety of the slave-holding South.

My decision to share works like Ovid's 'Philomela', Shakespeare's *Titus Andronicus*, Julie Taymor's *Titus* and Tarantino's *Django Unchained* raises the obvious question of content or trigger warnings. Essential as they have become in the American educational context – and I do provide them for these materials – I have come to feel that the debate about trigger warnings is to some extent a red herring. On the one hand, there are those who refuse to acknowledge that 'being triggered is more than merely being offended by content or feeling uncomfortable with ideas that contradict someone's beliefs; it is a physiological response to external stimuli caused by past trauma, seemingly uncontrollable and often unpredictable'.[29] The existence of post-traumatic stress disorder is not up for debate, and it is well known that trauma changes the biochemistry of the body. It is therefore medically as well as emotionally true that, as Charlene Smith puts it, 'there are productive ways to make an audience uncomfortable, and there are harmful ways to make an audience uncomfortable'.[30] Besides misrepresenting humane consideration as 'cancel culture', the attack on trigger warnings is also ahistorical, obliterating the fact that Shakespearean plays have been modified and adapted in response to audience demand for as long as they have existed. A century's worth of spectators did not witness Cordelia's death. Enlightenment snowflakes? Serious approaches to trigger warnings therefore must distinguish the work they do from forms of ideological policing, infantilizing or avoidance of challenging or uncomfortable ideas. Indeed, given the ways that many early modern texts do not just record historical traumas but also continue to cause harm – by, for example, perpetuating racist language – the term 'trigger' is actually not comprehensive enough to account for the varied forms of troubled engagement that go beyond a bodily, involuntary stress response. For this reason, a content note can initialize engagement rather than undermine it, empowering students to wrestle with difficult texts on their own terms. As Kirsten Mendoza puts it, 'trigger warnings themselves advocate for social justice since they challenge ableist norms about the people who belong in our classrooms and put communal care and responsibility in action.'[31] They signal our regard and concern to our students, establishing the kind of trust required to actually enable serious engagement in the first place.

At the same time, however, it has long been my concern that trigger warnings may not actually *do the work* that we invoke them to do, and indeed might short-circuit more subtle forms of engagement and preparation on both students' and professors' parts. In the absence of real structural and cultural change – not only in our societies but also in our universities – they are not themselves efficacious of anything; in fact, they can easily be uttered by those who have no training or interest in social justice pedagogy.[32] Some studies find that they are only 'trivially helpful';[33] others, more troublingly, suggest that 'trigger warnings may increase acute anxiety by fostering an expectancy of harm'.[34] This seems anecdotally as well as experientially compelling: many of us have had the experience of being warned that 'what we are about to see is disturbing', and experienced anticipatory stress. Such announcements, however well-intentioned, can 'lead the witness', producing overdetermined responses. When treated reductively, they risk reducing complex texts to dangerous materials that require monitoring, misdirecting their original intentions for the purposes of censorship and the stifling of academic freedom.[35] For those who came of age in the 1980s and 1990s, such assessments may be redolent of the PMRC (Parents Music Resource Center), which put 'Parental Guidance: Explicit Lyrics' warning labels on ostensibly obscene punk, heavy metal and hip-hop records. Such moralistic and top-down impositions do more to police art than to protect listeners.

We have seen the dangers of these top-down models play out in academia. My own institution, for example, briefly circulated a 'Sexual Offense Resource Guide' which included the suggestion to 'remove triggering material when it does not contribute directly to the course learning goals' and warned that 'anything could be a trigger'.[36] Since the document was presented by an administrative office (The Office of Equity Concerns) and compiled with little faculty input, it felt intrusive to many faculty and also garnered a good deal of criticism nationally.[37] The trouble was not in the several legitimately useful resources provided in the guide but rather in its positioning faculty as needing to justify the inclusion of any materials that might upset readers. As scholars know, not just plays by Shakespeare but almost an infinite number of literary works and films – indeed entire historical fields – are minefields of potentially disturbing material, for the simple reason that the human experience itself is filled with challenge and trauma. The solution is surely not identifying some texts as kryptonite, lest we become wary of tackling urgent social problems altogether. As one of my students warned, the trauma of rape is compounded by its elision by a society that 'squirms away from being faced head-on with the tragedy of it', and a special class of fraught texts has too often produced a special class of fraught silence. Indeed, as Barbara Baines asserts, 'the reluctance to acknowledge the history of rape *is* the history of rape'.[38] In the classroom, tactical evasions of the topic of sexual violence – like similarly gingerly treatments of racism – ultimately privilege the fragility of those who do not want to bear witness.[39] Teachers who care about social justice need to take responsibility for not perpetuating harm by obfuscating its presence.[40]

Alerting students to challenging content provides a way of setting a tone of trust and care, so that I have at least some chance of taking the next steps. It tells my students that I am invested in their well-being, that I will respect their boundaries, and that I value them seeking the forms of redress or reparation that the world too often denies. But then, I have to *do* the actual work of making that investment. In other words, the warning is not a get-out-of-jail-free card for me, and it is not a magic wand for them. Instead, I try to reverse engineer the ingredients that let my students understand themselves as agents who can change their worlds, and that starts with showing them that their needs co-create our shared space in the classroom. But my content note is also always an invitation – even a rallying cry – to engage. I model the conviction that resilience and agency are not only possible but a beacon, and that we can harness the intellectual and transformational power of discomfort towards transformative ends. My content note ends by offering that 'to respond on an aesthetic and intellectual level to difficulty is to increase our internal resources, and to deepen our capacity for knowledge, growth, and pleasure'.[41] I try to offer a pathway towards fierce engagement rather than self-protective withdrawal.

An essential component of a successful process should be an assignment structure designed to augment students' resilience and sense of agency. Over time, I have come to create space in each of my classes for at least one low-stakes 'student choice' assignment, usually chosen from a small menu of options (recitation, response to a film, that sort of thing). But in this class, fully 60 per cent of assignments are determined by each student. I require them all to write an analytical essay, and I retain 15 per cent for assessment of their engagement in discussions and the class overall. But beyond that, they need to determine, in consultation with me, what their own learning goals for the course are. The process of determining this is all about making way for intentionality and responsibility, wherein they alone can decide: Is this a semester in which you really want to focus on your analytical skills, say by tackling a series of short essays with ongoing feedback? Is this the semester in which you want to try bringing together your English and creative writing majors by writing your *own* myth? Are you interested in working on your research skills, and therefore want to develop an annotated bibliography? Do you need more practice giving in-class presentations, and can we set up a schedule for those? In each case students meet with me and discuss their accomplishments in college so far, the skills they hope to develop this semester, the rubric that they would like applied to their work and the deadlines they think they can manage. It almost goes without saying that by asking them to take responsibility for what they most wanted to work on, they are more likely to achieve it. But beyond that, the growing confidence and sense of ownership of their learning process centres their own agency even as we confront materials that could potentially be destabilizing for some of them.

The work produced within this framework is some of the most extraordinary I have ever received, from a site-specific installation which reimagined the town green as an allegorical landscape (the student hung poems on trees, with a tip of the hat to both Ovid and *As You Like It*, and composed a musical score you could listen to as you walked through the space) to a full-length 'newspaper' recording the goings-on of Greek Gods and Renaissance characters (crime beat: Romeo and Juliet commit suicide). One assignment in particular stands out: a project my student Maddie Hinkle simply titled 'ASL Philomel'.

Combining her longstanding love of classical myths, passion for social justice and ongoing study of American Sign Language (Maddie is now a master's student at Gallaudet), she first transcribed the myth into American Sign Language (ASL), and then recorded a video of her signing the myth. Of course, it would have been an ambitious and intriguing project applied to any myth. But to render Philomela in ASL – when the myth itself so poignantly foregrounds questions of voice, access, and meaning-making – was remarkable.

I contacted Maddie for this essay, and asked her if she could tell me about the motivation behind this project, and she shared this with me:

> The rate of abuse (neglect, physical, and sexual) is about 25 percent higher for d/Deaf and Hard of Hearing youth than it is for hearing youth. How can you get the help you need, how can you ask for support, if no one understands you or you don't have the language to reach out? This is the Philomela concept. Her tongue is removed because if she can't speak, she can't fight back. She is silenced and no one will be able to help her. We are in a society that is incredibly phonocentric and we look down on people who don't speak 'properly' and, even more so, on people who don't speak at all. We take spoken language to be a sign of intelligence and the lack of it to display a lack of any kind of intellect. So both these things come into play with my Philomela project, right? Tereus 'silences' her and he abuses her and then he absolutely takes for granted that, because she can no longer speak, she no longer has any agency or power against him. But she proves him wrong. She uses the tools at her disposal in the form of the tapestry she weaves and, in my version, the power of American Sign Language. Not having a spoken voice doesn't mean you have no voice at all. She fights back, makes a plan, gets help, all using *her* language. What could be more powerful than that?[42]

What adds to the poignancy of the experience is that Maddie was, of all students in the class, the one perhaps least reconciled to the value of teaching *Titus Andronicus*, most concerned that its production might simply do more harm than good.[43] Feminists are not wrong to raise these concerns, although they are unlikely to agree about which plays, if any, just go too far. But Maddie did something more important than boycott or resist material that she found troubling. Instead, her transliterated explication of every utterance and gesture gave a new language to Philomela, a new life to Ovid's myth, and enacted new forms of justice. It did all this with intellectual and aesthetic precision ('ASL is a wonderful medium for storytelling because of the facial expressions and animated body language inherent in the language') that did honour both to the d/Deaf community and to our early modern and classical sources. And this must always be our primary goal: for our students to draw on the best of the texts we share with them, to create new structures, art forms and possibilities in the world.

So how did I teach *Titus Andronicus* during the week of the Brett Kavanagh hearings? I let students ask, and I asked them, lots of questions. Some of them wondered if art that dramatizes rape and suffering is itself a form of violation. When does it cross over into exploitation (e.g. are we confident that Quentin Tarantino doesn't make his films partially to give himself 'permission' to broadcast the N-word hundreds of times?).[44] Is the ugliness only worth it if the art is good enough? Is *Titus Andronicus* good enough? Or is it unjustified because it contributes to suffering, and is just a hatchet job, in all senses? Although I relish some of his films, I probably wouldn't go to the mat for Tarantino. But *Titus Andronicus*? That play, I think, can save your life, because that work of fiction actually tells the truth. This is what rape is. Here is no equivocation. Here are no metaphors. Just awful, brutal, brilliant actualizations. My students and I talked about how these ethical questions come to bear in different ways for drama than for myth, but regardless, 'Lavinia' is just stuff for the playwright to work with, not any more real than the props on the stage; and if we think otherwise, that is not only a testament to drama but also an opportunity to reflect on literary form.[45] But also, I told them, you each have to decide: what to watch, what to support, what to teach, and there will never be one easy answer, but you must articulate your answer with reference to as much complexity and care as possible. And when in doubt, err on the side of art.

Titus Andronicus, with its demonized villain buried up to his neck, its arrows shot up to an empty sky, its embodied characters of Rape and Murder, its tragical farce of proliferating body parts, its savagery, its biblical legions of murdered sons, its rapacious juggernauts of war, its narcissistic older generation, its Senecan excess, its cruellest perpetrators baked into a pie, its mutilated and brutalized Lavinia turned into an emblem of sacrifice: it is precisely the play's too muchness, its uberviolence and its refusal to compromise that reveals this revenge tragedy's ethical core. In its allegorical excess it is one of the few things ever written about rape that does not lie to your face. Its very *raison d'être* is 'making visible the disturbing'. This is part of the extravagant grammar by which revenge tragedy articulates a desire for justice, and our classrooms can speak its language.

I offer this chapter as a flare of encouragement. To my fellow teacher-scholars who are never sure whether to avoid or dive into these really tough issues – the deaths, the national tragedies, the scandals, the crises on-campus and off – I admit it is partly a matter of temperament and ethical orientation that I prefer to dive into the wreck.[46] But isn't there always a wreck, really? And where are we going, exactly, if we won't go there? My first day in a classroom was the day after 9/11, and there has been no shortage of crises since that time – from the sudden death of a beloved student to an insurrection on the US Capitol. I have, to varying degrees, made space for all these serious happenings, for they are the reason we even *have* literature. As I told my students on 13 March 2020, as we hastily left campus in the midst of an exfoliating pandemic: we don't get to choose when we were born. We don't get to choose the natural disasters, epidemiological emergencies, stock market crashes, tyrannical regimes or wars our generations face. We only get to choose how we react. If my students saw value in reading *Titus Andronicus* in the midst of the Kavanaugh hearings, it was partly because we collaboratively agreed on the value of 'diving into the wreck'. And here I had a final bit of help from Ta-Nehisi Coates's *Between the World and Me*, with which I ended the class, and which I also want to give the last word to here:

> I began to see discord, argument, chaos, perhaps even fear, as a kind of power. I was learning to live in the disquiet I felt ... in the mess of my mind. The gnawing discomfort, the chaos, the intellectual vertigo was not an alarm. It was a beacon. It began to strike me that the point of my education was a kind of discomfort, was the process that would not award me my own especial Dream but would break all the dreams, all the comforting myths of Africa, of America, and everywhere, and would leave me only with humanity in all its terribleness.[47]

Acknowledgement

This chapter was inspired by the brave and brilliant students of several iterations of my class, 'Shakespeare and Metamorphosis'. Special thanks to Anna Kozler, Maddie Hinkle, Carolyn Leibovich and Jenna Hoover for permission to share their words. Em Gormley, thank you for more than one important conversation and your meaningful comments on the revised chapter; and thanks to Liz Fox, another former student and now colleague who generously responded to an early draft. Beth M. Shapiro also provided important insight into the therapeutic framework for trauma recovery. Amanda Bailey encouraged me to think more deeply about race and aesthetic violence; my thanks, too, to Seo-Young Chu and Kirsten Mendoza, who have written provocatively about race, sexual violence and literary form in ways I have tried to show my indebtedness to. I am grateful to Sandra Young and Christopher Thurman for excellent feedback and the initial invitation to present this work at the Shakespeare and Social Justice conference in Cape Town, South Africa (2019), and for the many productive conversations with colleagues at that event, including David Sterling Brown, Kirsten Dey, Colette Gordon, Linda Gregerson, Derrick Higginbotham, Jonathan Hsy, Thulisile Fortunate Mngomezulu, Steven Mullaney, Lisa Barksdale Shaw and Ayanna Thompson. Thanks to the generous invitation of Hanh Bui and Will Tosh, I also gave a version of this chapter at the Women and Power Symposium hosted remotely by the Globe Theatre in 2021. Some of my thoughts on alternative assignment structures appeared as 'Choose your own adventure: New Approaches to Assignments', for the Oberlin College Center for Teaching Innovation and Excellence website, and were presented at a remote roundtable on Shakespeare and Social Justice for the Shakespeare Association of America in 2021.

Notes

1 These public events have generated a massive amount of coverage. For a review of their cultural significance, see Haley Sweetland Edwards, 'How Christine Blasey Ford's Testimony Changed America', *Time Magazine*, 4 October 2018; Masha Gessen, 'An NYU Sexual-

Harassment Case has Spurred a Necessary Conversation About #Metoo', *The New Yorker*, 25 August 2018; Colleen Flaherty, 'Junot Díaz, Feminism and Ethnicity', *Chronicle for Higher Education*, 29 May 2018. Although I focus here on the impact of high-profile rape cases in the United States, obviously it is a form of violence that knows no national boundaries.

2 More than one hundred people reportedly fainted, for example, at a 2014 production at the Globe Theatre (https://www.independent.co.uk/arts-entertainment/theatre-dance/news/globe-theatre-takes-out-100-audience-members-with-its-gory-titus-andronicus-9621763.html). A 2013 RSC production at the Swan also caused audience members to become physically ill, according to Thomas Dixon's survey of extreme reactions to the play: https://emotionsblog.history.qmul.ac.uk/2013/10/violence-vomit-and-hysteria-an-interview-with-rose-reynolds/.

3 For another account of teaching *Titus Andronicus* with a feminist (and especially anti-racist) lens in the Fall of 2018, see Ambereen Dadabhoy, '#MeToo Shakespeare at Harvey Mudd College', written as an entry on the author's blog: https://ambereendadabhoy.com/2019/12/17/metoo-shakespeare-at-harvey-mudd-college/.

4 Anna Kozler, 'Symbolic Violence: The Mythologization of Lavinia's Rape in *Titus Andronicus*' (unpublished essay submitted for ENG 304, Summer 2019).

5 Hillary Eklund and Wendy Beth Hyman, eds, *Teaching Social Justice Through Shakespeare: Why Renaissance Literature Matters Now* (Edinburgh: Edinburgh University Press, 2019).

6 As Deborah Willis notes, 'In *Titus Andronicus* Shakespeare provides a powerful exploration of the multiple yet related ways in which revenge can provide an emotional container for traumatic loss and humiliation ... by enabling them [survivors] to reenact elements of the traumatic scene with the roles reversed, reestablishing agency and a position of mastery.' '"The gnawing vulture": Revenge, Trauma Theory, and *Titus Andronicus*', *Shakespeare Quarterly* 53, no. 1 (2002): 50–1.

7 nsvrc.org/statistics.

8 Rape Statistics by Country, https://worldpopulationreview.com/country-rankings/rape-statistics-by-country.

9 I also taught the play again a few months later, in the Summer of 2019, and again in the Spring of 2021. I discuss teaching strategies used, and student work received, during each of these iterations of the course.

10 The term entered scholarly literature via the work of R. G. Tedeschi and L. G. Calhoun in their book *Trauma and Transformation: Growing in the Aftermath of Suffering* (Thousand Oaks, CA: Sage Publications, 1995); Jane Shakespeare-Finch and Janine Beck examine the relationship between trauma and adaptive development in 'A Meta-analytic Clarification of the Relationship Between Posttraumatic Growth and Symptoms of Posttraumatic Distress Disorder', *Journal of Anxiety Disorders* 28, no. 2 (2014): 223–9.

11 Seo-Young Chu, 'A Refuge for Jae-in Doe: Fugues in the Key of English Major', *Entropy Magazine*, 3 November 2017 (online).

12 For the complex relationship between the two figures, and particularly for the ways that references to Philomel 'activate a violent causal force within' Shakespeare's play (146), see Jennifer Waldron, 'Lavinia is Philomel', *Object Oriented Environs*, ed. Jeffrey Jerome Cohen and Julian Yates (Earth: Punctum Books, 2016); and William W. Weber, '"Worse Than Philomel": Violence, Revenge, and Meta-Allusion in *Titus Andronicus*', *Studies in Philology* 112, no. 4 (Fall, 2015): 698–717.

13 The evolution of Shakespeare's treatment of rape is brought home for my students when we read *Cymbeline*. They recognize Lavinia as the palimpsest behind Imogen, a woman for whom assault is *not* a lived event but an aesthetically mediated dream. In that late play, the would-be rapist Iachimo refers to himself as Tarquin, but ultimately sates himself on fictions of ravishment. In this sense the arc of Shakespeare's career demonstrates his own process of choosing to metamorphose brute literalism into metaphor. The playwright clearly continued to think seriously about rape, but increasingly demurs from subjecting his female characters to staged assault.

14 Lisa Starks-Estes, *Violence, Trauma, and Virtus in Shakespeare's Roman Poems and Plays: Transforming Ovid* (New York: Palgrave Macmillan, 2014), 93.

15 Although it is outside the scope of this chapter, the suffering of the entire Andronicus family can be understood not only (as many critics understandably do) as the selfish appropriation of Lavinia's suffering by her male relatives, but contrarily as a legitimate expression of what Sara Ahmed calls the 'sociality of pain'. See 'The Contingency of Pain', *Parallax* 8, no. 1 (2002): 17–34, 22. I am grateful to Lina Perkins Wilder for suggesting a consideration of Ahmed's work in the context of this essay.

16 See for example David Sterling Brown, '"Is Black so Base a Hue?": Black Life Matters in Shakespeare's *Titus Andronicus*', in *Early Modern Black Diaspora Studies*, ed. Cassander L. Smith, Nicholas R. Jones, and Miles P. Grier (New York: Palgrave Macmillan, 2018), 137–55.

17 Kozler, 'Symbolic Violence', n.p.
18 For the ways in which Tamora and the 'uber white' Goths are also racially marked as outsiders, see Francesca Royster, 'White-Limed Walls: Whiteness and Gothic Extremism in Shakespeare's *Titus Andronicus*', *Shakespeare Quarterly* 51, no. 4 (Winter 2000): 432–55.
19 Jenna Hoover; informal Slack post, March 3, 2021.
20 Andrew Van Dam, 'Less Than 1% of Rapes Lead to Felony Convictions. At Least 89% of Victims Face Emotional and Physical Consequences', *Washington Post*, 6 October 2018 (accessed online). Based on analysis of the 2010–14 Justice Department figures compiled by the Rape, Abuse, Incest National Network, Van Dam reports that 'just 5.7 percent of incidents end in arrest, 0.7 percent result in a felony conviction and 0.6 percent result in incarceration'. Almost nine out of ten sexual assault victims 'experienced some level of distress, with 46% experiencing severe distress. . . . As many as 82 percent of victims experience fear and anxiety'.
21 Quotations from *Titus Andronicus* are taken from Richard Proudfoot, Ann Thompson, David Scott Kastan and H. R. Woodhuysen, eds, *The Arden Shakespeare Complete Works, Third Series* (London and New York: The Arden Shakespeare, 2021).
22 This haunting permanence is a feature of diagnosed PTSD; using strikingly similar language, R. J. Lifton describes traumatic memory as a kind of '"indelible image" or "death imprint"' in 'The Concept of the Survivor', in *Survivors, Victims, and Perpetrators: Essays on the Nazi Holocaust*, ed. J. E. Dimsdale (New York: Hemisphere Press, 1980), 113–26; quoted here from Deborah Willis, '"The Gnawing Vulture": Revenge, Trauma Theory, and *Titus Andronicus*', *Shakespeare Quarterly* 53, no. 1 (Spring 2002): 21–52, 26.
23 The statement about what was "indelible in the hippocampus" came from during the questioning and was widely reported. See for instance Jamie Ducharme, '"Indelible in the Hippocampus Is the Laughter': The Science Behind Christine Blasey Ford's Testimony", *Time Magazine*, 27 September 2018. https://time.com/5408567/christine-blasey-ford-science-of-memory/. The full transcript of Ford's opening statement can be found in the 9.26/2018 Politico. https://www.politico.com/story/2018/09/26/christine-blasey-ford-opening-statement-senate-845080.
24 Kozler, 'Symbolic Violence', n.p.
25 See also Anna Waymack, 'Teaching de Raptu Meo: Chaucer, Chaumpaigne, and Consent in the Classroom', *Medieval Feminist Forum* 53, no. 1 (2017) 150–75. 'I place "Trigger Warning: Breakfast"

next to the Reeve's Tale because I find it hard to read them as separate works' (158). My thanks to Penelope Geng for pointing me to this important essay.

26 Sandra Young, opening remarks at the Shakespeare and Social Justice Conference, Cape Town, South Africa, 16 May 2019.

27 Willis, '"The Gnawing Vulture", 52. Although the role of comedic excess in revenge narratives is outside the scope of this chapter, it is a timeless feature of the genre. See, for example, Emerald Fennell's 2020 film *A Promising Young Woman*, a rape revenge movie which weaves together retribution fantasy, macabre comedy and an aesthetic that might best be described as bubblegum grotesque.

28 Quentin Tarantino, *Django Unchained* (Columbia Pictures, 2012).

29 Christin Essen, 'Provoked and Triggered: Content Warnings and Student Spectators', *Howlround Theatre Commons*, 21 July 2019; online, n.p. In the North American context, dismissal of trigger warnings often but not always comes from cultural conservatives. See for example Jack Halberstam, 'You're Triggering Me: The Neoliberal Rhetoric of Harm, Danger, and Trauma' (2014). Halberstam lampooned how his own queer and progressive community 'made adjustments, curbed their use of deodorant, tried to avoid patriarchal language, thought before they spoke, held each other, cried, moped, and ultimately disintegrated into a messy, unappealing morass of weepy, hypo-allergic, psychosomatic, anti-sex, anti-fun, anti-porn, pro-drama, pro-processing post-political subjects'. https://www.beaconbroadside.com/broadside/2014/07/you-are-triggering-me.html.

30 Charlene Smith, 'Staging Sexual Assault Responsibly: Lessons from *The Changeling*', *Howlround Theatre Commons*, 10 July 2019; online, n.p. Smith continues, 'We must consider the effect a violent scene will have on those who have experienced such violence in real life. Too often we over-exalt violence in storytelling for being "real" and "gritty". Theatre allows for more powerful choices. There are limitless – and more interesting – options beyond realism.'

31 Kirsten N. Mendoza, 'Sexual Violence, Trigger Warnings, and the Early Modern Classroom', in Eklund and Hyman, 97–105, 98.

32 Instead, we might ask with Kandice Chuh, '[H]ow do and might the knowledge and teaching principles and practices we elaborate, occupy, and employ be recruited toward the broadly ethicopolitical aims of something like greater justice? Of lessening the determinative effects of the circumstances of the accidents of birth?' *The Difference Aesthetics Makes: On the Humanities After 'Man'* (Durham: Duke University Press, 2019), 14.

33 Mevagh Sanson, Deryn Strange, Maryann Garry, 'Trigger Warnings Are Trivially Helpful at Reducing Negative Affect, Intrusive Thoughts, and Avoidance', *Clinical Psychological Science* 7, no. 4 (2019). The abstract summarizes that 'to better estimate trigger warnings' effects, we conducted mini meta-analyses on our data, revealing trigger warnings had trivial effects – people reported similar levels of negative affect, intrusions, and avoidance regardless of whether they had received a trigger warning. Moreover, these patterns were similar among people with a history of trauma. These results suggest a trigger warning is neither meaningfully helpful nor harmful' (n.p.).

34 Benjamin W. Bellet, Payton J. Jones and Richard J. McNally, 'Trigger Warning: Empirical Evidence Ahead', *Journal of Behavior Therapy and Experimental Psychiatry* 61 (December 2018): 134–41, 139. However, it is worth noting that unlike the Sanson, Strange and Garry study cited earlier, this one did not distinguish among subjects those who had previously suffered traumatic events.

35 See the statement by the AAUP (American Association of University Professors) on trigger warnings, which offers the following critique: 'The presumption that students need to be protected rather than challenged in a classroom is at once infantilizing and anti-intellectual. It makes comfort a higher priority than intellectual engagement and . . . singles out politically controversial topics like sex, race, class, capitalism, and colonialism for attention. Indeed, if such topics are associated with triggers, correctly or not, they are likely to be marginalized if not avoided altogether by faculty who fear complaints for offending or discomforting some of their students. Although all faculty are affected by potential charges of this kind, non-tenured and contingent faculty are particularly at risk.' https://www.aaup.org/report/trigger-warnings

36 'I think this guidance also, in a way, misunderstands the nature of trauma and triggers. It's true that anything can be a trigger, but that doesn't mean all triggers are to be avoided at all costs. Avoidance can and does cause the world of trauma survivors to continually narrow if they work to persistently avoid triggers. Part of the work of trauma therapy is to establish safety by supporting the person in re-developing their own sense of agency, capacity to care for themselves when they are activated, and re-teach themselves (and their nervous system) that they're safe / not actually experiencing a threat when having a trauma response. It is counterproductive in this work to constantly avoid triggers in perpetuity, *and* a content or trigger warning does ideally allow the person to decide how they want to engage (and maybe what supports they need to do so) without being blindsided. But the suggestion that faculty remove all potentially

triggering material not relevant to learning goals was patently ridiculous, impossible, and I think also potentially disempowering to trauma survivors by taking away agency to decide to engage with potentially challenging material' (Em Gormley, personal correspondence, 26 September 2021).

37 See, for example, Colleen Flaherty, 'Trigger Unhappy', *Chronicle of Higher Education*, 14 April 2014. The AAUP statement also refers explicitly to the way these charged conversations played out on Oberlin's campus.

38 Barbara J. Baines, 'Effacing Rape in Early Modern Representation', *English Literary History* 65, no. 1 (Spring 1998): 69–98, 69. She is responding here to the encapsulated claim by Sylvana Tomaselli that the erasure of rape is a relatively modern phenomenon. See also Judith Herman, *Trauma and Recovery: The Aftermath of Violence – From Domestic Abuse to Political Terror* (New York: Basic Books, 1995), which opens on this note: 'The ordinary response to atrocities is to banish them from consciousness. Certain violations of the social compact are too terrible to utter aloud: this is the meaning of the word unspeakable. Atrocities, however, refuse to be buried. Equally as powerful as the desire to deny atrocities is the conviction that denial does not work. Folk wisdom is filled with ghosts who refuse to rest in their graves until their stories are told. Murder will out. Remembering and telling the truth about terrible events are prerequisites both for the restoration of the social order and for the healing of individual victims' (1).

39 Carolyn Leibovich, personal conversation, 10 March 2021. Her comment alluded to Robin DiAngelo's controversial *White Fragility: Why It's So Hard for White People to Talk about Racism* (Beacon, 2018). Carolyn elaborated on her thoughts in a class Slack post: 'A rape victim's pain is generally unseen, and rarely spoken about . . . What Shakespeare does here, to me at least, is to show the violence and trauma of this act in full detail. The mutilation of the woman exists the moment rape occurs, Shakespeare merely makes it visual, and forces his audience to address it. "Look", he says, "look at how terribly you have wronged this woman". It is powerful, and righteous' (4 March 2021).

40 This issue is fundamental to issues of translation, as well, as in the very long history of Ovidian translators 'turning assault into a consensual encounter'. In the face of this almost ubiquitous erasure, Stephanie McCarter insists, 'we must think carefully about why translators have mitigated, even erased [Ovidian] rape. Their hedging in many ways reflects . . . our tendency to gloss over rape with language

that mitigates and obscures it'. Stephanie McCarter, 'Rape: Lost in Translation', *Electric Lit*, 1 May 2018. https://electricliterature.com/rape-lost-in-translation/. McCarter has recently produced a full-length translation of the *Metamorphoses* for Penguin (2022), the second only by a female translator. Leo Curran's foundational article, 'Rape and Rape Victims in the "Metamorphoses"', *ISIS* 11, no. 1–2 (Spring 1978): 213–41, helped shift the critical conversation, but the majority of translations still evade a frank rendering of the original source.

41 The full text of content note is as follows: '*Omnia praeclara tam difficilia quam rara sunt.* The great early modern Jewish philosopher Baruch Spinoza's words can be translated this way: "all things supremely splendid are as difficult as they are rare." Although hopefully we have all experienced moments of delight that were not necessarily hard-earned, I take his words to mean that many of the most precious things we experience in life – and the most beneficial knowledges we arrive at – might emerge out of suffering, difficulty, and discomfort. Some of the material we are reading this semester is about suffering, and some of it may be difficult to read. I cannot always anticipate every reader's reactions (you may not even anticipate your own!), and I want you to take excellent care of yourself in all circumstances. But it is my conviction that to respond on an aesthetic and intellectual level to difficulty is to increase our internal resources, and to deepen our capacity for knowledge, growth, and pleasure.'

42 I am grateful to Maddie Hinkle for sharing these perspectives with me. She also wanted to note the following: 'While I am fairly fluent in ASL and currently in grad school for Deaf Studies, I am hearing and not a native signer so the language doesn't belong to me. I wanted to give back some of the agency to Philomela but I don't want to do so at the expense of the Deaf community. This kind of project, this kind of work, has been done by the Deaf community for decades and I want to be sure that I don't laud myself for their predating work and their language without acknowledgement. ASL belongs to the Deaf, as do their stories, their Philomela-esque traumas, their responding displays of agency' (Personal correspondence, 26 August 2020).

43 A similar argument has been made about *Othello*, *Merchant of Venice* and *Taming of the Shrew* by Ayanna Thompson, who argues that these plays are important to think about and teach, but damaging to enact. She has shared these thoughts in several venues, but most publicly in the Codeswitch episode 'All That Glisters Is Not Gold', 21 August 2019. See also Ayanna Thompson and Laura Turchi, *Teaching Shakespeare with a Purpose: A Student-Centred Approach* (London: Arden, 2016).

44 Roxanne Gay speaks astutely that Tarantino's pretense of using the word for the purpose of historical accuracy is belied by his slim interest in other forms of verisimilitude. See 'Surviving "Django"', *Buzzfeed*, 4 January 2013. She notes that the film deploys the N-word 110 times in 3 hours, while *Roots* 'manages to depict the realities of slavery without using the N-word once and it's nearly ten hours long'.

45 See Eileen Joy's reference in 'You Are Here: A Manifesto', in *Animal, Vegetable, and Mineral: Ethics and Objects*, ed. Jeffrey J. Cohen (New York: Punctum, 2012), to the ways in which Ovid's myth utilizes figures as a kind of 'activation device' (165). Quoted in Waldron, 146.

46 I am, of course, paying homage to Adrienne Rich's book and poem, 'Diving into the Wreck', *Diving into the Wreck: Poems 1971–1972* (W. W. Norton, 1973).

47 Ta-Nehisi Coates, *Between the World and Me* (New York: Spiegel & Grau, 2015), 52.

INDEX

Note: Page numbers in *italics* refer to figures. Page numbers followed by "n" refer to notes.

1572 'Acte for the punishment of Vacabondes' 50
'1619 Project, The' 13–14 n.2
1971 Act of Parliament 49
1971 Immigration Act 57 n.17

Aaron, C. 210
abandonment 47
Adelman, J. 124–5
advertising trends 63, 64
Aeneid 38
Africa 22, 27
African National Congress (ANC) 158, 165 n.28
Africanus, L.
Geographical Historie of Africa 38
agaciro 105
Ahmed, S. 109
'Alchoran' (the Qur'an) 132
Al-Mansur, A. 130
Althusser, L. 219
American Association of University Professors (AAUP) 251 n.35
American Civil Liberties Union (ACLU) 82
American Sign Language (ASL) 243, 244
anaphora 110
ANC, *see* African National Congress (ANC)

Anderson, C. 103
Anglocentrism 20, 28, 29
Anglophone 167
 cultural production 71
 culture, hegemony of 6
al-Annuri, Abd al-Wahid bin Masoud bin Muhammad 130–1
anti-immigrant populism 62
anti-immigration 2
Antony and Cleopatra (Shakespeare) 147
Aosailuo 72–3
apartheid 150
appropriation 31
 acts of 63
Arabian Peninsula 22
Arden Research Handbook of Shakespeare and Social Justice (Ruiter) 5
Arden Shakespeare (Bloomsbury) 26
Aristotle
 Politics 151
artistic transgression 59
Art of English Poesie, The (Puttenham) 88
Asia 22, 27
Asian Shakespeare Intercultural Archive (A-S-I-A) 27
ASL, *see* American Sign Language (ASL)

ASL (American Sign Language) Shakespeare Project 31
As You Like It (Shakespeare) 59, 146, 147, 153–6
Auden, W. H.
  Dyer's Hand, The 54
Austen, J. L. 218
Australasia 27
  Indigenous Studies 28
Australia 22, 26
Avital Ronnell scandal 230

Bank of China 25
Banks, J. 53
barbarism 84–6, 91, 94
Battle of Alcácer Quibir 129
BBC 26, 59
Beloved (Morrison) 96 n.2
Bennett, S. 5–6, 60–1
Berg, L. W. 207
Between the World and Me (Coates) 245
Bevington, D. 86
Bhardwaj, V. 29
Bhattacharjee, P. 58
Bigelow, K.
  Zero Dark Thirty 136
biological sex 219
BIPOC (Black, Indigenous, and People of Colour) 65
Black Codes post-Emancipation 87
Black death 87
Black femininity 94
Black freedom 91
Black Jacobins (James) 43
#BlackLivesMatter 2–3, 52, 115, 236
Black Madness :: Mad Blackness (Pickens) 90
blackness 84, 85, 87–90, 92–4, 100 n.37, 123, 139 n.17
Black nothingness 91
Black Panther 72

Black theory 63
Boccaccio
  Decameron 192
Bodies That Matter (Butler) 217
Bodin, J.
  Methods for the East Comprehension of History 124
Bohannan, L. 60
Booke of Battaile, The 130
Bourdieu, P. 173
Bovilsky, L. 123
Branagh, K. 59, 146
Brathwaite, E. K.
  'Caliban' 36
Brazil 24
Brechtian alienation 217
British Commonwealth 57 n.17
British Council 26, 62
British Library 22–3
British Museum 71
British Sign Language 31
Britton, D. 127
Brokaw, K. S. 30–1
Brotton, J. 130
Brown, D.S.
  'Shakespeare and Social Justice in Contemporary Performance' 4 n.14
Brown, J. P. 89
Broyhill, S. 211
Bulman, J. 217
  Oxford Handbook of Shakespeare and Performance, The 22, 30
Burge, S. 72
Burton, J. 121
Butler, J. 12, 89, 209, 216–17, 221
Butlerian discursivity 219
Byrd, D. A. 208

Calbi, M. 169
Caliban 36–57

INDEX

'Caliban' (Brathwaite)   36
Caliban Codex, The
   (Durham)   36
'Calibanic lineage' (Nixon)   41
calmness   110–16
*Cambridge Companion to
   Shakespeare, The* (de Grazia
   and Wells)   21
*Cambridge Guide to the Worlds
   of Shakespeare, The*
   (Smith)   21
Canada   26
   Indigenous Studies   28
   pedagogical instrumentality
      of global Shakespeare
      adaptations   61
Canker, L.   122
Captain America: Civil War   72
Captive Audience (Jewkes)   176–7
Caribbean Commonwealth   49
Caroll, T.   64
Carson C.   24
Carthaginian control   37
Castro, F.   41
Catholicism   133
Cavalli, F.   167
censorship   240
Césaire, M. A.   41, 162
   *Tempest: Adaptation for a
      Black Theatre, A*   36
Cesare deve morire   167, 169
Charon, R.   71
Chiang, D.   62
Choi, S.   29
Christian social code   91
Christian Turn'd Turk, A
   (Daborne)   134
Chu, S.-Y.
   'Refuge for Jae-in Doe: Fugues
      in the Key of English Major,
      A'   235
citation   216–20
   acting   220–6
   theory of   218

Citizen: An American Lyric
   (Rankine)   89
Clark, J. P.   41
Classic Stage Company   59
Clean Break   167
climate change   37
#ClimateStrike   2
Coates, Ta-Nehisi
   *Between the World and
      Me*   245
Cold-War Europe   22
colonial displacement   44
colonial objectification   100 n.37
colour-blind casting   65
colourblindness   62
colour-conscious practice   65
Comedy of Errors (Roy-e-Sabs
   Company)   62
communal care   32, 240
*Companion to Shakespeare and
   Performance, A* (Hodgdon
   and Worthen)   21–2
'Conflicting Fields of Vision:
   Performing Self and Other
   in Two Intercultural
   Shakespeare Productions'
   (Tompkins)   22
Cooks, C. M.   8, 81–3, 89, 94
Cooper, S.   157
Correa, Y.   212, 212
Cosby, B.   230
cosmopolitanism   61
Crewe, B.   172
cross-dressing   211, 217, 220
'cross-gender' casting   12,
   226 n.4
cultural appropriation   1, 54, 59
cultural capital   1, 2, 11, 24, 169
cultural self-determination   149
cultural signifier   121
cultural subordination   47
Cymbeline (Shakespeare)   11,
   189, 192–6, 200, 203, 248
   n.13

Daborne, R.
  Christian Turn'd Turk, A 134
D'Amico, J. 130
Daniel, N. 71
Deafinitely Theatre 31
de Belleforest, F.
  Histoires Tragiques 84
Decameron (Boccaccio) 192
decolonization 5–6, 26, 27, 29, 73, 149
de-communization 105
de Grazia, M.
  Cambridge Companion to Shakespeare, The 21
Deleuze, G. 61
democracy 105
depredation 36, 48
De Providentia (Seneca) 156
Derrida, J. 152, 159
deterritorialization 61
  economic 75 n.9
deterritorializing effect of global arts 7
Dey, K. 11
Dhaka Theatre 31
Diamond, E. 218, 228 n.16
Dickson, A. 25
  'From Globe to Global' 24
Different Romeo and Juliet, A 31
Digging Up Stories (Thompson) 168–9
Digital Theatre+ 27
Dimmock, M. 133
disability
  and race, relationship between 90
  rights 31
  white 89
displacement 37, 38, 44, 46, 47, 55
Django Unchained 238, 239
Dobson, M.
  Oxford Companion to Shakespeare, The 22, 23, 29

Donkey Show, The 216
Doran, G. 64
double vision 217
drag 216–20
dramaturgical choices 210–16, 212, 214
dreamscape 25
Dromgoole, D. 24–5
Drouin, J. 211
Dubow, S. 150, 158
Durham, J.
  Caliban Codex, The 36
Dustagheer, S.
  'Global Shakespeare for Anglophone Audiences' 24
Dyer's Hand, The (Auden) 54

economic
  deterritorialization 75 n.9
Edinburgh Festival 60
Edited Approach 210–14
Eklund, H. 232
  Teaching Social Justice Through Shakespeare 5, 30
elitism 2
Elizabeth I 23, 130
Elliott-Newton, D. 8
emotional vulnerability 171
epistemic evaluation 72
Erickson, P. 121
Esien, J. J. 208
Espinosa, R. 103
Estill, L. 23, 26
ethics
  site-specific 72–3
  theory of 71
Europe 27
European colonialism 28, 30
European
  Commonwealth 57 n.17
exclusion 2

fairness 139 n.26
Fanon, F. 28, 41, 90

#FeesMustFall 2
fierce 105–10
Finland 22
Flinders, M. 53
Floyd-Wilson, M. 125
forced abortion 47
Ford, C. B. 230, 237–8
Foreign Shakespeare
   (Kennedy) 20–2, 27, 28
fragility 105–10, 118 n.15
Framed Approach 210, 213–14
France, Shakespeare scholarship
   and performance in 21
freedom 4, 219
   academic 240
   Black 91
free-market economy 63
'From Global London to
   Global Shakespeare'
   (Mancewicz) 24
'From Globe to Global'
   (Dickson) 24
The Fugard Theatre 3, 4, 70

Gallowfield Players
   Julius Caesar 166–84
Gang, F.
   Revenge of Prince Zi Dan,
     The 60
Garbo, G. 217
Garner, S. 122, 123, 133, 134
Gartree Therapeutic Community
   (GTC) 175, 176
Gates, H. L., Jr. 63
GBV, *see* gender-based violence
   (GBV)
gender 12
   diversity 63
   gender-based violence (GBV) 5,
     11, 13, 187–206
Gender Trouble (Butler) 216–17,
   228 n.19
genocide ideology 105
genre theory 231

Geographical Historie of Africa
   (Africanus) 38
geopolitical identity 131
Germany, Shakespeare scholarship
   and performance in 21
Gillen, K. 85
   'Recovering Shakespeare's
     Racial Genealogies' 83
Global North, race/racism
   in 8
Global Shakespeare
   as exercise in ethics 58–77
   pedagogical
     instrumentality 60–3
   to the rescue 65–72
   site-specific ethics 72–3
   for social injustice 1–13,
     19–35
   uneven valuation 63–5
'Global Shakespeare for
   Anglophone Audiences'
   (Dustagheer and
   Sakowska) 24
Global South 62
   race/racism in 8
Globe Player 27
Globe productions 64
Globe Theatre 23, 30, 247 n.2
Globe to Globe Festival 24, 31,
   61–2
Graeae 31
Gregerson, L. 4, 6–7
Grewal, Z. 122, 135
GTC, *see* Gartree Therapeutic
   Community (GTC)
Guattari, F. 61

Habib, I. 130
habitus 173
Halberstam, J. 250 n.29
Hall, K. F. 88, 94, 103, 121
Hamlet (Shakespeare) 24–5, 29,
   60, 61, 83, 146, 147, 156–9,
   207

Hamlet's Dreams: The Robben Island Shakespeare (Schalkwyk) 146
Hannah-Jones, Nikole 13–14 n.2
Hardt, M. 28
Harlem Shakespeare Festival 208
Harris, C. 85
Hartman, S. 87–8
Hassim, K. 153
Henry IV (Shakespeare) 208
Henry V (Shakespeare) 146, 147, 156–9
Her Majesty's Inspectorate of Prisons Annual Report 2018–19 175
Her Majesty's Prison and Probation Services (HMPPS) 168
heterosexual normativity 217
Higginbotham, D. 8, 9
Highlife for Caliban (Johnson) 36
Hinkle, M. 242
Histoires Tragiques (de Belleforest) 84
HMPPS, *see* Her Majesty's Prison and Probation Services (HMPPS)
Hodgdon, B.
  Companion to Shakespeare and Performance, A 21–2
Hofmeyr, I. 162
Holland, P. 21
Honigmann, E. A. J. 198
Huang, A. 29, *see also* Joubin, A. A.
Hulme, P. 39
humoral corollary 125
Hunter, K. 208, 211–12
Hyman, W. B. 12–13
  Teaching Social Justice Through Shakespeare 5, 30
Hytner, N. 166

illiberal humanities 98 n.22
Indigo (Warner) 6, 36, 47–55, 57 n.16
inequality 3
inequity 1–2
injustice 115, 202
  historical 4
  social 1–13, 19–35, 123, 188
Institute of Social Security for Employees in Mexico (ISSSTE) 31
intellectual vulnerability 171
intimate partner violence 187, 189
Islam, racialization of 4, 10, 120–41
  concealing and confirming differences 124–8
  'Moorish' identity 128–35
Islamophobia 136–7
ISSSTE, *see* Institute of Social Security for Employees in Mexico (ISSSTE)

Jackson, A. 166
Jackson, G. 207–8
Jackson, R. 21
James, C. L. R.
  Black Jacobins 43
Javid, S. 25
Jewkes, Y.
  Captive Audience 176–7
Johnson, L.
  Highlife for Caliban 36
Jones, B. 210
Jones, I. 92
Jonson, B.
  Masque of Blackness, The 8, 83, 92
Josephine, C. 208
Joubin, A. A. 4, 7–8, 22, 23, *see also* Huang, A.
Joyce, J.

INDEX

Ulysses 146
J.P. Morgan 25
Julius Caesar (Shakespeare) 10, 147, 148, 166–84, 208, 209, 212–16, 220, 222–6
justice 30, 102–19
   social 2, 3, 5, 19, 63
   system 11
Justinus, M. J. 56 n.5

Kagame, P. 104–5
Kani, J. 72, 73
Kaplan, M. L. 123
Kathrada, A. 156–7, 165 n.28
Kavanaugh, B. 230
Kemp, S. 64
Kennedy, D. 24
   Foreign Shakespeare 20–2, 27, 28
   'Shakespeare Worldwide' 21
Khan, I. 58
King Lear (Shakespeare) 60, 146, 147, 153–6
King of Marocco, The 130
Kingsley-Smith, J. 156
Kipling, R. 151
knowledge dissemination 71
knowledge production 71
Kontyo, A. J. 208
Koslin, D. 85
Kriegel, L.
   'Uncle Tom and Tiny Tim' 90
Kurosawa, A. 59
   Throne of Blood 58
Kyd, T. 134
   Spanish Tragedy, The 133

Lamming, B. G. 41
   Pleasures of Exile, The 43–6, 55
   Water with Berries 6, 36, 42–7, 52, 53, 55, 56 n.14, 162

Lan, Y. L.
   'Shakespeare and the Fiction of the Intercultural' 22
Latin America 22
Leahy, P. 237
Leibovich, C. 252 n.39
LePage, R. 36
Levenson, J.
   Shakespearean World, The 21
Levinas, E 71
Lew, M.
   Teenage Dick 31, 35
liberation 4, 10, 42, 67, 91, 95, 98 n.22
liberty 3, 167, 172
Libonati, A. 216
Litvin, M.
   'Middle Eastern Shakespeares' 21
Lloyd, P. 166–7, 208
Loomba, A. 121, 128
   Postcolonial Shakespeares 28
   'Shakespeare and the Possibilities of Postcolonial Performance' 22, 28
Lorber, J. 227 n.13
Love's Labour's Lost (Shakespeare) 31
Lucas, A. 167

Macbeth (Shakespeare) 29, 59, 65, 147, 170, 176, 177
McCarter, S. 252–3 n.40
MacDonald, J. G. 91
Mackenzie, R. 10
McLynn, P. 208
Magnússon, S. 83
Mama, B. *214*
Mamdani, M. 122
Mancewicz, A.
   'From Global London to Global Shakespeare' 24
#MarchForOurLives 2

marginalization 98 n.22
Market Theatre,
    Johannesburg 72
masculinity 221
*Masks of Conquest:
    Literary Study and
    British Rule in India*
    (Viswanathan) 13 n.1, 28
Masque of Blackness (Jonson) 8,
    83, 92
Matar, N. 130, 131
Matchinske, M. 86–7
materialization 228 n.21
Mazzocco, P. J. 65
Measure for Measure
    (Shakespeare) 86–7, 208
Meer, N. 122
Memorandum of Understanding
    (MoU) 31
Mendoza, K. 240
mental health 174–5
mental illness 83–5, 90
Mercedes Benz 25
Merchant of Venice, The
    (Shakespeare) 8, 9, 83,
    85–7, 89–91, 93, 102–19,
    147, 175
    calm and wild 110–16
    concealing and confirming
        differences 124–8
    fragile and fierce 105–10
    Islam, racialization of 120–41
    Prince of Morocco 120–41
metapoesis 235
metatheatricality 215, 217, 220
*Methods for the East
    Comprehension of History*
    (Bodin) 124
#MeToo 2
Metzger, M. J. 123
'Middle Eastern Shakespeares'
    (Litvin, Oz and
    Partovi) 21

Midsummer Night's Dream, A
    (Shakespeare) 26, 29, 147,
    216
migration
    forced 6
    mass 36–57
Miller, G. 210
Mirren, H. 208
miscegenation 91
Mish Mash Media
    Productions 208
misogyny 2, 13, 44, 47, 235
misshapenness 89
MIT, Global Shakespeare 27
Mnouchkine, A. 61
Modenessi, A. M.
    'Shakespeare in Iberian
    and Latin American
    Spanishes' 21
Modood, T. 122
Moosa, H. 4, 8–10
Morkinskinna 8, 83–7, 89–91,
    93
Morocco, as a Muslim 128–31
    profiling 131–5
Morrison, T.
    Beloved 96 n.2
MoU, *see* Memorandum of
    Understanding (MoU)
Much Ado about Nothing
    (Shakespeare) 11, 58–9,
    189–92, 203
Muslim identity 10, 121, 129,
    131–6
Mwambari, D. 105
mythopoesis 231

Nabirye, A.-M. 208
Nafisi, A. 169
Nair, B. 148–9
nationalism 156–9
National Sexual Violence
    Resource Center 233

National Theatre of China 29
Negga, R. 207
Negri, A. 28
Neill, M. 202
neocolonialism 25, 41, 63
neurodivergence 90
New Zealand
  Indigenous Studies 28
Ninagawa, Y. 59
Nixon, R. 54, 55, 57 n.22
  'Calibanic lineage' 41
North America 27
Norton Shakespeare
  (Shakespeare) 26
Nosworthy, J. M. 192

oeuvre 28, 123
Off-Broadway 59
Office of Equity Concerns,
  The 240
Oldenburg, S. 57 n.18
ontological terror 91
open-gendered casting 12,
  207–29
oppression 4, 28, 46, 47, 52, 53,
  55, 65, 152, 157, 173
  political 65
Oregon Shakespeare Festival 62
Orientalism (Said) 122
Orkin, M.
  Postcolonial Shakespeares 28
Ormsby, R.
  Shakespearean World, The 21
Orphan of Zhao, The 64
Osborne, G. 26
Othello (Shakespeare) 11, 22,
  29, 46, 73, 131, 189–90,
  196–203, 208
Othello: A Woman's Story 208
Other/otherness 71, 122
  racial 91
  religious 91
Ottoman Empire 38

*Oxford Companion to
  Shakespeare, The*
  (Dobson) 22, 23, 29
*Oxford Handbook of Shakespeare
  and Performance, The*
  (Bulman) 22, 30
Oz, A.
  'Middle Eastern
    Shakespeares' 21

Painter, W.
  *Second Tome of the Palace of
    Pleasure, The* 130
Parents Music Resource Center
  (PMRC) 240
Paris Is Burning 217
Partovi, P.
  'Middle Eastern
    Shakespeares' 21
patriality 57 n.17
patriarchal authority 99 n.35
Peake, M. 207
pedagogical instrumentality 60–3
pedagogy 32, 93, 230
  language 88
  obscene 85, 88
  radical 13
  social justice 240
  transformative 13
  trauma-informed 231
people of colour 65
Perez, J. J. 64, 214, 215, 216,
  220
performativity 218
*Performing Race and Torture on
  the Early Modern Stage*
  (Thompson) 93
Peterson, H. 212, *212*
Petrarchan slander 187–206
Petrarchism 188–9, 196
phallogocentrism, self-
  aggrandizing gesture of 23
physical exploitation 47

Pickens, T. A.
    Black Madness: Mad Blackness 90
Pleasures of Exile, The (Lamming) 43–6, 55
    'Caliban Orders History' 43
    'Monster, A Child, A Slave, A' 43
PMRC, *see* Parents Music Resource Center (PMRC)
Poesie 90
police brutality 82, 89
Politics (Aristotle) 150
politics of oppositionality 210
Porter, G. 208
postcolonialism 6, 8, 27–9, 36, 41, 46, 55, 73, 147, 159–63
postcoloniality 28, 29
postcolonial Shakespeares 8, 27–9
Postcolonial Shakespeares (Loomba and Orkin) 28
postcolonial theory 28
'post-gender' casting 64
post-traumatic growth 235
power 31
Prison Reform Trust 171
psychiatric disorders 175
psychological manipulation 47
psychological trauma 236
Puttenham, G. 89–90, 98 n.22
    Art of English Poesie, The 88

quasi-prostitution 47
queer theory 225

race/racism 3, 44, 109, 122
    and disability, relationship between 90
    gendered 99 n.29
    in Global North 8
    in Global South 8
    Islam, racialization of 4, 10, 120–41

Jews, racialization of 97 n.13
    pre-modern 122
    racecraft 102–19
    racial contempt 47
    racial difference 103, 120, 127
    racial diversity 63
    racial identity 59, 105, 121, 129
    racialized whiteness 104
    racial otherness 91
    racial sameness 126–8
    racist discourse 2
    racist violence 3, 5, 236
radical listening 71
rage 112
Rana, J. 122
Rankine, C. 98 n.23
    Citizen: An American Lyric 89
rape 42, 44, 47, 85, 100 n.42, 151, 230–4, 236, 237, 241, 244, 245, 247 n.1, 248 n.13, 250 n.27, 252–3 nn.38–40
realpolitik *vs.* benignant utopianism 40
reconciliation 46–7
'Recovering Shakespeare's Racial Genealogies' (Gillen) 83
'Refuge for Jae-in Doe: Fugues in the Key of English Major, A' (Chu) 235
religion/religiosity, *see also* Islam
    religious defiance 132
    religious difference 120
    religious identity 121–3, 131
    religious language 127
    religious otherness 91, 121
    rhetoric 126
representation 31
reterritorialization 61, 73
Revenge of Amleth, The 84
Revenge of Prince Zi Dan, The (Gang) 60

INDEX

Rhodes, C. 150–1
#RhodesMustFall 2
Richard II (Shakespeare) 61, 147
Richard III (Shakespeare) 29, 31, 61
right of abode 57 n.17
Robben Island 'Bible' 10, 71
Robben Island Shakespeare
    exile and nationalism 156–9
    exile in and on one's own land 153–6
    method 147–8
    politicized reading and performative writing in 145–65
    and postcolonial rewritings 159–63
    symbolic undoing of exile 148–53
Rolex 25
Romeo and Juliet (Shakespeare) 31
Royal Shakespeare Company (RSC) 25, 26, 46, 58, 60, 61, 64, 166, 208
RSC, *see* Royal Shakespeare Company (RSC)
Ruiter, D.
    Arden Research Handbook of Shakespeare and Social Justice 2
RuPaul's Drag Show 217
Rwanda 116
    genocide 104–5
    Rwandan Patriotic Front 105
Rylance, M. 64

Said, E. 28, 158, 160
    Orientalism 122
Sakowska, A.
    'Global Shakespeare for Anglophone Audiences' 24
Salter, N. 64

Saraf, S. 210
Schalkwyk, D. 160, 163 n.6, 188
    Hamlet's Dreams: The Robben Island Shakespeare 146
Schandl, V.
    'Shakespeare in Eastern Europe' 21
Seacole, M. 57 n.21
Sealey, J. 31
Second Part of the Booke of Battailes, The 129
Second Tome of the Palace of Pleasure, The (Painter) 130
self-loathing 47
self-Orientalizing 59
Selod, S. 122, 123, 133, 134
Seña y Verbo (Sign and Verb) theatre 31
Seneca
    De Providentia 156
sex 12, 87
    biological 219
    sexual deviance 86
    sexual exploitation 47
    sexual revenge 44
    sexual violence 11, 12, 88, 91, 94, 230, 231, 233, 236, 241, 246
'Sexual Offense Resource Guide' 240
Shakespeare, W.
    Antony and Cleopatra 147
    Cymbeline 11, 189, 192–6, 200, 203, 248 n.13
    Hamlet 24–5, 29, 60, 61, 83, 146, 147, 156–9, 207
    Henry IV 208
    Henry V 146, 147, 156–9
    Julius Caesar 10, 147, 148, 208, 209, 212–15, 220, 222–6

King Lear 60, 146, 147, 153–6
Love's Labour's Lost 31
Macbeth 29, 59, 65, 147, 170, 176, 177
Measure for Measure 86–7, 208
Merchant of Venice, The 8, 9, 83, 85–7, 89, 90, 93, 102–41, 147, 175
Midsummer Night's Dream, A 26, 147, 216
Much Ado about Nothing 11, 58–9, 189–92, 203
Norton Shakespeare 26
Othello 11, 22, 29, 46, 73, 131, 189–90, 196–203, 208
Richard II 61, 147
Richard III 29, 31, 61
Romeo and Juliet 31
Shakespeare's Sonnets 188
Taming of the Shrew, The 188
Tempest, The 6, 36–9, 42, 48, 50, 54, 59, 73, 146–53, 172, 208
Titus Andronicus 12, 230–54
Twelfth Night 62, 64, 147, 209, 211, 214–15, *214*, 220–2, 224, 225
Two Gentlemen of Verona, The 146
Venus and Adonis 188
Winter's Tale, The 62
As You Like It 59, 146, 147, 153–6
'Shakespeare and Social Justice' conference (2019) 3–4, 177
'Shakespeare and Social Justice in Contemporary Performance' (special issue, *Shakespeare Bulletin* 39, no. 4, 2021, ed. David Sterling Brown and Sandra Young) 4 n.14
'Shakespeare and Social Justice in South Africa' (special issue, *Shakespeare in Southern Africa* 34, 2021, ed. Chris Thurman) 4 n.14
'Shakespeare and the Fiction of the Intercultural' (Lan) 22
'Shakespeare and the Possibilities of Postcolonial Performance' (Loomba) 22, 28
Shakespearean World, The (Levenson and Ormsby) 21
Shakespeare Beyond English (Bennett and Carson) 24
'Shakespeare in Africa' (Young) 21
Shakespeare in the Global South: Stories of Oceans Crossed in Contemporary (Young) 70, 73, 77 n.30, 77 n.37
'Shakespeare in Eastern Europe' (Schandl) 21
'Shakespeare in Iberian and Latin American Spanishes' (Modenessi) 21
Shakespeare's Sonnets (Shakespeare) 188
'Shakespeare: Staging the World' exhibition (2012) 161
Shakespeare studies 19
Shakespeare Theatre Company, Washington, DC 64
'Shakespeare Worldwide' (Kennedy) 21
Shanty Productions 62
Shapiro, J. 123
Simba, C. 211, *214*, 220–1
Singh, J. 28, 29
Sino-British trade 33 n.13
site-specific ethics 72–3
skin colour 124–5
slavery 3

slums 87
Smith, B.
  Cambridge Guide to the Worlds of Shakespeare, The 21
Smith, I. 92–3
social injustice 1–13, 19–35, 123, 188
social justice 2, 3, 5, 19, 63, 74
  pedagogy 240
Solomon, A. 217
Soul on Ice 52
South Africa 22, 149–52, 162
  National Party 150, 152, 153, 158
  Natives Land Act of 1913 149, 150, 155
South America 27
South Sudan 24
sovereignty 40, 42, 57 n.15
Spanish Tragedy, The (Kyd) 133
speech act theory 218
Spiller, E. A. 125
Spinoza, B. 253 n.41
Spivak, G. 28
Starks-Estes, L. 236
stereotyping 65
Stoll, A. 11–12
student activism 3
Substance Abuse and Mental Health Services Administration (SAMHSA) 171
supplement 152
Suzman, J. 72
Syal, M. 58
Syro-Mesopotamian cultures 85
systemic inequity 224

Tamburlaine 132
Taming of the Shrew, The (Shakespeare) 188
Tarantino
  Django Unchained 238, 239
Taymor, J. 59
  Titus 239

Teaching Social Justice Through Shakespeare (Eklund and Hyman) 5, 30, 32
Teenage Dick (Lew) 31, 35 n.28
Tempest, A (Césaire) 36
Tempest, The (Shakespeare) 6, 36–9, 42, 48, 50, 54, 59, 73, 146–53, 172, 208
Terry, M. 64, 207, 210
Theater Wit 35 n.28
Theatre Journal 218
Thompson, A. 32, 65
  Performing Race and Torture on the Early Modern Stage 93
Thompson, J.
  Digging Up Stories 168–9
Throne of Blood (Kurosawa) 58
Thurman, C
  'Shakespeare and Social Justice in South Africa' 4 n.14
Titus (Taymor) 239
Titus Andronicus (Shakespeare) 12, 230–54
Tommy, L. 64, 65
Tompkins, J.
  'Conflicting Fields of Vision: Performing Self and Other in Two Intercultural Shakespeare Productions' 22
trans community 64
transvestitism 217
trauma-informed pedagogical practices 231
Tristia (Ovid) 156
Truong, N. 223–4
Turkey 22
Twelfth Night (Shakespeare) 62, 64, 147, 209, 211, 214–15, 214, 220–2, 224, 225
Two Gentlemen of Verona, The (Shakespeare) 146

UK, *see* United Kingdom (UK)
Ukraine 22, 116
Ulysses (Joyce) 146
Unacknowledged
   Approach 210–11
'Uncle Tom and Tiny Tim'
   (Kriegel) 90
United Kingdom (UK)
   pedagogical instrumentality
     of global Shakespeare
     adaptations 61
   race/racism in 8
   Robben Island 'Bible' 10, 71
United Nations Refugee
   Agency, on mass
   migration 37
United States 26, 71
   Black death 87
   Indigenous Studies 28
   National Sexual Violence
     Resource Center 233
   pedagogical instrumentality
     of global Shakespeare
     adaptations 61
   race/racism in 8
   War on Terror 122, 135,
     139 n.17
University of San Diego
   Old Globe Theater 12, 208,
     209
   Shirley Graduate Theater
     Program 12, 208

Vammer, J. 211, 215
Varnado, C. 103
venereal disease 47
Venkatrathnam, S. 145, 153, 160
Venus and Adonis
   (Shakespeare) 188
victimization 106
violence 2, 82, 95 n.1, 96 n.2,
   99 n.29, 106, 236
   comedic 94

gender-based 5, 11, 13,
   187–206
intimate partner 187, 189
normalization of 9, 94
physical 88, 89
racist 3, 5, 236
rhetorical 88, 89
sexual 11, 12, 88, 91, 94, 230,
   231, 233, 236, 241, 246
Viswanathan, G.
   *Masks of Conquest: Literary
   Study and British Rule in
   India* 13 n.1, 28

Walter, H. 41, 208, 213–14
Ward, J. 134
Warner, M.
   Indigo 6, 36, 47–55,
   57 n.16
War on Terror 122, 135,
   139 n.17
Warren, C. 91
Water with Berries (Lamming) 6,
   36, 42–7, 52, 53, 55,
   56 n.14, 162
Wayne, V. 173, 192
wealth, redistribution of 103
Weinstein, H. 230
Welles, O. 64
Wells, S.
   *Cambridge Companion to
   Shakespeare, The* 21
Western Europe 95
Western imperialism 65
white
   Christianity 93
   disability 89
   femininity 93
   melancholia 85
   monarchy 93
   patriarchalism 92
   patriarchy 93
   rage 103

white Christian fragility 118 n.15
whiteness 81–101, 111
Wiegman, R. 210
Wilde, O. 71
wildness 110–16
Willis, D. 238, 247 n.6
Wilson, E. 210
Windrush Generation 49, 50
Winter's Tale, The
  (Shakespeare) 62
Wonder Woman 223
World Health Organization 187
World Shakespeare Bibliography
  (WSB) 27
World Shakespeare Festival 62
Worthen, A. 219–20
  *Companion to Shakespeare
  and Performance, A* 21–2
Worthen, W. B. 219
WSB, *see* World Shakespeare
  Bibliography (WSB)

xenophobia 57 n.18

Yohangza Theatre Company 29
Yong'an, M. 72
Young, S. 73
  'Shakespeare and Social
  Justice in Contemporary
  Performance' 4 n.14
  'Shakespeare and Social
  Justice Conference,'
  Cape Town 2019, opening
  remarks 250 n.26
  'Shakespeare in Africa' 21
  *Shakespeare in the Global
  South: Stories of
  Oceans Crossed in
  Contemporary* 70,
  73, 77 n.30, 77 n.37

Zero Dark Thirty (Bigelow) 136
Zhaohua, L. 61

www.ingramcontent.com/pod-product-compliance
Lightning Source LLC
Chambersburg PA
CBHW071813300426
44116CB00009B/1297